B2
FIRST

FORMULA

FOR EXAM SUCCESS

EXAM TRAINER

with key

and **Interactive eBook**

CONTENTS

The first page of each exam part begins with a section entitled ABOUT THE TASK. This provides key information about this exam task and its key testing aims.

The first TEST section starts with a mini exam PRACTICE TASK, which is a reduced version of what you will find in the actual B2 First exam.

The TEACH section provides detailed practice of the strategies and skills required to perform well in the exam part. You are guided through in a systematic, step-by-step way, building on each skill as you progress.

READING AND USE OF ENGLISH - Part 3 Word formation

ABOUT THE TASK

- In Reading and Use of English Part 3, you read a short text with eight gaps. The missing words are shown in capital letters at the end of the sentence containing the gap, but are in the base form. You have to change the form of the word so that it fits correctly into each gap.
- You can change the form by adding a prefix or suffix, for example by changing **art** to **artist**, or by changing **able** to **unable**.
- Sometimes you need to make more significant changes to the word, for example by changing **deep** to **depth** or by changing **choose** to **choice**.
- You might have to make a compound word, for example by changing **note** to **notebook**.
- It may be necessary to make a noun plural after you have changed it.
- Each question is worth one mark.

Practice task

1 Read the first paragraph of a text about beauty. Use the word given in capitals at the end of some of the lines to form a word that fits in the gap in the same line. There is an example at the beginning (0).

SIMPLE BEAUTY

The **(0)** <u>MANUFACTURERS</u> of beauty products would like us to believe that we can only look good if we spend money on expensive creams, gels and lotions. However, **(1)** _____ research provides some much simpler solutions. Experiments suggest that diet, exercise and sleep can have a huge effect on our **(2)** _____ . In one experiment, people who had slept well the previous week were judged as more attractive than those whose sleep was limited. Other studies have shown that people who eat **(3)** _____ get higher scores for attractiveness than those who don't. Of course, these findings are **(4)** _____ to prove conclusively. But following a healthy lifestyle is certainly a cheaper way to look good!

MANUFACTURE

SCIENCE

APPEAR

HEALTHY

POSSIBLE

How did you do?

2 Check your answers.

3 Look at the four answers again.
1 In which answer do you need to form an adjective from a noun?
2 In which answer do you need to form an adverb from an adjective?
3 In which answer do you need to form a noun from a verb?
4 In which answer do you need to add a prefix to give a negative meaning?

The practice task is followed by a series of 'How did you do?' questions that encourage you to reflect on how you performed.

15

READING AND USE OF ENGLISH - Part 3 Word formation

Strategies and skills
Negative prefixes

Sometimes the word in capitals is an adjective, and you have to add a prefix to give an opposite meaning.

1 Make negative adjectives from the words in the box and add them to the table.

accurate	certain	formal	legal
organised	patient	pleasant	precise
regular	relevant	satisfied	

un-	in-	im-	ir-	il-	dis-

SPEAKING BOOST
Discuss or answer.
1 What kinds of health and beauty products or services are worth spending money on? Why?
2 'Beauty is in the eye of the beholder.' What does this mean? Do you think it's true?

Noun suffixes

We often use suffixes to form nouns from verbs and adjectives.

2 Form nouns from the words in the box by adding the correct suffix and add them to the table. Can you add any more nouns?

TIP: Remember, sometimes other spelling changes may be necessary.

agree	appear	assist	collect	decide
destroy	employ	encourage	explain
happy	ill	improve	independent
kind	nervous	perform	popular	safe
similar	vary			

-ance/-ence	-ment	-ness	-ion	-y/-ity

16

3 Write the nouns for people from these words. What suffixes can we use to form nouns for people?

1	music	5	economy	8	science
	musician				
2	assist	6	employ	9	politics
3	consume	7	instruct	10	tour
4	comedy				

4 Some nouns are irregular and aren't formed using a suffix. Match the verbs and adjectives (1–10) with the related nouns (a–j).

TIP: There is no rule for these nouns - you need to learn them!

1	choose	6	deep	a	depth	f	pride
2	high	7	please	b	success	g	weight
3	short	8	lose	c	choice	h	loss
4	weigh	9	proud	d	pleasure	i	shortage
5	grow	10	succeed	e	height	j	growth

5 Read the text about the Silver Snipers. Complete it with nouns formed from the words in capitals at the end of some of the lines.

TIP: When you are completing gaps with nouns, remember to think about whether they should be singular or plural.

We tend to associate computer games with young people, and it is true the majority of **(0)** <u>gamers</u> are young. However, a group from Sweden is showing that reaching the age of **(1)** _____ doesn't mean that you stop having fun. With an average age over 60, the Silver Snipers are the oldest team to take part in professional gaming **(2)** _____ . And don't be put off by their elderly **(3)** _____ . They take their playing very seriously! Although they don't enjoy much **(4)** _____ in terms of winning trophies, they get enormous **(5)** _____ from taking part. They have a website, and many loyal **(6)** _____ who cheer them on. They even have a professional coach to help improve their **(7)** _____ . But their main **(8)** _____ is to show that gaming is for everyone, old and young!

GAME

RETIRE

COMPETE
APPEAR

SUCCEED
SATISFY
SUPPORT

PERFORM
AMBITIOUS

The practice task is followed by a series of 'How did you do?' questions that encourage you to reflect on how you performed.

In Reading and Use of English and Listening exam parts, you can find optional Speaking boost tasks. These provide questions to prompt speaking practice in class, or individually at home, to help develop your communicative skills.

READING AND USE OF ENGLISH - Part 3 Word formation

Adjective suffixes 1
We often use suffixes to form adjectives from nouns and verbs.

6 Form adjectives from the words in the box and add them to the table. You can use some words more than once. Can you add any more adjectives for each suffix?

TIP: Think about the spelling carefully. Sometimes you need to make small spelling changes. Your answer is only correct if you have spelled the word correctly.

> ambition care create danger dare effect
> embarrass excite help impress nature
> stress success tradition wonder

-al	-ful	-ing	-ive	-less	-ous

We form some adjectives with less common suffixes. With some other adjectives, we need to change the form of the word slightly when we add a suffix.

7 Complete the sentences with adjectives formed from the word in capitals.

1 She came from a very _____ family. **ART**
2 There is no _____ proof for this. **SCIENCE**
3 The product became a huge _____ success. **COMMERCE**
4 I'm an _____ football supporter. **ENTHUSIASM**
5 The fireworks were really _____ . **SPECTACLE**
6 He was one of the most famous athletes of the _____ century. **TWENTY**

Sometimes, you need to decide whether to use an adjective ending in *-ed* or *-ing*.

8 Complete the sentences with the correct *-ed* or *-ing* adjectives formed from the word in capitals.

TIP: An **-ed** adjective describes how you feel; an **-ing** adjective describes a thing that gives you this feeling.

1 It was a _____ exhibition. **FASCINATE**
2 I was _____ to be accepted onto the course. **DELIGHT**
3 We were _____ at his speed. **AMAZE**
4 The show was lively and _____ . **ENTERTAIN**
5 We were _____ by the score. **DISAPPOINT**
6 The first few exercises were very _____ . **CHALLENGE**
7 The children were _____ to see their cousins after so long. **EXCITE**
8 The book was not as _____ as I expected it to be. **INTEREST**
9 I no longer feel _____ about the same kinds of things as when I was a teenager. **EMBARRASS**
10 The article about the actor was extremely _____ . **REVEAL**

SPEAKING BOOST

Discuss or answer.

1 If you could go to any major sports event, which would it be?
2 Are you a competitive person? In what ways?

Adjective suffixes 2
Adjectives can be formed in a variety of ways using suffixes. It's important that you remember the different suffixes and the rules you need to apply when you use them.

9 Form adjectives from the words in the box and add them to the table. Can you add any more adjectives for each suffix?

TIP: Remember to think about whether you need to make any spelling changes.

> comfort confidence employ health
> noise patience please profit rely taste

-able/-ible	-ant/-ent	-y

10 Complete the sentences with the correct positive or negative adjectives formed from the word in capitals.

TIP: Sometimes you have to form an adjective AND add a negative prefix. Think about how to form the adjective first, then decide if the meaning is positive or negative.

1 I enjoyed the film, despite the _____ seat. **COMFORT**
2 The trip didn't go as planned, and there were some _____ difficulties. **EXPECT**
3 It was _____ that the train was a few minutes late, so we managed to catch it. **FORTUNE**
4 I try not to eat _____ foods like cakes and chocolate. **HEALTH**
5 Emojis are not an _____ way to communicate how we feel. **EFFECT**
6 We were very _____ that we didn't win the game. **LUCK**

READING AND USE OF ENGLISH - Part 3 Word formation

Adverbs
Some gaps require an adverb. You may have to form an adverb from an adjective, or you may have to form it from a noun or verb.

11 Complete the table with the adjectives and adverbs formed from each noun or verb.

TIP: When you have to form an adverb from a noun or a verb, it can help to think about the adjective first, then make this into an adverb.

noun or verb	adjective	adverb
1 increase		
2 comfort		
3 despair		
4 occasion		
5 tradition		
6 accident		
7 origin		
8 person		
9 success		
10 imagine		

12 Complete the sentences with adjectives or adverbs formed from the word in capitals.

1 Only a few people held him _____ responsible for the accident. **PERSON**
2 The _____ documents no longer exist. **ORIGIN**
3 Very few people have _____ completed this challenge. **SUCCESS**
4 I realised that I had _____ deleted the file on my computer. **ACCIDENT**
5 There was a _____ end to the race. **DRAMA**
6 These sweets are _____ eaten at special occasions. **TRADITION**
7 Online shops such as this one are becoming _____ popular. **INCREASE**
8 She was praised for her _____ designs. **IMAGINE**

Verb suffixes and prefixes
Most gaps in Reading and Use of English Part 3 tasks are nouns, adjectives or adverbs. But sometimes the missing word is a verb.

13 Complete the sentences with verbs formed from the word in capitals.

TIP: Where the gap is a verb, remember to think about the correct form and tense.

1 They decided to _____ the event online, to encourage more people to come. **ADVERT**
2 I knew they were just trying to _____ us. **FRIGHT**
3 No one enjoys being _____ when they are doing their best. **CRITICISM**
4 The financial support they received _____ them to continue with the research. **ABLE**
5 We soon _____ that we had made a mistake. **REAL**
6 The handle was a bit loose, so we had to _____ it. **TIGHT**

EXAM TASK

Read the text about coral reefs. Use the word given in capitals at the end of some of the lines to form a word that fits in the gap in the same line. There is an example at the beginning (0).

CORAL REEFS

We are all familiar with images of coral reefs, with their colourful rock **(0)** _FORMATIONS_ created from the shells of sea creatures. Maya Beach in Thailand became famous after it was used as the **(1)** _____ for the Hollywood movie *The Beach*. Its **(2)** _____ as a tourist destination increased dramatically and, as a result, the coral began to suffer **(3)** _____ amounts of damage. The Thai authorities responded by closing the beach. **(4)** _____ now think they have found a solution. They have found it is possible to collect up broken pieces of reef and **(5)** _____ fix them back in place, using normal household glue! Specialist **(6)** _____ swim down to carry out the repairs. The technique has so far proved extremely **(7)** _____ , and the coral has started to regrow. It is hoped that the beach will be reopened one day, but the number of visitors will be **(8)** _____ controlled to protect the coral.

FORM

LOCATE
POPULAR

SUBSTANCE

SCIENCE

CARE
DIVE

EFFECT

STRICT

18

There are TIP boxes which give targeted advice on how to approach the particular exam part.

Each strategy, skill or language focus is clearly labelled, and there is a variety of exercise types throughout.

All the full exam tasks are clearly flagged like this in every exam paper and part.

The final TEST section is a full-length exam task. This provides an opportunity to put the strategies and skills you have studied into practice. You should apply the strategies and skills that you have practised when you do the task to perform well. Completing the full exam task also gives you valuable experience of the kind of task you can expect to find in the Cambridge B2 First exam.

An Answer Key for all tasks is provided, either in the back of your book or via the Digital resources.

All audioscripts are printed in the back of the book.

What is *Formula*?

Formula is a brand-new exam preparation course that provides teachers and learners with unrivalled flexibility in exam training. The course offers complete and extensive preparation for the Cambridge B1 Preliminary, B2 First and C1 Advanced exams. The core materials provide thorough, step-by-step targeted exam training, helping learners to develop a deeper understanding of the strategies and skills needed to succeed. Comprehensive practice of these skills and strategies for each exam task type is systematically provided through engaging, contemporary topics.

The course comprises two core components: the **Coursebook** and the **Exam Trainer**. These can be used as stand-alone components, or together, depending on the learning environment.

Both course components are suitable for the standard and 'For Schools' versions of the Cambridge English exams.

What is the *Formula* B2 First Exam Trainer?

The **Formula B2 First Exam Trainer** is a book specially designed to maximise your chances of success in the Cambridge B2 First or B2 First for Schools examinations.

It can work either as a standalone component or in combination with the **Formula B2 First Coursebook**. Its structure follows the Cambridge B2 First exam, working systematically through each Paper and Part, from Reading and Use of English Part 1 to Speaking Part 4. Each Paper is introduced with a detailed overview of the exam task format, followed by a 'Test, Teach, Test' approach, to improve understanding and performance.

The Test, Teach, Test approach

TEST: A mini 'practice task' that reflects the Cambridge B2 First exam task for that Part, with a 'How did you do?' reflection activity. This helps learners familiarise themselves with the task type and quickly highlights any obvious focus for improving performance.

TEACH: An extensive series of explanations, tips and targeted tasks to practise the strategies and skills for improving performance in the exam. The skills are organised in priority order, so students with little time know which sections to focus on first to make the most progress.

TEST: A full-length, authentic-style exam task to put the exam training to the test, with a full, 'smart' answer key.

At the back of the Exam Trainer there is also a full, authentic-style Cambridge B2 First exam, with accompanying audio. We advise that this exam is taken under exam conditions when the training phase is complete.

All audio for the Exam Trainer is available via the App and Digital resources. The audio is available for download so you can save it to your device to listen offline.

How can I use the *Formula* B2 First Exam Trainer?

The **Formula B2 First Exam Trainer** is a flexible component and can be used effectively in a number of different learning environments. Here are some typical situations:

You are studying for the Cambridge B2 First exam with other students in a classroom scenario, probably over an academic year.

You are using the **Formula B2 First Coursebook** in class. Sometimes you will also do the related exercises or even a whole exam part from the **Formula B2 First Exam Trainer** in class, though your teacher will ask you to do exercises from it at home as well. You will use the entire **Exam Trainer** or you will use it selectively, depending on your needs and the time available.

You have already completed a Cambridge B2 First exam course or a general B2-level English course. You are enrolled on an intensive exam preparation course with other students to do targeted exam practice.

You may have already worked though the **Formula B2 First Coursebook** or perhaps another Cambridge B2 First coursebook. You will use the **Formula B2 First Exam Trainer** in class to give you a concentrated and highly focused short exam course. This will provide systematic, teacher-led exam training paper by paper, with Speaking boosts for communicative activities in class. You may focus on the exam sections in class, and the skills and strategies at home, or the reverse. There is also a full, authentic-style Practice Exam included in the title, which you can sit under exam conditions prior to taking the exam.

You only have a short time available to prepare for the Cambridge B2 First exam and are not enrolled in an exam preparation course.

You have been attending general English classes and your level of English is already nearing Cambridge B2 First exam standard. You now need targeted exam skills practice. You will use the **Formula B2 First Exam Trainer** independently to work through each of the exam papers in order, so that you are familiar with the exam tasks and equipped with key strategies for improving your performance. The Speaking boost sections provide valuable speaking practice and the full, authentic-style Practice Exam can be sat under exam conditions prior to taking the exam.

You only have a short time available and are preparing for the exam on your own.

Maybe you are not attending English classes at present but wish to take the Cambridge B2 First exam and prepare for it independently. You will use the **Formula B2 First Exam Trainer** independently to work through each of the exam papers in order, so that you are familiar with the exam tasks and equipped with key strategies for improving your performance. The Speaking boost sections provide valuable speaking practice and the full, authentic-style Practice Exam can be sat under exam conditions prior to taking the exam.

ABOUT THE TASK

- In Reading and Use of English Part 1, you read a short text with eight gaps.
- There are four multiple-choice options for each gap.
- You choose the word or phrase that best fits each gap.
- The gaps can test your understanding of differences in meaning between similar words, for example, **found**, **invent** and **discover**. They can also test your knowledge of words that collocate with particular prepositions, or words that occur in fixed phrases.

- They also test your knowledge of verb patterns, for example whether a verb is followed by an infinitive or a clause.
- Some gaps test your knowledge of phrasal verbs and linking words.
- Each question is worth one mark.

Practice task

1 Read the first paragraph of a text about micro homes and decide which answer (A, B, C or D) best fits each gap. There is an example at the beginning (0).

Micro homes

Most people **(0)** _____ B _____ of owning their own home, but for many young people this is not a realistic possibility. House prices are **(1)** _____ , and renting is also expensive, which **(2)** _____ that saving enough money for a deposit is often out of reach. In recent years, **(3)** _____ , the micro house movement has started to grow. Micro homes are small, compact homes that are cheap to build and need very little space. If the idea **(4)** _____ off, it could offer an alternative to more traditional homes.

How did you do?

2 Check your answers.

3 Look at the four answers again.

1 Which answer needs you to use linking words correctly?

2 Which answer needs you to understand typical collocations?

3 Which answer needs you to know the meaning of a phrasal verb?

4 Which answer needs you to understand differences in meaning between words with similar meanings?

4 Look at the four sets of words from the options (1–4) in Ex 1 in context. What do you notice about how each one is used? Then look at the gaps in the Ex 1 text again. Can you see why the answers are correct?

1 The film was a **great success**.
   The new TV arrived in a **big box**.
   We were delayed by the **severe weather**.
   They charge very **high prices**.

2 Pollution in cities **causes** a lot of health problems.
   Working with children **demands** a lot of patience.
   He has no job, and this **means** that he has very little money.
   Living in a micro home would **allow** us to save more money.

3 **Although** he's only young, he's a brilliant player. / He's a brilliant player, **although** he's only young.
   Her sister, **however**, isn't interested in sport at all. / **However**, her sister isn't interested in sport at all.
   Despite her young age, she is determined to go to the USA.
   You should study more **instead of** chatting to friends online.

4 I'm sure the idea will **take off**.
   I can't **get** the lid **off**.
   You can't **put off** the decision any longer.
   A thief **made off** with the money.

0	A	hope	B	dream	C	intend	D	wish
1	A	great	B	big	C	severe	D	high
2	A	causes	B	demands	C	means	D	allows
3	A	although	B	however	C	despite	D	instead
4	A	takes	B	gets	C	puts	D	makes

Strategies and skills

Phrases with prepositions

The correct choice for a gap often depends on matching the correct option with the preposition after the gap.

1a Read the sentences and look at the highlighted prepositions. Choose the word that is followed by each preposition and fits the context.

1 I'm very **interested / curious / keen / attracted in** music.

2 I wasn't sure how to **arrive / find / reach / get to** the restaurant.

3 I'm not **informed / interested / familiar / knowledgeable with** his books.

4 James is still **mending / recovering / improving / gaining from** his operation.

5 I felt very **pleased / satisfied / proud / content of** myself.

6 It wasn't clear whether she **approved / liked / agreed / accepted of** what we had done.

7 The wet weather had a very damaging **result / solution / effect / end on** tourism.

8 I hadn't **recognised / noticed / realised / heard of** this artist before.

1b What prepositions are the other words followed by? Which words are not usually followed by a preposition?

Prepositions are also used before nouns, in fixed phrases or collocations. It is important to learn and recognise these. Sometimes the preposition may be the gap.

2 Look at the prepositions and nouns (A–D) carefully. Then choose the ones which form fixed phrases or collocations to complete the sentences.

1 It was really exciting to finally meet her in
   _____ .
   A end   B life   C person   D face

2 She was a doctor by _____ .
   A job   B profession C work   D employment

3 We soon found that we had a lot _____ common.
   A as   B for   C between D in

4 _____ my surprise, they offered me the job as a photographer.
   A For   B In   C To   D Against

5 The police soon arrived on the _____ .
   A location B place   C situation D scene

6 He could play the whole piece of music by
   _____ .
   A memory B mind   C heart   D feeling

Discuss or answer.

1 Describe your perfect home.

2 What are the challenges when you move to a new home/ location?

Phrasal verbs

Some questions test your knowledge of phrasal verbs. Sometimes the whole phrasal verb is missing, or sometimes just the verb or the particle.

> **TIP:** Make sure you learn as many phrasal verbs as you can. It's important to remember which need an object, which can be separated and which have three rather than two parts.

3 Choose the correct words or phrases to complete the sentences.

1 The book was popular and quickly sold **in / off / out / after**.

2 There were fears that robots would **take / give / get / make** over our lives.

3 Other members of the group **made up for / got through to / went over to / came up with** some good ideas.

4 I decided to **take / get / make / put** up his offer of a job with the company.

5 I hoped I might pick **off / up / out / over** some useful tips.

6 I always **shut down / put off / take off / shut up** my computer before I go home from work.

4 Choose the correct verb (A–D) to complete the sentences.

1 We've decided to _____ ahead with our plans for a new office.
   A take   B go   C put   D bring

2 They've _____ the meeting off until next week.
   A got   B stopped   C put   D taken

3 Food prices have _____ up a lot recently.
   A changed B got   C taken   D gone

4 Do you think we should _____ together for a meeting?
   A get   B bring   C take   D make

5 All the lights suddenly _____ off.
   A moved   B got   C put   D went

6 I was ill last week, so I _____ a bit behind with my work.
   A went   B came   C got   D turned

7 We don't like the temporary office location but we will have to _____ up with it until June.
   A live   B put   C take   D turn

8 Everyone says I _____ after my father because we look alike and both love jazz.
   A look   B go   C take   D do

Verb patterns

Sometimes you need to think about what kind of pattern follows a verb, for example an infinitive, a noun, an *-ing* form or a *that* clause.

5 Choose the correct verb pattern to complete the sentences.

1 Finally, I managed **reserving / to reserve** a table at the popular new bistro.

2 It was very hard to accept **to lose / that we had lost** the game.

3 I had never considered **moving / that I move** to another country before.

4 I urged **Sam to be / Sam that he should be** careful.

5 Some of my friends agreed **helping / to help** us.

6 I couldn't imagine **working / me to work** in a busy restaurant kitchen all day.

6 Choose the correct verbs (A-D) to complete the sentences.

1 We _____ to go ahead with the event despite the concerns.
   A considered   B thought   C decided   D insisted

2 I had always _____ studying very difficult.
   A found   B experienced   C believed   D realised

3 Our manager _____ that we should postpone the show for a few weeks.
   A urged   B suggested   C told   D persuaded

4 Natalie _____ to think of herself as an artist.
   A insists   B imagines   C likes   D stresses

5 I really _____ what everyone did for me.
   A benefited   B approved   C agreed   D appreciated

6 Some friends _____ me to apply to a TV baking show.
   A suggested   B proposed   C said   D encouraged

SPEAKING BOOST

Discuss or answer.

1 Talk about what drinks you have in a typical day and where you have them.

2 What do you think of fair trade products?

Easily confused words

Some words have very similar meanings and are easy to confuse. Think carefully about the particular meaning each word has, and also think about the prepositions, collocations and patterns each word is used with.

7 Choose the correct words (A-D) to complete the sentences.

1 I've always taken loads of photos and _____ them online.
   A sent   B posted   C mailed   D delivered

2 She _____ her first album in 2016.
   A brought   B displayed   C released   D presented

3 The pack _____ posters and leaflets for the environmental campaign.
   A contains   B combines   C composes   D consists

4 You can see the _____ of the sun reflected on the solar panels.
   A bars   B rays   C lights   D flashes

5 Prague is an extremely popular _____ for tourists.
   A visit   B intention   C aim   D destination

6 From the hill, you can get a wonderful _____ of the whole city.
   A scene   B sight   C view   D glance

Verb collocations

A lot of common verbs such as *get, have, make, put, take*, etc. are used in collocations or fixed phrases. It is important to learn as many of these as you can.

8 Complete the sentences with the verbs from the box.

> come   do   go   get   have   keep
> make   play   spend   take

1 I knew I needed to _____ this secret from everyone.

2 I wondered how I could _____ advantage of the situation.

3 A bit of string should _____ the job and hold everything together.

4 What he said didn't _____ sense to me.

5 I took Ewa to one side to _____ a quiet word with her.

6 I hope your dreams will _____ true.

7 I don't _____ a lot of time watching TV.

8 We decided to _____ a trick on Jack.

9 You should _____ rid of those old trainers – they are disgusting!

10 I don't think anything will _____ wrong because you have prepared so carefully.

Linking words

Some questions test your knowledge of linking words and phrases.

9 Look at the bold linking words in the sentences (1–6). Match them to the synonyms (a–f).

1 We had the party at home **rather than** hiring a hall.
2 We'll go ahead, **as long as** you're happy with that.
3 The plane was late **owing to** the bad weather.
4 Everyone was early, **apart from** Leon.
5 He is still a formidable opponent, **despite** his age.
6 I turned the music down **so as to** hear him better.

a because of, due to, thanks to
b in spite of
c instead of
d in order to
e except
f if, provided that

10 Choose the correct linking words (A–D) to complete the sentences.

> **TIP:** Make sure the word you choose fits with the words that come after the gap as well as those that come before.

1 We decided to take our own picnic, _____ than eating out.
  A instead   B whereas
  C rather   D by contrast

2 We needed to hurry up, _____ we would be late.
  A otherwise   B however
  C although   D except

3 The product was a success _____ its problems.
  A except   B in spite of
  C however   D although

4 I won't call you _____ there's a problem.
  A unless   B provided that
  C except   D owing to

5 The shop sold cards and magazines _____ books.
  A in addition   B in particular
  C as well as   D what's more

6 _____ the first experiments failed, she never thought about giving up.
  A However   B Nevertheless
  C In spite of   D Although

EXAM TASK

Read the text about preparing for a possible emergency and decide which answer (A, B, C or D) best fits each gap. There is an example at the beginning (0).

Preparing for the worst

We all depend on supermarkets for food and we **(0)** _____D_____ it for granted that the shelves will always be full. But some people believe it's best to be prepared **(1)** _____ there's an emergency and normal life is disrupted for a while. They say there is a risk from extreme weather or an outbreak of flu, **(2)** _____ more serious natural disasters. People who prepare in this way are informally **(3)** _____ as 'preppers', and more and more people are now listening to their **(4)** _____ . Alison Jones from Cambridge, UK, is a typical example. She keeps a month's **(5)** _____ of food in a cupboard, along with bottled water and medicines that her family needs. She is aware that some people would **(6)** _____ her to be slightly odd, but says that, for her, it makes perfect **(7)** _____ to be prepared. 'We keep just enough to see us through a few weeks, so we can then **(8)** _____ our normal lives. Why would anyone not do that?'

0	**A** get	**B** have	**C** make	**D** take
1	**A** even if	**B** in case	**C** provided that	**D** whereas
2	**A** although	**B** as well as	**C** in spite of	**D** in contrast
3	**A** known	**B** called	**C** named	**D** entitled
4	**A** views	**B** wishes	**C** requests	**D** decisions
5	**A** donation	**B** number	**C** supply	**D** delivery
6	**A** decide	**B** accept	**C** realise	**D** consider
7	**A** sense	**B** reason	**C** idea	**D** judgement
8	**A** go through with	**B** put up with	**C** get on with	**D** get away with

ABOUT THE TASK

- In Reading and Use of English Part 2, you read a short text with eight gaps. You have to think of the word that best fits each gap.
- There are no options to choose from.
- You have to think about the structure of the language in the text and the meaning of the text.
- The word you write must be spelled correctly, and must fit the gap grammatically.
- You cannot write contractions such as **don't** or **won't**, but you can write the word **cannot**.
- The gaps test your understanding of different kinds of grammar, for example, parts of verbs, dependent prepositions and articles.
- They also test your knowledge of phrasal verbs, linking words and fixed phrases.
- The answer is always a single word.
- Occasionally, there is more than one correct answer.
- Each question is worth one mark.

Practice task

1 Read the first paragraph of a text about power naps. Think of the word which best fits each gap. Use only one word in each gap. There is an example at the beginning (0).

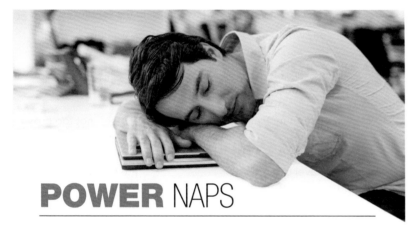

POWER NAPS

Short sleeps, or 'power naps', are regarded by many **(0)** _____AS_____ a good way to recharge your batteries during the day. I have **(1)** _____ taking regular afternoon naps for a while now, and couldn't do without them. Experts used to think a quick power nap could make up for a bad night's sleep, but **(2)** _____ is now being questioned. It seems that for people **(3)** _____ sleep is disrupted at night, an afternoon nap can help to some extent, but it is far **(4)** _____ important to get the right amount of sleep at night.

How did you do?

2 Check your answers.

3 Look at the answers to the four questions in Ex 1 again.

1 Which answer is part of a verb tense? Which tense is it? Why is this tense correct here?

2 Which answer is a relative pronoun? What noun does it refer back to? Why is this pronoun correct here?

3 Which answer is part of a comparative structure? Which word before the gap helps you decide it should be a comparative structure? Why is *less* not correct?

4 Which answer is a reference word, which refers to an earlier idea? What idea does it refer back to? Why is *these* not correct here?

4 Which gap can be filled by two possible words? Why?

Strategies and skills

Present tenses

The gaps often test your knowledge of the present and present perfect verb tenses. The gapped word is often an auxiliary verb, for example a form of the verbs *be*, *do* or *have*. The verb may be in the active or passive form.

1 Complete the sentences with one word in each gap.

1 I have _____ training for a marathon recently.

2 Nowadays, a good diet _____ believed to be extremely important for health.

3 These days, people _____ beginning to realise that we need to take climate change seriously.

4 Some people think that cooking is a chore, but I _____ not agree.

5 The competition _____ been held in the town for the last 15 years.

6 It's now six o'clock in the morning and the sun _____ just come up.

> **SPEAKING BOOST**
>
> Discuss or answer.
>
> 1 Where's the funniest place you have fallen asleep?
>
> 2 Describe a dream that you had recently.

Future forms

The gaps sometimes test your knowledge of future forms, such as the future continuous, future perfect and future perfect continuous. The gapped word is usually an auxiliary verb, for example a form of the verbs *be* or *have*. They may also test your knowledge of future forms of *be able to* and *have to*.

2 Choose the correct words to complete the future forms in the sentences.

1 My knee is nearly better, so I hope I **be able / will be able** to go on my walking holiday.

2 Next week's World Cup Final will **watch / be watched** by millions of people all over the world.

3 Hurry up, or the train **will have left / will have been leaving** by the time we get to the station!

4 In June we **will be travelling / going to travel** around India.

5 It will be too far to walk, so you **have to / will have to** get a taxi.

6 By next summer I will **have been living / be living** in Cádiz for five years.

3 Complete the sentences with one word in each gap.

1 Tomorrow I will _____ flying to New York for my gap year.

2 The festival will _____ started by the time we get back from our trip to Tuscany.

3 I hope you will _____ able to join us for the meal.

4 We will be tired when we get home because we will have _____ walking for ten days.

5 The new sports centre will _____ opened by a TV celebrity next month.

6 I think we will _____ to work harder if we want to get everything finished.

Conditional forms

The gaps sometimes test your knowledge of conditionals. Make sure you know the zero, first, second and third conditional forms, and learn the difference between *if* and *unless*. The gaps may also test your knowledge of structures with *wish*.

4 Choose the correct words (A–C) to complete the sentences.

1 The holiday would have been more fun if the weather _____ been better.
   A had   B was   C would

2 If I had more free time, I _____ love to join a choir.
   A will   B would   C can

3 We'll meet for lunch next week if I _____ not too busy at work.
   A am   B will   C was

4 I usually travel by tram if I _____ the choice.
   A had   B have   C got

5 I knew that I wouldn't have any chance of winning _____ I could improve significantly.
   A if   B because   C unless

6 It was getting late now, and I was starting to wish that we _____ caught an earlier train.
   A would   B have   C had

7 It is worth upgrading to a first-class ticket _____ you want to be certain of getting a seat.
   A if   B although   C unless

8 I wish my brother _____ let me borrow his car!
   A will   B would   C can

> **SPEAKING BOOST**
>
> Discuss or answer.
>
> 1 What changes will there be in the car industry over the next 20 years?
>
> 2 What's the oldest thing you own? Why do you still have it?

Relative clauses

Some gaps test your knowledge of relative pronouns in relative clauses.

> **TIP:** Remember, we use **when** for places, **where** for times and **whose** for possession. Remember also that we use **which** (not **that**) in non-defining relative clauses.

5 Look at the words before and after the gaps in these sentences. How do you know that a relative pronoun is missing from each gap? Which sentence is different?

1 Istanbul is a city _____ East and West come together.

2 I have always thought of myself as someone _____ loves a challenge.

3 Hans was looking forward to the day _____ he could finally set off on his travels.

4 I decided to talk to Ana, _____ job involved a lot of contact with different kinds of art projects.

5 The show had already started when we arrived, _____ was a bit disappointing.

6 The creative writing course _____ I had originally intended to do was already full.

6 Complete the sentences in Ex 5 with one word.

Comparative forms

Gaps sometimes test your knowledge of comparative forms. As well as basic comparatives and superlatives, make sure you know how to use *so*, *such* and *how*. Try to learn phrases with comparatives and superlatives, too.

7 Match the beginning of each comparative or superlative sentence (1–6) to its ending (a–f).

1 Sara commented on how

2 When I got home, I was so

3 It was by far

4 The dinosaur skeleton was far

5 I didn't expect her to be such

6 The bigger the challenge, the

a the most terrifying experience of my life.

b a good actor.

c bigger than I thought it would be.

d tired that I went straight to bed.

e more determined he was to succeed.

f delicious the food was.

8 Complete the sentences with the words from the box.

> by   how   more   most   so   such

1 I'm sure he would be far _____ successful if he put in a bit more effort.

2 I didn't realise it would be _____ a big event.

3 She is now one of the nation's _____ respected chefs.

4 I was surprised at _____ keen he was to join us.

5 I knew she was _____ stubborn that it would be hard to change her mind.

6 It was _____ far the biggest cake I had ever seen!

Reference words and impersonal structures

Gaps sometimes test the use of words such as *this*, *that*, *these*, *those*, *it*, *what*, *that* and *there*.

> **TIP:** For this kind of gap, you need to read the whole sentence or context so you can understand the meaning.

9 Choose the correct word to complete the sentences.

1 There is no doubt **that / what / there** online shopping is now the first option for many people.

2 I opened the email. Most of her emails had been quite friendly, but **these / it / this** one had a different tone.

3 **There / It / This** is difficult to convey quite how important this decision was.

4 I have read the report and **what / that / there** it seems to show is that pollution is definitely getting worse.

5 Paul and Johanna looked troubled, and I could see that **it / there / that** was definitely something going on.

6 Marta had failed to answer her phone, and **that / there / what** was worrying.

Quantifiers

The gap may be a quantifier, for example *many*, *much*, *few*, etc. Make sure you know the difference between *much/many* and *little/few*, and try to learn phrases that express quantity, for example *plenty of*, *very few*, *a great deal of*, *well over*, etc.

10 Complete the sentences with one word in each gap.

1 After a _____ hours of delay, it became clear that there was a problem with the plane.

2 I realised that I didn't have _____ choice in the matter, and I would have to accept.

3 They don't have regular jobs, and they seem to survive on very _____ money.

4 I hoped to find a biscuit in the tin, but there were _____ left.

5 There must have been well _____ a hundred people in the room.

6 Don't worry, we've got plenty _____ time.

Linking words and expressions

Some gaps are linking words. For these, you will need to think carefully about the meaning.

> **TIP:** Think about the linking words you know that fit the meaning, then see which one also fits the grammar in the sentence.

11 Look at the gaps in the sentences (1–6). Answer the questions (a–c).

a Which ones need a word to express contrast?

b Which ones need a word to introduce a similar idea?

c Which one needs a time expression?

1 _____ travelling by bus in Peru is sometimes slow, it can also be an interesting experience.

2 I wasn't keen to go to the festival as it was such a long way away. _____ , I couldn't really afford it.

3 The visit to the museum was rewarding _____ the crowds.

4 The winter months are characterised by cold nights and heavy rainfall. _____ , the summer months are gloriously hot and sunny.

5 There are lots of different kinds of food on offer at the market, and there are often cookery demonstrations, _____ .

6 He continued to work on his painting _____ we were chatting.

12 Choose the correct linking words (A–C) to complete the sentences (1–6) in Ex 11.

1 A Although   B But   C However
2 A But   B Besides   C Too
3 A however   B whereas   C despite
4 A Whereas   B However   C Also
5 A too   B plus   C however
6 A while   B whereas   C but

There are also a lot of common linking expressions that are made up of more than one word.

13 Complete the linking expressions in the sentences with one word in each gap.

1 She had suffered from pains in her legs ever _____ the accident.

2 I felt relaxed and happy even _____ we hadn't managed to reach the summit.

3 I knew the championship was within my grasp if _____ I could keep myself motivated.

4 There were monkeys in the trees, as _____ as many kinds of brightly coloured birds.

5 He continued to work in _____ of his poor health.

6 We decided to travel by train _____ than flying.

7 Everyone was happy _____ from George, who continued to complain.

8 Our boat trip was cancelled _____ to the severe weather.

9 I took my phone with me in _____ anyone tried to call me.

10 The islands are closed to visitors during the breeding season in _____ to protect the birds.

EXAM TASK

Read the text below and think of the word which best fits each gap. Use only <u>one</u> word in each gap. There is an example at the beginning (0).

Fix it with friends

We have all got used **(0)** ___TO___ buying new things, using them for a while and then throwing them away. But it **(1)** _____ become clear in recent years that this is not sustainable, as we are generating huge amounts of waste. **(2)** _____ response to this, many people are setting up informal cafés **(3)** _____ people can bring broken items for repair. The cafés provide tools, help from volunteers and plenty **(4)** _____ friendly chat. Dan, twenty-two, works at a repair café in Bristol. 'Many modern devices are difficult to repair **(5)** _____ you have the correct tools and a bit of knowledge,' he says. 'I don't have any qualifications, so I've just picked things **(6)** _____ as I've gone along.' The emphasis is on teaching people. 'We don't repair things *for* people,' Dan says. 'What we do **(7)** _____ help them to repair things themselves.' So, the next time you have something that's broken, why not look out **(8)** _____ a repair event near you?

- In Reading and Use of English Part 3, you read a short text with eight gaps. The missing words are shown in capital letters at the end of the sentence containing the gap, but are in the base form. You have to change the form of the word so that it fits correctly into each gap.

- You can change the form by adding a prefix or suffix, for example by changing **art** to **artist**, or by changing **able** to **unable**.

- Sometimes you need to make more significant changes to the word, for example by changing **deep** to **depth** or by changing **choose** to **choice**.

- You might have to make a compound word, for example by changing **note** to **notebook**.

- It may be necessary to make a noun plural after you have changed it.

- Each question is worth one mark.

Practice task

1 Read the first paragraph of a text about beauty. Use the word given in capitals at the end of some of the lines to form a word that fits in the gap in the same line. There is an example at the beginning (0).

SIMPLE BEAUTY

The **(0)** <u>MANUFACTURERS</u> of beauty products would like us to believe that we can only look good if we spend money on expensive creams, gels and lotions. However, **(1)** _____ research provides some much simpler solutions. Experiments suggest that diet, exercise and sleep can have a huge effect on our **(2)** _____ . In one experiment, people who had slept well the previous week were judged as more attractive than those whose sleep was limited. Other studies have shown that people who eat **(3)** _____ get higher scores for attractiveness than those who don't. Of course, these findings are **(4)** _____ to prove conclusively. But following a healthy lifestyle is certainly a cheaper way to look good!

MANUFACTURE

SCIENCE

APPEAR

HEALTHY

POSSIBLE

How did you do?

2 Check your answers.

3 Look at the four answers again.

1 In which answer do you need to form an adjective from a noun?

2 In which answer do you need to form an adverb from an adjective?

3 In which answer do you need to form a noun from a verb?

4 In which answer do you need to add a prefix to give a negative meaning?

Strategies and skills

Negative prefixes

Sometimes the word in capitals is an adjective, and you have to add a prefix to give an opposite meaning.

1 Make negative adjectives from the words in the box and add them to the table.

> accurate certain formal legal
> organised patient pleasant precise
> regular relevant satisfied

un-	in-	im-	ir-	il-	dis-

SPEAKING BOOST

Discuss or answer.

1 What kinds of health and beauty products or services are worth spending money on? Why?

2 'Beauty is in the eye of the beholder.' What does this mean? Do you think it's true?

Noun suffixes

We often use suffixes to form nouns from verbs and adjectives.

2 Form nouns from the words in the box by adding the correct suffix and add them to the table. Can you add any more nouns?

TIP: Remember, sometimes other spelling changes may be necessary.

> agree appear assist collect decide
> destroy employ encourage explain
> happy ill improve independent
> kind nervous perform popular safe
> similar vary

-ance/ -ence	-ment	-ness	-ion	-y/-ity

3 Write the nouns for people from these words. What suffixes can we use to form nouns for people?

1 music
   _____musician_____

2 assist
   _____

3 consume
   _____

4 comedy
   _____

5 economy
   _____

6 employ
   _____ ,

7 instruct
   _____

8 science
   _____

9 politics
   _____

10 tour
   _____

4 Some nouns are irregular and aren't formed using a suffix. Match the verbs and adjectives (1–10) with the related nouns (a–j).

TIP: There is no rule for these nouns – you need to learn them!

1	choose	6	deep
2	high	7	please
3	short	8	lose
4	weigh	9	proud
5	grow	10	succeed

a	depth	f	pride
b	success	g	weight
c	choice	h	loss
d	pleasure	i	shortage
e	height	j	growth

5 Read the text about the Silver Snipers. Complete it with nouns formed from the words given in capitals at the end of some of the lines.

TIP: When you are completing gaps with nouns, remember to think about whether they should be singular or plural.

We tend to associate computer games with young people, and it is true the majority of **(0)** _____gamers_____ are young. **GAME**
However, a group from Sweden is showing that reaching the age of **(1)** _____ doesn't mean that you **RETIRE**
stop having fun. With an average age over 60, the Silver Snipers are the oldest team to take part in professional gaming **(2)** _____ . And don't be put off by **COMPETE**
their elderly **(3)** _____ .They take their playing **APPEAR**
very seriously! Although they don't enjoy much
(4) _____ in terms of winning trophies, they **SUCCEED**
get enormous **(5)** _____ from taking part. They **SATISFY**
have a website, and many loyal **(6)** _____ who **SUPPORT**
cheer them on. They even have a professional coach to
help improve their **(7)** _____ . But their main **PERFORM**
(8) _____ is to show that gaming is for everyone, **AMBITIOUS**
old and young!

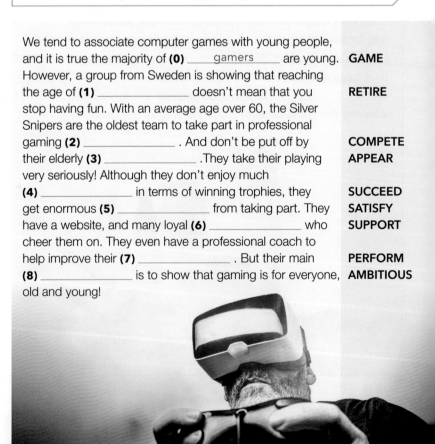

Adjective suffixes 1

We often use suffixes to form adjectives from nouns and verbs.

6 Form adjectives from the words in the box and add them to the table. You can use some words more than once. Can you add any more adjectives for each suffix?

TIP: Think about the spelling carefully. Sometimes you need to make small spelling changes. Your answer is only correct if you have spelled the word correctly.

> ambition care create danger dare effect
> embarrass excite help impress nature
> stress success tradition wonder

-al	-ful	-ing	-ive	-less	-ous

We form some adjectives with less common suffixes. With some other adjectives, we need to change the form of the word slightly when we add a suffix.

7 Complete the sentences with adjectives formed from the word in capitals.

1 She came from a very _____ family. **ART**
2 There is no _____ proof for this. **SCIENCE**
3 The product became a huge _____ success. **COMMERCE**
4 I'm an _____ football supporter. **ENTHUSIASM**
5 The fireworks were really _____ . **SPECTACLE**
6 He was one of the most famous athletes of the _____ century. **TWENTY**

Sometimes, you need to decide whether to use an adjective ending in -ed or -ing.

8 Complete the sentences with the correct -ed or -ing adjectives formed from the word in capitals.

TIP: An **-ed** adjective describes how you feel; an **-ing** adjective describes a thing that gives you this feeling.

1 It was a _____ exhibition. **FASCINATE**
2 I was _____ to be accepted onto the course. **DELIGHT**
3 We were _____ at his speed. **AMAZE**
4 The show was lively and _____ . **ENTERTAIN**
5 We were _____ by the score. **DISAPPOINT**
6 The first few exercises were very _____ . **CHALLENGE**
7 The children were _____ to see their cousins after so long. **EXCITE**
8 The book was not as _____ as I expected it to be. **INTEREST**
9 I no longer feel _____ about the same kinds of things as when I was a teenager. **EMBARRASS**
10 The article about the actor was extremely _____ . **REVEAL**

SPEAKING BOOST

Discuss or answer.

1 If you could go to any major sports event, which would it be?
2 Are you a competitive person? In what ways?

Adjective suffixes 2

Adjectives can be formed in a variety of ways using suffixes. It's important that you remember the different suffixes and the rules you need to apply when you use them.

9 Form adjectives from the words in the box and add them to the table. Can you add any more adjectives for each suffix?

TIP: Remember to think about whether you need to make any spelling changes.

> comfort confidence employ health
> noise patience please profit rely taste

-able/-ible	-ant/-ent	-y

10 Complete the sentences with the correct positive or negative adjectives formed from the word in capitals.

TIP: Sometimes you have to form an adjective AND add a negative prefix. Think about how to form the adjective first, then decide if the meaning is positive or negative.

1 I enjoyed the film, despite the _____ seat. **COMFORT**
2 The trip didn't go as planned, and there were some _____ difficulties. **EXPECT**
3 It was _____ that the train was a few minutes late, so we managed to catch it. **FORTUNE**
4 I try not to eat _____ foods like cakes and chocolate. **HEALTH**
5 Emojis are not an _____ way to communicate how we feel. **EFFECT**
6 We were very _____ that we didn't win the game. **LUCK**
7 He's so _____ I'm surprised he can find anything! **ORGANISE**
8 My application was _____ so I don't have an interview for the job. **SUCCESS**

Adverbs

Some gaps require an adverb. You may have to form an adverb from an adjective, or you may have to form it from a noun or verb.

11 Complete the table with the adjectives and adverbs formed from each noun or verb.

> **TIP:** When you have to form an adverb from a noun or a verb, it can help to think about the adjective first, then make this into an adverb.

noun or verb	adjective	adverb
1 increase	_____	_____
2 comfort	_____	_____
3 despair	_____	_____
4 occasion	_____	_____
5 tradition	_____	_____
6 accident	_____	_____
7 origin	_____	_____
8 person	_____	_____
9 success	_____	_____
10 imagine	_____	_____

12 Complete the sentences with adjectives or adverbs formed from the word in capitals.

1 Only a few people held him _____ responsible for the accident. **PERSON**

2 The _____ documents no longer exist. **ORIGIN**

3 Very few people have _____ completed this challenge. **SUCCESS**

4 I realised that I had _____ deleted the file on my computer. **ACCIDENT**

5 There was a _____ end to the race. **DRAMA**

6 These sweets are _____ eaten at special occasions. **TRADITION**

7 Online shops such as this one are becoming _____ popular. **INCREASE**

8 She was praised for her _____ designs. **IMAGINE**

Verb suffixes and prefixes

Most gaps in Reading and Use of English Part 3 tasks are nouns, adjectives or adverbs. But sometimes the missing word is a verb.

13 Complete the sentences with verbs formed from the word in capitals.

> **TIP:** Where the gap is a verb, remember to think about the correct form and tense.

1 They decided to _____ the event online, to encourage more people to come. **ADVERT**

2 I knew they were just trying to _____ us. **FRIGHT**

3 No one enjoys being _____ when they are doing their best. **CRITICISM**

4 The financial support they received _____ them to continue with the research. **ABLE**

5 We soon _____ that we had made a mistake. **REAL**

6 The handle was a bit loose, so we had to _____ it. **TIGHT**

EXAM TASK

Read the text about coral reefs. Use the word given in capitals at the end of some of the lines to form a word that fits in the gap in the same line. There is an example at the beginning (0).

CORAL REEFS

We are all familiar with images of coral reefs, with their colourful rock **(0)** <u>FORMATIONS</u> created from the shells of sea creatures. Maya Beach in Thailand became famous after it was used as the **(1)** _____ for the Hollywood movie *The Beach*. Its **(2)** _____ as a tourist destination increased dramatically and, as a result, the coral began to suffer **(3)** _____ amounts of damage. The Thai authorities responded by closing the beach. **(4)** _____ now think they have found a solution. They have found it is possible to collect up broken pieces of reef and **(5)** _____ fix them back in place, using normal household glue! Specialist **(6)** _____ swim down to carry out the repairs. The technique has so far proved extremely **(7)** _____ , and the coral has started to regrow. It is hoped that the beach will be reopened one day, but the number of visitors will be **(8)** _____ controlled to protect the coral.

FORM
LOCATE
POPULAR
SUBSTANCE
SCIENCE
CARE
DIVE
EFFECT
STRICT

- In Reading and Use of English Part 4, you read six pairs of sentences. The sentences in each pair have a similar meaning, but they are expressed in different ways.

- There is a gap in the second sentence which you have to fill in, using between two and five words. Contractions count as two words.

- You are given one of the words (called the key word) which you must use, and you can't change this word in any way.

- This part tests your knowledge of both grammar and vocabulary by testing your ability to express the same ideas using different grammatical forms and different words.

- You need to show that you can express a sentence in a different way, without changing its meaning.

- The answer for each sentence is divided into two parts, and there is one mark for each correct part.

Practice task

1 Read the fact file about false science beliefs in the past. Then read sentences 1–3. Complete the second sentence so that it has a similar meaning to the first sentence, using the word given. Do not change the word given. You must use between two and five words, including the word given.

Here is an example:

0   In the past, there were some scientific theories that people don't believe in now.

LONGER

People __NO LONGER BELIEVE IN__ some scientific theories from the past.

Crazy science beliefs from the past

1 In the Middle Ages, people believed it was possible to make gold from other metals.

2 In the nineteenth century, people believed you could tell someone's personality from the bumps on their head. This was called phrenology.

3 In the past, people thought the Earth was slowly growing in size.

1   People no longer try to make gold from other metals.
GIVEN
People _____ to make gold from other metals.

2   People stopped using phrenology in the nineteenth century.
USED
People have _____ the nineteenth century.

3   In the past, people thought the Earth was slowly getting bigger.
BELIEVED
In the past, the Earth _____ slowly getting bigger.

How did you do?

2 Check your answers.

3 Look at the three answers again.

1   In which answer do you need to change an active verb to a passive one?

2   In which answer do you need to use a phrasal verb?

3   In which answer do you need to use the present perfect with *since*?

TEACH

Strategies and skills

Past tenses

It is important to understand the meaning of all the main verb tenses, including continuous forms, *would* and *used to*. Make sure you know how to use *for* and *since* with the present perfect, too.

1 Look at the pairs of sentences. Decide if they have a similar meaning (S) or different meanings (D).

1 A When I was at college, I played tennis a lot.
   B I used to play a lot of tennis at college.

2 A Paris has been my home since 2012.
   B I have been living in Paris since 2012.

3 A We first became friends ten years ago.
   B We had first become friends ten years earlier.

4 A I was always told by my father to do my best at school.
   B My father would always tell me to do my best at school.

5 A I haven't seen George for two years.
   B It's been two years since I last saw George.

6 A Joan prepared a meal for us when we got home.
   B Joan was cooking a meal for us when we got home.

2 Complete the second sentence so that it has a similar meaning to the first.

1 I first came to live here five years ago.
   LIVING
   I _____ five years.

2 We visited our grandparents every weekend.
   WOULD
   We _____ weekend.

3 I didn't enjoy music lessons as a child.
   USE
   I _____ music lessons as a child.

4 This was the first time I had ever met Charles.
   NEVER
   I _____ before.

5 My nephew no longer tries to do well at school.
   STOPPED
   My nephew _____ to do well at school.

6 It's been five months since I last took an exam.
   TAKEN
   I _____ for five months.

SPEAKING BOOST

Discuss or answer.

1 What would you tell your 12-year-old self?

2 What was the last excuse you made up to avoid doing something you didn't want to?

Reported speech

You may need to rewrite direct speech as reported speech. Make sure you know the patterns with different reporting verbs, and how to report questions.

3 Complete the reported speech sentences.

1 'Sam, I think you should check your computer for viruses,' said Rami.
   Rami advised _____ his computer for viruses.

2 'Don't sit on that chair! It's wet!' Jodie said to me.
   Jodie warned _____ on that chair because it was wet.

3 'You stole the money!' Ellie said to Marta.
   Ellie accused _____ the money.

4 'Would you like to come to the cinema with me?' Amber asked me.
   Amber invited _____ to the cinema with her.

5 'What are you doing at the weekend?' Josh asked me.
   Josh asked me _____ the weekend.

6 'Can I use your pen?' Nadia asked Leo.
   Nadia asked Leo if _____ his pen.

Comparative forms

You may have to use comparatives, superlatives and phrases which express comparisons. Make sure you know how to use *so* and *such* correctly.

4 Choose the correct words or phrases to complete the second sentence so that it has a similar meaning to the first.

1 I expected the film to be longer than it was.
   The film **was longer than / wasn't as long as** I expected.

2 Marlon can't run as fast as his brother.
   Marlon's brother is **a faster runner than / not such a fast runner as** Marlon.

3 The second film was less successful than the first.
   The first film **wasn't as successful as / was more successful than** the second.

4 I didn't realise their house was so big.
   I didn't realise they lived in **a much bigger / such a big** house.

5 Which exhibition did you enjoy the most?
   Which was **such an interesting / the most interesting** exhibition?

6 This hotel is far more expensive than the last one.
   The last hotel was **much cheaper than / just as expensive as** this one.

SPEAKING BOOST

Discuss or answer.

1 What is the point of celebrity culture?

2 How important is it for your social media to be popular? Why?

Passive forms

The second sentence often uses the passive form of a verb. Make sure you know the passive forms for all verb tenses, and how to use *have/get something done*. Learn how to use impersonal structures like *He is thought to be … , It is believed to have been …* .

> **TIP:** Remember, we use **by** + agent to say who does the action of a passive verb.

5 Complete each second sentence with the correct passive form of the verb.

1 They are opening a new supermarket here.

BEING

A new supermarket _____ here.

2 A woman at the gate gave me a ticket.

GIVEN

I _____ a woman at the gate.

3 Someone had decided that the museum would have to close.

BEEN

It _____ the museum would have to close.

4 We will inform you when your order has been sent.

BE

You _____ when your order has been sent.

5 People think the show will start at eight o'clock.

EXPECTED

The show _____ at eight o'clock.

6 It is said that eating fish is good for your brain.

SUPPOSED

Eating fish _____ good for your brain.

7 People believe the play was written in 1578.

HAVE

The play is _____ written in 1578.

8 My computer needs repairing again.

GET

I need to _____ again.

Conditionals and *wish*

Some sentences may use first, second or third conditionals. Make sure you are confident with all the conditional forms, and learn how to use alternatives to *if*, such as *unless, in case* and *as long as*.

6 Which second sentence matches the meaning of the first sentence? Write A, B or 'both'.

1 She will only come to the party if she can get a taxi home.
   A She has refused to come to the party unless she can get a taxi home.
   B She has agreed to come to the party as long as she can get a taxi home.

2 You can use my computer, but you mustn't download any films.
   A You can't use my computer in case you download any films.
   B You can use my computer as long as you don't download any films.

3 Lily arrived late because her train was delayed.
   A If Lily's train had been late, she wouldn't have arrived on time.
   B If Lily's train had been on time, she wouldn't have arrived late.

4 It was snowing, so we didn't go shopping.
   A We would have gone shopping if it hadn't been for the snow.
   B If it hadn't been snowing, we would have gone shopping.

5 Petra regretted spending so much money.
   A Petra wished she hadn't spent so much money.
   B Petra didn't think she would have spent so much money.

6 It's a shame that it's raining today.
   A I wish it wouldn't rain so much!
   B I wish it wasn't raining!

Grammar and vocabulary changes

You often have to make grammatical changes to the second sentence and also use a word or phrase with a similar meaning. Think about the grammar patterns of the word in capitals, and think about other changes you need to make so the meaning stays the same.

7 Correct one or two mistakes in each completed second sentence.

1 It isn't necessary to take a coat.

POINT

There is _____no point to take_____ a coat.

2 Paula arrived late because her flight was delayed.

TIME

If Paula's flight _____was in time_____ , she wouldn't have arrived late.

3 The exam was too difficult for me to do.

SO

The exam was _so too difficult that I could_ not do it.

4 Nabil started learning French two years ago.

FOR

Nabil _was learning French for_ two years.

5 The journey wasn't as boring as I expected.

MORE

The journey was _____more interesting as_____ I expected.

6 Emma said that we shouldn't stay too late.

ADVISED

Emma _____advised us don't stay_____ too late.

Paraphrasing

As well as making grammatical changes to the second sentence, you usually have to change other words to words or phrases with similar meanings. It is important to recognise words, phrases and phrasal verbs that have similar meanings to familiar words.

8 Choose the word or phrase (A–C) that matches the meaning of the bold words in the sentences (1–6).

1 They decided to **postpone** the match.
   A put out   B put off   C put down

2 Are you going to **go in for** the competition?
   A take part in   B get part of   C give part of

3 Max **didn't accept** her offer.
   A turned away   B turned off   C turned down

4 He **left** his job as an accountant.
   A gave up   B gave away   C gave out

5 **It isn't worth** going into town now.
   A There's no   B There isn't a   C There's a
      point in   point of   point for

6 Abi has **stopped** singing now.
   A given off   B given in   C given up

9 Decide if the pairs of sentences (A and B) have a similar meaning (S) or different meanings (D).

1 A I'm never going to speak to Carol again.
   B My intention is never to speak to Carol again.

2 A I'm sure he broke it by accident.
   B I'm sure he meant to break it.

3 A They didn't let people park on the beach.
   B People were allowed to park on the beach.

4 A They had no money left.
   B They had run out of money.

5 A We finally managed to escape.
   B We finally succeeded in escaping.

6 A Brad took no notice of the children.
   B Brad paid attention to the children.

EXAM TASK

Complete the second sentence so that it has a similar meaning to the first sentence, using the word given. Do not change the word given. You must use between two and five words, including the word given.

Here is an example:

0 People think that the coins are Roman.

BELIEVED

The coins _____ARE BELIEVED TO BE_____ Roman.

1 'You're lying!' Marissa said to me.

ACCUSED

Marissa _____ the truth.

2 It was careless of her to leave her keys on the table.

SHOULD

She _____ her keys on the table.

3 Carl does not dance as well as Jack.

DANCER

Jack is _____ than Carl.

4 People think that singing is good for your health.

THOUGHT

Singing _____ good for your health.

5 I'm sorry I didn't go to the cinema with the others.

WISH

I _____ to the cinema with the others.

6 I can't wait to meet all your friends.

FORWARD

I am really _____ all your friends.

ABOUT THE TASK

- In Reading and Use of English Part 5, you read a long text.
- There are six multiple-choice questions with four options. You have to choose the correct options, based on information in the text.
- The questions can be about the general meaning of the text or details in the text.
- Questions can also be about the writer's attitude, opinion or purpose.
- Some questions test your understanding of unfamiliar words and expressions in context and the use of reference words in the text.
- Each question is worth two marks.

Practice task

1 Read the first two paragraphs of an article about scientists in Antarctica. Ignore the highlighting. For questions 1 and 2, choose the answer (A, B, C or D) which you think fits best according to the text.

1 What point does the writer make about Antarctica in the first paragraph?
  - A It is an increasingly important place for scientific studies.
  - B It is a unique place.
  - C It shows us that we are not the most important thing on Earth.
  - D It is mostly British scientists who carry out research there.

2 The writer thinks that it was difficult for women to get jobs in Antarctica because
  - A only men had the physical strength to live in the extreme weather conditions.
  - B women were not attracted to the idea of living in such a remote place.
  - C women generally accepted the excuses they were given too easily.
  - D most people found it impossible to believe that women could live there.

How did you do?

2 Check your answers.

3 Look at the four highlighted parts of paragraph 1 of the article.

1 Match each highlighted part (1–4) with an option (A–D) in Ex 1 question 1.

2 Read the options and highlighted parts carefully. Which one matches the meaning exactly?

3 Why don't the others match?

4 Look at paragraph 2 in the article and the options in Ex 1 question 2 again.

1 Highlight the part of the text that relates to each option.

2 Read the options and highlighted parts carefully. Which one matches the meaning exactly?

3 Why don't the others match?

Flying over Antarctica is an unforgettable experience. [1]In all directions, there is nothing for thousands of kilometres except snow and ice. No houses, no inhabitants, just a vast wilderness [2]which serves to remind us that we are only a tiny part of the life on this planet of ours. Anja Davidson arrived there in a small, noisy aeroplane last October to take up her position as a researcher at Rothera, [3]the main British research station on the continent. Here, [4]scientists study, among other things, the effects of climate change, and Anja is one of a growing number of women who are slowly gaining access to this traditionally male-dominated environment.

Britain first established research stations in Antarctica in the 1940s, and, from the start, a no-women rule was strictly followed. As late as the 1960s, female scientists who applied for posts in Antarctica were banned from joining male colleagues on trips to the continent. Unbelievably, one female scientist received a rejection letter stating that there were no facilities for women in Antarctica, including no shops or hairdressers! This trivial-sounding excuse revealed a deeper, widely held belief that somehow Antarctica was only for men. This is not surprising when you consider that the history of the continent is made up of heroic accounts of adventurers like Robert Scott and Ernest Shackleton, tales in which courageous men relied on their strength and determination in a battle to survive. It was only in the 1980s that women finally overcame these prejudices and joined the teams of researchers in the remote stations.

TEACH

Strategies and skills
Identifying attitude and opinion

Questions often ask about the opinion, attitude or feelings of the writer. This is not usually stated directly in the text, but is expressed using different words.

1 Look at the extracts from reading texts and answer the questions.

> Although we were determined to give our all in the game, we were only too aware of the difficulty of beating our heavily favoured opponents.

1 Was the writer confident of winning? How do you know?

> When the band stepped out onto the stage a few minutes later, I couldn't believe the volume of noise the fans created as they cheered and screamed almost with one voice.

2 Was the writer surprised by the reaction of the audience? How do you know?

> After so many months of planning this once-in-a-lifetime trip, I couldn't help feeling that the reality didn't quite live up to my expectations.

3 Was the writer disappointed by the trip? How do you know?

> As the train journey continued, the child's behaviour became more and more outrageous, causing even more embarrassment to his mother and father. But I must admit I felt more sorry for the other passengers than I did for the parents, whose efforts to control their child seemed far from adequate.

4 Was the writer sympathetic to the parents? How do you know?

> The narrow bridge stretched across the valley, with a drop of around 20 metres to the river below. Although made only of wood and rope, the bridge looked reasonably solid, and I didn't hesitate to follow my fellow travellers across it.

5 Was the writer worried about crossing the bridge? How do you know?

2 Read the sentences (1–6) and choose the word (A–C) that best expresses the writer's opinion, attitude or feeling. Which words or expressions in the sentences confirm this?

1 After my third fall, I was beginning to think that maybe skiing wasn't for me and I should stick to something I was good at, like reading or cooking.
   A discouraged   **B** ashamed   **C** relieved

2 We sat through the play until the end out of a sense of duty, although by the time the final curtain fell the plot was as much of a mystery to us as it had been at the beginning.
   A annoyed   **B** suspicious   **C** confused

3 As we headed out away from the coast and into deeper water, and the small boat started to rock heavily with the movement of the waves, I began to wonder what the experience would be like.
   A determined   **B** unsure   **C** excited

4 Working in a small restaurant in Los Angeles definitely has its moments, like the day I walked out of the kitchen and was delighted to find that two well-known Hollywood actors were sitting at one of my tables, waiting to be served!
   A thrilled   **B** concerned   **C** proud

5 It was day five of the holiday, and, although the activities were interesting and fun, I must admit that some of the group members were definitely beginning to get on my nerves.
   A bored   **B** annoyed   **C** worried

6 As Ela started to talk about her qualifications and experience, I had to revise my opinion of her. Not many people could claim such a varied and interesting work history.
   A fascinated   **B** impressed   **C** jealous

SPEAKING BOOST

Discuss or answer.

1 Would you rather live somewhere very hot or very cold? Why?

2 In what ways can we use the power of nature to improve our lives?

Deducing the meaning of unfamiliar vocabulary

Some questions ask about unfamiliar words and phrases in the text. To answer these, you need to use the context to guess the meaning.

3 Look at the sentences and answer the questions.

1 I was alarmed to see **hordes** of angry-looking rugby fans all heading for the same train as me.

   Does the word **hordes** indicate a large number or a small number? How do you know?

2 After ten years, I was no further on with my ambition to become a professional singer, and found myself becoming more and more **disillusioned** with the entire music industry.

   Does the word **disillusioned** describe a positive or a negative feeling? How do you know?

3 After ten minutes of **beating about the bush**, I decided to take a more direct approach and asked: 'Are you interested in investing money in the business?'

   Does the phrase **beating about the bush** suggest discussing something in a direct or indirect way? How do you know?

4 Losing in any sport is disappointing, and each time you lose it becomes more difficult to **pick yourself up** and approach the next game with confidence and optimism.

   Does the verb **pick yourself up** refer to feeling better or feeling worse? How do you know?

5 Although I loved the educational side of university life, I found the social life difficult as I had a very limited amount of money to live on and couldn't keep up with my more **prosperous** friends.

   Does the word **prosperous** relate to money or educational ability? How do you know?

6 The final hotel we stayed in had its own gym and sauna, as well as much more comfortable rooms and an excellent restaurant, so it was definitely **a cut above the rest**.

   Does the phrase **a cut above the rest** indicate something positive or something negative?

4 Look at the extracts and choose the correct answers (A-D). How do you know?

> The stalls were crammed with attractive souvenirs, but I knew from the guidebook that we would find better bargains elsewhere, so I kept my wallet firmly in my pocket to avoid being ripped off.

1 The phrase 'ripped off' indicates that the writer
   A suspects that the prices in the market are too high.
   B does not feel safe in the market.
   C does not trust the advice given in the guidebook.
   D is keen to buy souvenirs.

> As I approached the kitchen, I could hear the muffled voices of Hugh and Dona coming from behind the closed door, but they were too unclear for me to tell whether they were arguing or just chatting.

2 The word 'muffled' suggests that the voices
   A sounded angry.
   B were very loud.
   C weren't easy to hear.
   D weren't in the kitchen.

> The company did well. Our products were new and innovative, and proved instantly popular. But we knew that we had to establish our brand quickly because it wouldn't take long for others to jump on the bandwagon with their own versions.

3 The phrase 'jump on the bandwagon' suggests that
   A the company's products would continue to be popular.
   B other companies would copy their ideas.
   C the company needed to keep developing new ideas.
   D their company would continue to grow quickly.

> I hadn't seen my aunt and uncle for at least 15 years, so I wasn't exactly thrilled when I was told they were coming to visit my city and I would have the dubious pleasure of showing them around.

4 The word 'dubious' suggests that the writer
   A was looking forward to seeing her aunt and uncle.
   B wasn't sure she would enjoy seeing her aunt and uncle.
   C felt bad about not meeting her aunt and uncle.
   D felt very excited at the thought of meeting her aunt and uncle.

Matching meaning

It is important to read the relevant part of the text very carefully to match the exact meaning in the text to the meaning in the correct answer.

5 Read the extracts carefully and decide if the sentences (A-D) are true or false, according to the text. How do you know?

> **TIP:** If an answer option mentions something that does not appear in the text, it cannot be the correct answer (or true, according to the text).

1   As we prepared for the race across the desert, one of our biggest challenges was to find suitable team members. Not only did they have to be physically fit, but they also had to have personalities and habits that wouldn't drive us mad.

   A   The writer wanted to find people to take part in a race.
   B   It was easy to find team members.
   C   Team members had to be strong and healthy.
   D   They needed team members that they could get on well with.

2   The Isle of Skye, off the northwest coast of Scotland, is fast becoming a victim of its own success. Having advertised its beautiful and remote landscape in an attempt to attract visitors, it now faces a crisis. Tourists are now flocking to the island in such numbers each year that they risk destroying the very peacefulness they hope to enjoy.

   A   The Isle of Skye never encouraged tourists.
   B   A lot of tourists now come to the island.
   C   The problem of too many visitors is now very serious.
   D   Tourists are damaging the beautiful landscape on the island.

3   The first indication we had that there were flying fish in the water was the occasional 'plop' as they dropped back below the surface. It was only a few moments later that Joe caught sight of some and called out excitedly to me. I turned my head to see a small group of them, as clear as day as they emerged from beneath the waves and then quickly returned.

   A   The writer was very excited to see the flying fish.
   B   The writer couldn't see the flying fish very clearly.
   C   They heard the flying fish before they saw them.
   D   The flying fish stayed out of the water for a long time.

4   It was her passion for landscape photography that first took Amber to Canada, and it was only a chance day trip on a sailing boat that gave her a first sighting of humpback and minke whales. But this encounter changed her life, and she resolved to play whatever part she could in bringing these magnificent creatures back from the verge of extinction.

   A   Amber's visit to Canada gave her an interest in photography.
   B   Amber travelled to Canada in order to see whales.
   C   Amber discovered a new interest during her time in Canada.
   D   Amber managed to take some wonderful photos of whales.

6 Read the first paragraph of an article about Jack Thomson's experience of studying an active volcano. Answer the questions (1-5).

VOLCANO **WATCH**

It was February 2012. I'd flown from London to Rwanda, driven nearly 200 kilometres through the Democratic Republic of the Congo on rough tracks, then fought my way on foot through eight exhausting kilometres of hot and humid rainforest to reach the Nyamuragira Volcano. I was a young researcher and this was my first experience of an active volcano. The thrill of finally arriving was mixed with a certain nervousness on realising the awesome natural power of what was in front of us. There was a fierce energy somehow in the air, and the low, steady rumble of explosions was accompanied by occasional terrifying bursts of smoke and flames. I was very relieved that I wasn't alone.

1   What do we learn about the writer's journey to the volcano?

2   Does the writer say how he felt during the journey?

3   What do we learn about the writer's background?

4   What emotions did the writer experience when he arrived at the volcano?

5   What signs were there that the volcano was active?

7 Now read the exam question about the paragraph in Ex 6 and choose the correct answer (A, B, C or D).

TIP: Words or ideas in the options often occur in the text, but this does not mean that the option is correct. They may be distractors, placed there to catch you out if you don't read the text carefully enough. Read the relevant part of the text very carefully to see if the meaning matches.

What was the writer's main impression when he arrived at the volcano?
A how uncomfortable the weather conditions were
B how relieved he was to finally be there
C how powerful and dangerous the volcano was
D how lonely he felt

Understanding reference words

Some questions ask about reference words in the text. To answer these, you need to read the part of the text before the reference word very carefully to find out which noun or verb the reference word refers back to.

TIP: The reference word is usually the subject or object of a verb. Think about which nouns make sense as the subject or object.

8 Look at the bold reference words in the extracts (1–3). Then look at the highlighted words. Answer the questions (A–C).

1 There were customers at all the tables, waiting patiently as skilful waiters hurried around handing **them** large plates of delicious-looking food.
A Who was handing out plates?
B Who were they handing the plates to?
C Which highlighted word does '**them**' refer to?

2 There was a slight mist in the air as we headed for the truck to go on our tiger-watching trip, but **that** only added to the sense of excitement that we felt.
A How does the writer feel about the trip?
B What made that feeling stronger?
C Which highlighted word does '**that**' refer to?

3 Young people queue up each year to take part in TV talent shows, dreaming of the chance to become celebrities, but very **few** ever achieve their ambitions.
A Who wants to become celebrities?
B Who wants to achieve their ambitions?
C Which highlighted word does '**few**' refer to?

9 Look at the extracts and choose the correct answer (A–D).

TIP: Reference words always refer back to earlier nouns or verbs, not to later nouns or verbs.

Working as a newly qualified teacher can be daunting. Lesson preparation seems to take forever, and marking students' work is even more demanding on time. Then there is the huge issue of learning how to keep control of an uninterested and often unwilling class of teenagers. It takes years to achieve **this** and become a confident and effective teacher.

1 What does '**this**' refer to?
A preparing lessons
B keeping control of the class
C marking students' work
D becoming a confident and effective teacher

'How do I get to your house?' I asked. 'Just go along the main road until you get to the traffic lights, then turn left. **It**'s simple,' Ana replied. 'You could get the bus if you don't want to walk.'

2 What does '**it**' refer to?
A getting to Ana's house
B going along the main road
C turning left
D getting the bus

Life is not easy for young actors. Well-paid jobs are few and far between, and most theatre companies don't offer regular contracts. For this reason, **many** give up and turn to alternative careers.

3 What does '**many**' refer to?
A careers
B theatre companies
C actors
D contracts

The ultimate challenge

The ultramarathon in the Amazon is one of the toughest footraces in the world. You run 230 kilometres over four days through dense jungle, carrying your kit on your back, in temperatures up to 30 degrees. Why would anyone want to do this? Of course, there's a competitive element, and most runners have at least some desire to win. There's also the personal satisfaction of pushing your body to its limits. But these are secondary to the main motivation, which is simply the pleasure of running. This is what really drives people to compete in these extreme events.

My running career had followed a fairly established path, graduating from a relaxed 5k in my local park to a half marathon and, finally, what I saw at the time as my ultimate challenge, the New York Marathon. Except that when I crossed the finish line, **it** didn't feel like such a big achievement. I'd trained so well and got so fit that running 42 kilometres no longer felt like a big deal, and I felt I needed more. A friend suggested an ultramarathon, so I signed up for one in the Amazon.

My training programme involved running in the heat and rain as well as building up my fitness. One challenge was to get used to running with a backpack. I knew I would have to carry at least 2.5 litres of water every day, and that's a lot of weight! Luckily, the human body can adapt quickly. Covering more kilometres in a day wasn't a huge problem for me. But the tough thing about ultra-running is getting up day after day and persuading your tired, aching body to perform again. This was what really tested me.

> ## "Why would anyone want to do this?"

I arrived at the base camp on 31 May, three days before the start of the race. My journey there had been long but fairly straightforward, and I had got a reasonable amount of rest along the way. The tents provided for us were quite big and fairly comfortable. The weather wasn't brilliant, but the forecast was good, so it wasn't a huge concern. I spent a lot of time over those few days chatting to the other competitors, comparing notes about training and experience. They were all very friendly and keen to offer help and support, which I hadn't expected. Then it was time for the race itself.

I knew I would have to deal with running over rough ground, with lots of ups and downs and sometimes in the dark. I was also well prepared for the psychological highs and lows, the inner battle that all runners experience, with one voice in your head telling you to just give up and go home, while the other urges you forward. What I **hadn't bargained for** was the physical effect of running with wet feet, due to the many streams we had to cross. My feet were sore and bleeding by the end of day one. In the end, though, it was my legs that let me down. On the third day, they simply couldn't do any more and I had to stop.

Of course, failing at anything is not as good as winning, but, to my mind, having a go at one of the toughest challenges in the world, even if it ends in failure, is hardly something to be ashamed of. I travelled home with no medal, but by no means defeated. And when friends asked me, 'Are you going to try an ultramarathon again?' I had no hesitation in saying 'no'. I am not sorry that I took part, but have accepted that I have my limits and in future I will be happy to stick to standard marathons!

You are going to read an article about a woman's experience of preparing for an extreme marathon. For questions 1–6, choose the answer (A, B, C or D) which you think fits best according to the text.

1 According to the writer, people take part in ultramarathons mainly because
   A they are determined to win.
   B they find them enjoyable.
   C they want to see how much their body can achieve.
   D they want to prove that they can do it.

2 The word 'it' in line 20 refers to
   A the writer's running career.
   B a big achievement.
   C completing the New York Marathon.
   D training so well.

3 Which part of training for the ultramarathon did the writer find the most difficult?
   A learning to run while carrying a heavy weight
   B running much longer distances
   C learning to run even when she was exhausted
   D practising running in difficult weather conditions

4 How did the writer feel at the base camp, before the race?
   A tired after a difficult journey
   B surprised at the attitude of other runners
   C disappointed about the accommodation
   D worried about the weather conditions

5 The phrase 'hadn't bargained for' (line 57) suggests that running with wet feet
   A caused some unexpected problems.
   B was not a particularly difficult challenge.
   C had been part of the writer's training.
   D was not as unpleasant as the writer expected.

6 What feeling does the writer have now?
   A determination to succeed in an ultramarathon one day
   B pride at having taken part
   C disappointment at having failed to complete the race
   D regret at trying to do something too challenging

ABOUT THE TASK

- In Reading and Use of English Part 6, you read one long text with six gaps.
- The missing sentences that fill these gaps are written below the text, but not in the correct order.
- There is also a seventh sentence which does not fit any of the gaps in the text – this is called a distractor.

- You have to decide which of the seven sentences fits each of the six gaps.
- To do the task, you need to understand the flow of a text, and understand how sentences refer back to earlier ideas in the paragraph or the text and forward to the next ideas.
- Each question is worth two marks.

Practice task

1 Read part of an article about education outdoors. Two sentences have been removed from the article. Choose from the sentences A–C the one which fits each gap. There is one extra sentence which you do not need to use.

How did you do?

2 Check your answers.

3 Look at the article again with the missing sentences added. Match the bold parts of the highlighted sentences to words and ideas they refer back to in the previous sentence.

Getting out of the classroom

A group of excited children run along the beach, enthusiastically collecting pieces of wood and other rubbish. But this isn't the summer holidays, and the adults accompanying them aren't their parents, but their teachers. The kids are attending a beach school. **(1)** _____ Children learn about the beach environment and also do a range of fun activities like building fires and producing art from whatever the tide has washed onto the shore.

The idea of outdoor learning is not new. Forest schools have been popular since they were first introduced in the 1990s. And outdoor learning is about a lot more than just having fun in the fresh air. Parents and teachers have observed that children who learn outdoors become more confident and independent. **(2)** _____ Forest and beach schools are so far limited to primary-age children. But there are many opportunities for teenagers to enjoy similar experiences and benefits at summer camps.

A group of excited children run along the beach, enthusiastically collecting pieces of wood and other rubbish. But this isn't the summer holidays, and the adults accompanying them aren't their parents, but their teachers. The kids are attending a beach school. **This new kind of outdoor teaching establishment** started recently in some parts of the UK and is already proving popular. Children learn about the beach environment and also do a range of fun activities like building fires and producing art from whatever the tide has washed onto the shore.

The idea of outdoor learning is not new. Forest schools have been popular since they were first introduced in the 1990s. And outdoor learning is about a lot more than just having fun in the fresh air. Parents and teachers have observed that children who learn outdoors become more confident and independent. **They** are **also** more likely to pay attention and achieve good results academically. Forest and beach schools are so far limited to primary-age children. But there are many opportunities for teenagers to enjoy similar experiences and benefits at summer camps.

A They are also more likely to pay attention and achieve good results academically.

B There are, however, some disadvantages to attempting to conduct classes outside.

C This new kind of outdoor teaching establishment started recently in some parts of the UK and is already proving popular.

Strategies and skills

Understanding reference devices

To decide whether a sentence fits a gap, you need to understand pronouns and other words that refer back to words or ideas earlier in the text.

1 Look at the bold words in the extracts. Match them to the words or ideas they refer back to in the previous sentence.

> **TIP:** Some pronouns and reference words can refer back to a whole idea, not just a single word.

1 The population of urban foxes in London is now estimated to have reached over 30,000. Although **they** are a familiar sight in all parts of the city centre, not everyone feels comfortable with their presence.

2 In 1768, Captain Cook set off on his first voyage of exploration, to the South Pacific island of Tahiti. It was **here** that he carried out observations on the stars, designed to help calculate the distance of the Sun from the Earth.

3 There are many popular myths concerning diet and exercise. **One of the most widely believed** is that limiting food intake to the first half of the day only will help with faster weight loss.

4 One useful tip for travellers is to keep your money, valuables and documents in different places. **Doing so** means that you reduce your risk of losing all of them at the same time.

5 By this time, there were hundreds of tons of crude oil covering the beach and the race was on to clear it all up. **This** was far too challenging a task for the small coastal community alone.

2 Look at the bold words in Ex 1 again. Which ones refer to

1 a place? _____
2 an idea? _____
3 people or animals? _____
4 an action? _____ , _____

3 Look at the pronouns and reference words in sentences A and B. Decide which one can follow on from each extract (1–4). Why is the other sentence incorrect?

1 Two commonly held beliefs about sleep were that it was more important for the body than the mind, and that people could train themselves to need less sleep.

A Both of these turned out to be wrong.
B Their ideas didn't stand up to scientific investigation, however.

2 It is thought that ice cream was first made by the ancient Persians in about 500 BCE, when ice was combined with flavours to produce a sweet treat.

A This one was very popular in Europe in the 1500s.
B It first reached Europe in the 1500s.

3 One strategy for finding wild mushrooms is to identify suitable places through the summer, when the weather is fine.

A You can go back there in the autumn, when mushrooms are likely to appear.
B This is the perfect place to find them once autumn comes around.

4 Cross-country skiing has the advantage that you see a lot more of the mountains, rather than being confined to a few well-worn ski runs.

A Here, you can enjoy skiing for less money, and without the dangers.
B It is also easier and cheaper, and there is less risk of accidents.

SPEAKING BOOST

Discuss or answer.

1 How do you improve your mood when you feel a bit down?
2 In what ways does social media make us happy and unhappy?

Text structure and cohesion

A sentence that fits a gap often adds more information to something that has been mentioned before, or may introduce a new idea which is mentioned again in the following sentence.

4 Match each second sentence (a–f) to the sentence it follows (1–6).

> **TIP:** The correct sentence for a gap often adds a similar or contrasting idea to the previous sentence.

1 His talent for acting has propelled him to fame and made him a household name.

2 June is a great time to visit because the sea is warm and the weather is generally settled.

3 The downstairs rooms had been completely modernised and redecorated.

4 Robots can certainly help children with learning in the classroom.

5 The island is dotted with a number of fascinating ancient sites.

6 From a distance, the rock looks completely bare.

a September is equally beautiful, and a little less crowded, too.

b However, upstairs, much of the original décor was still intact.

c It has also won him ten awards.

d Yet on closer inspection, you can see it is actually covered in tiny plants.

e But can they ever cope with the complexities of managing a large group of children?

f As well as these attractions, it is also home to many rare species of birds.

5 Look at sentences a–f in Ex 4 again. Which ones add a similar idea, and which add a contrasting idea? Which words tell you this?

6 Read the sentences (1–6) about plastic pollution. Choose the correct similar or contrasting idea (a–f) to follow each one. Use pronouns and reference words to help you.

1 For the last 40 years, plastic has been accumulating in the oceans.

2 It is possible to recycle some kinds of plastic.

3 Understanding of the issue of plastic pollution has certainly increased recently.

4 Plastic is widely used in packaging and in everyday items that we buy.

5 Many people now choose reusable drinks bottles rather than disposable ones.

6 Alternatives to plastic are available for manufacturers.

a However, this awareness has done little to resolve the actual problems.

b They increasingly choose to buy from packaging-free shops, too.

c It has also begun washing up on our beaches.

d But these materials tend to be more expensive and more difficult to work with.

e In addition to this, plastic fibres form part of many of the clothes that we wear.

f Other kinds, however, cannot be reprocessed into new products.

It is important to recognise how different phrases link ideas in texts.

7 Choose the correct words to link the second sentence to the first.

> **TIP:** The missing sentence may add extra details about something that has been mentioned before, or it may give a reason for something.

1 When choosing the best university for you, location and price are obviously extremely important. **Other factors to consider are / The next one is** the range of courses on offer and the number of teaching hours per week.

2 The fear of heights is not restricted to a feeling you get when peering over the edge of a very tall building. **This is because / In extreme cases**, it can prevent people from doing simple everyday things like going upstairs.

3 Chess has been shown to improve concentration levels in children and teenagers. **Instead of this / This is why** some schools are introducing it as part of their weekly lesson plans.

4 Young people with hearing difficulties often find it difficult to hear well in noisy environments such as cafés. **Other problems include / This means that** they can find themselves unable to join in normal social activities.

5 It is definitely a good idea to avoid screen time for an hour before you go to bed. **This is because / Doing so means** the blue light that screens give off can interfere with your body's natural urge to sleep.

8 Link the sentences with the phrases from the box.

TIP: Before you decide if a sentence is correct, read it carefully with the sentences that come both before and after. Do the sentences all make sense together?

> In some cases   My favourite is   That is why
> This is because   What fascinated me more was

1 We are far more likely to laugh when we are with other people than when we are alone. _____ laughter is essentially a social activity.

2 There are ten main museums in the city. _____ the Museum of Fashion because of the range of clothing and accessories it has on display.

3 These spiders can give a very nasty bite. _____ , it can even prove fatal.

4 I found his reluctance to talk a little odd. _____ his apparent lack of interest in the people around him.

5 Dolphins are highly intelligent animals. _____ many people believe it is wrong to keep them in captivity.

Rephrasing, exemplifying and commenting

A sentence that fills a gap sometimes rephrases something that has been said in a previous sentence, or it may add an example or a comment about something that has been mentioned.

TIP: Writers can use adverbs or adjectives to show their attitude. For example, they might use a comment adverb such as **unfortunately**, or they might use a phrase such as **It was unfortunate that …**

9 Choose the correct phrase to link the second sentence to the first.

1 After six months, the business was still struggling to make even a small profit and I was beginning to doubt whether it had a future. **In other words, / For example,** I realised it was time to move on.

2 I asked Jake many times to come walking with us but he always seemed to have an excuse. **Clearly, / Fortunately,** hiking wasn't his thing.

3 It is well known that colours can have a profound effect on our mood. **For instance, / It is lucky that** blue can make us feel calmer and more relaxed.

4 My brother was not at all like me, and our very different personalities often led to conflicts. **To put it simply, / Interestingly,** we didn't get on.

5 The number of people choosing to cycle to work has been increasing steadily. **For example, / Luckily,** in London the number has more than doubled in the last decade.

6 We continued our clean-up of the beach over the next few weeks, removing at least twenty bags of rubbish a day. **It was frustrating that / To put it another way,** more trash appeared on the beach with each incoming tide, and we felt our job would never be done.

10 Choose the sentence (A or B) which best follows each first sentence (1–5). What phrase helped you decide?

1 Coming up to the surface too quickly after a deep-sea dive can be dangerous.
   A But the most exciting thing is being alone in that underwater world.
   B In extreme cases, it can lead to death.

2 As well as being fun to drive, these compact electric scooters are light and easy to carry.
   A Other features include a powerful battery which lasts for at least ten hours.
   B For instance, cities like Paris have actively encouraged their use as a green form of transport.

3 I wasn't particularly keen to spend hours walking around the markets of Fez and trying to avoid buying cheap souvenirs.
   A What interested me more was the idea of visiting its public library, which is over 1,000 years old.
   B Unfortunately, we didn't get as much time for sightseeing as I would have liked.

4 Carl knew that an injury of this type would take at least two or three years to recover from, by which time he would be nearly 30 and unlikely to get back into the team.
   A Fortunately, treatments for such injuries have improved a lot in recent years.
   B In other words, he realised that his professional career was over.

5 After months of carefully studying maps and deciding on the best routes, we finally set out on our big adventure, armed with a selection of guide books and phrase books, and full of excitement for our round-the-world-trip.
   A Unfortunately, things didn't go quite according to plan, and the difficulties started as soon as we got to the airport.
   B For example, we found it incredibly difficult to decide which countries to visit and which to leave off the list.

> **SPEAKING BOOST**

Discuss or answer.

1 Are films getting better as technology develops? In what ways?

2 Talk about an animation film that you like.

You are going to read an article about computers and art. Six sentences have been removed from the article. Choose from the sentences A-G the one which fits each gap. There is one extra sentence you do not need to use.

Can COMPUTERS become ARTISTS?

Machines already perform a lot of tasks that used to be done by humans. They can build our cars and do complex calculations for us, even mark our exam papers. But now it seems that ever more intelligent machines are straying into areas where we never imagined they would go. We have always liked to think of ourselves as having a unique kind of intelligence that machines could never match, one which allows us to think of new ideas and produce creative and artistic works. But it seems that even here, computers are lining up to compete with us.

Of course, machines can easily be trained to do the physical work of producing art. **(1)** _____ It had been programmed to look at a photographic image and then reproduce this on paper as a painting, using a range of different brush strokes. But now it seems machines are going a step further.

In 2018, the New York auction house Christie's sold a painting for $432,000. The painting, entitled 'Portrait of Edmond de Belamy', shows a blurred image of a young man, and what made it unusual was that the idea, as well as the image itself, was produced entirely by a computer. There were of course humans giving instructions to the computer. **(2)** _____ Their aim was simply to show that computers can be creative.

So, how do you 'teach' a computer to be creative? In the case of art, it seems that the answer is fairly simple. You program it to search for and scan thousands of similar images online. **(3)** _____ It can then use this information to create something similar to, but distinct from, all the others it has scanned.

Some artists are now working with computers to produce a new kind of art. In one project, an artist programmed a computer to search for images of birds of the kinds that he saw regularly around the British coast. The computer, of course, did not know what species it was looking for, but it made a selection and formed these into a single image. **(4)** _____ It was then filmed in its natural surroundings, and the result is a work which shows how the real world and the machine world can work side by side.

These computer-generated works are certainly interesting, and they make us think about the limits of what machines can and cannot do. **(5)** _____ Some enthusiasts would argue they do, and the collectors willing to pay high prices for these works would suggest that there is definitely a market for computer art. Others, however, would disagree.

Many 'real' artists would claim that art is an expression of human intelligence and human emotions. **(6)** _____ These things, they argue, are part of being human and can never be produced by a machine. So the 'Portrait of Edmond de Belamy' may look convincing from a distance. But when you get closer, you can see that although it has the shape of a human, the eyes show no human feelings – because only a human can see and represent these.

A   This enables it to build up a store of data about the features the images have in common.

B   But not everyone would accept that they qualify as art.

C   In 2009, a painting robot known as e-David was created at the University of Konstanz in Germany.

D   They were a group of young French artists, who worked together under the collective name Obvious.

E   It is true to say that artists are becoming increasingly interested in working with computers to produce works of art.

F   More importantly, it is about a desire to communicate with other people.

G   This was taken and placed on the mud close to where the living ones feed.

ABOUT THE TASK

- In Reading and Use of English Part 7, you read one long text which is divided into different sections, or up to six shorter texts all on the same topic.

- There are ten questions to answer. These state information or ideas taken from the text or texts. You have to match each question or statement to the correct section of the long text, or the relevant short text.

- Questions can be about detailed information in the text, or about the writer's attitude or opinion. Remember, the information or opinions will be phrased in different ways in the questions and the text.

- Each question is worth one mark.

Practice task

1 Read the first two parts of an article about organising surprises for people. For questions 1–4, choose from the sections (A or B). The sections may be chosen more than once.

Which writer

1 was accused of breaking the law? _____

2 failed to persuade a family member to do things differently? _____

3 wishes she had been more forceful in expressing her concerns? _____

4 felt happier after revealing the secret? _____

SURPRISE!

Some people love surprises, but keeping a surprise secret isn't always easy. Two people tell us about their experiences.

A KATYA

It was my sister-in-law Tara's birthday, and my brother was keen to organise a surprise party for her. I tried to discourage him, on the grounds that most people actually prefer to know about these things in advance, but he refused to change his mind. So I was allocated the task of keeping Tara busy in town, while friends and family members prepared food and decorated the house. I thought it would be pretty straightforward, but Tara is a police officer and knows when people aren't telling the truth. After three hours of listening to excuse after excuse about why we should visit yet another shoe shop, she finally confronted me with: 'What's going on?' To my huge relief, I was forced to tell the truth. Once we'd had a good laugh, we thoroughly enjoyed the rest of the day, and I think she was secretly relieved not to have a party sprung on her out of the blue.

B HELEN

Everyone in my family loves surprises, including me. But things went horribly wrong when we tried to organise a surprise weekend in Paris to celebrate my cousin Jenna's graduation. My aunt had organised everything – someone would take Jenna to the airport, pretending that they were meeting a friend who was flying in. All I had to do was go into her flat, pick up her passport and pack a few suitable clothes, then join the others at the airport. It sounded simple, but I was uneasy at the idea of going into my cousin's flat when no one was there. I should have spoken up, because it turned out I was right to be worried. A neighbour spotted me searching through my cousin's wardrobe and reported what she thought was a break-in. Two hours later, I was finally released, but by this time we had all missed the flight. Luckily, everyone saw the funny side, and we had a big family meal together instead!

How did you do?

2 Check your answers.

3a Look at the two extracts (a and b) from Katya's story. Match each extract with an option (2 or 4) in Ex 1.

KATYA

a I tried to discourage him, on the grounds that most people actually prefer to know about these things in advance, but he refused to change his mind.

b To my huge relief, I was forced to tell the truth. Once we'd had a good laugh, we thoroughly enjoyed the rest of the day, and …

3b Check the answers to Ex 3a, then choose the correct words to complete sentences 1–3.

1 The extracts **use / don't use** the same words as the options.

2 The correct meaning is given in **a few words / a whole chunk** of the text.

3 You sometimes have to guess from **your own knowledge / the context** that the option matches.

4a Look at Helen's story again. Find the parts that match options 1 and 3 in Ex 1.

4b Check your answers to Ex 4a, then answer the questions (1–3).

1 Do the answers occur in the text in the same order as the options?

2 How do we know Helen 'wishes she had been more forceful'? What were her concerns?

3 What parts of the story suggest that she was accused of breaking the law?

Strategies and skills
Reading for specific information

To do this task, you don't need to read the whole text first. Read each option in turn and scan all the sections of the text to find a part that might match. Then read carefully to find the specific information you need.

> **TIP:** Practise scanning texts for particular words or ideas so you can find the part of a text that you need quickly.

1 Scan each text (1–3) quickly and find the specific information.

1 Read about preparing for sports events. Find a mention of **a mistake**.

> I've always been a fairly active person, so when a friend challenged me to enter a marathon with him, I decided to give it a go. I set about my preparations with great enthusiasm, drawing up schedules of training runs to increase my fitness and speed. I had done quite a bit of research on the physical and mental preparation necessary. But I forgot the most important rule: don't overtrain too early on. I picked up an injury on only my third week of training, and had to drop out, much to my disappointment.

2 Read about an experience of travelling. Find a mention of **an outdoor activity**.

> Spending three months travelling around Italy was an amazing experience. From the sleepy hilltop villages to the famous cities like Florence and Venice, everything had an unbelievable charm. I can honestly say I enjoyed every minute, from exploring the ancient ruins of Rome to spending three days hiking in the beautiful Tuscan landscape. And everywhere I went, the day would end with a delicious meal and an interesting conversation.

3 Read a story about performing in public. Find a mention of **a negative experience**.

> The curtain rose and the show got off to an excellent start. The opening songs went down well with the audience and no one put a foot wrong in the tricky dance routines. The applause encouraged us all, and we were beginning lose our pre-show nerves. Disaster struck when it came to my first solo number and the words completely went out of my head. Of course, everyone was very supportive, but I must say the memory of that put me off acting for months. Luckily, the audience didn't seem to mind.

2 Scan three extracts about popular cities to visit. Find the information 1–6 quickly.

> **TIP:** The information you are looking for does not necessarily occur in order in the texts.

Which text mentions

1 places to eat? _____
2 cultural activities? _____
3 an attraction outside the city? _____
4 a pleasant smell? _____
5 public transport? _____
6 taking photos? _____

A Paris is beautiful at all times of year, whether a sunny spring morning or a dull November afternoon. It's a city which just invites you to wander around, taking in the sights and sounds around you. And you'll be spoilt for choice when it comes to choosing somewhere to sit outside in the sunshine and enjoy a delicious lunch. Or, if you're looking for somewhere a bit quieter, why not try the Jardin des Plantes. If you're lucky enough to visit in June, you can take in the glorious scent of the roses.

B There are so many wonderful things to see in Barcelona that it's hard to know where to start. Of course, the amazing buildings are at the top of most visitors' lists, and rightly so. Make sure you take advantage of the excellent metro system to get around the city quickly. The other big attraction, especially in the summer, is the fact that Barcelona is on the coast. It's definitely worth considering a trip beyond the city limits for a day, to find some outstanding beaches.

C Exploring the well-known landmarks of New York can give first-time visitors the feeling of being on a movie set. So many of the squares, buildings and parks have featured in famous movies that it almost feels as if you already know the city. Make sure you get a few selfies to impress your friends! You also need to find time for the New York shopping experience, and, of course, there's no better city for an exciting evening out watching a play or a musical. I guarantee a long weekend will leave you feeling you must come back!

SPEAKING BOOST

Discuss or answer.

1 Describe the plot from a film or book that involves a lie.
2 What kinds of things do young children lie about?

Understanding implication

Sometimes, an exact meaning is not stated openly in the text: it is implied. However, you can infer the meaning (work out what is meant) from what the text says.

3 Look at the extracts (1–6) and choose the one thing (A–C) for each that you can infer from what the writer says.

1 I'd always loved sailing, so when I saw an advert asking for volunteers to work on a large yacht during the summer vacation, I jumped at the chance to apply.

The writer …
- **A** had no difficulty in getting a summer job.
- **B** found a summer job which suited her perfectly.
- **C** had always wanted to work on a yacht.

2 My website wasn't getting many hits, so I contacted a friend who was into film-making and asked if he'd help me make a few short videos to upload to it.

The writer …
- **A** was interested in film-making.
- **B** was very disappointed in the website.
- **C** made a decision to improve the website.

3 Preparing for a six-month backpacking trip requires some hard decisions, wherever you're planning to go. You have to look at everything you'd like to take with you and ask yourself: 'Do I really need this?'

The writer mentions …
- **A** the need to travel light when backpacking.
- **B** the importance of planning a route carefully.
- **C** the need for good decision-making when travelling.

4 A lot of my friends at university came from wealthy backgrounds, so had as much financial help as they needed. They could afford a decent place to live and expensive nights out whenever they wanted. It wasn't quite that simple for me.

The writer …
- **A** was extremely unhappy at university.
- **B** had some money worries as a student.
- **C** spent too much money socialising at university.

5 I realised I had just given up a steady job with a good income in order to throw myself into the world of acting, with all its uncertainties. What was I thinking?

The writer …
- **A** is confident of success as an actor.
- **B** has doubts about her decision to leave her job.
- **C** is aware of her lack of experience as an actor.

6 I opened the door and cast my eyes over the small, one-room flat with its hard bed and bare walls. Was this really going to be my home for the next six months? Still, at least I had my new job to look forward to.

The writer mentions …
- **A** a feeling of nervousness about a new job.
- **B** a feeling of disbelief about a new opportunity.
- **C** a feeling of disappointment about accommodation.

Paraphrasing in questions

The questions often use paraphrasing to express the exact meaning in the text in a different way.

> **TIP:** More than one extract or part of the text might mention an idea. Once you have scanned and found the ideas, you need to read those parts of the text carefully to match the exact meaning.

4 Read the pairs of extracts below carefully and answer the questions.

1 Read two extracts (A and B) about experiences of exciting sports.
- **a** Find a dangerous situation in each extract.
- **b** Find one dangerous situation which could have been avoided.

A Skiing is already an exciting sport, but getting away from the main ski runs and finding your own way back down the mountain raises the level even more. But you do have to be careful. Last year, I was out on the mountain with some friends when heavy snow started coming down. We were concerned about losing our way and getting stuck on the mountain overnight. This was when I realised I should have checked the weather forecast more carefully before we set out. Fortunately, it ended well and we got back to our base before dark.

B Nothing can beat the thrill of rock climbing – seeing a high cliff in front of you and knowing that you are going to use all your strength and skills to reach the top. It's important to remember the sport has risks. Last month, I was out with a group. We had all the proper safety equipment, and we all knew how to bang the metal pins into the rock to attach our ropes to. But we weren't sure of the best route to climb, and some parts of the rock looked too soft to hold our ropes securely. Luckily, our instructor made the decision to abandon the climb before we got too far up.

2 Read two extracts (C and D) about life at university.
- **a** Find a mention of social life in each extract.
- **b** Find one mention of social events which are less expensive than the person expected.

C I'd heard so many different accounts of university life before I went that I wasn't quite sure what to expect. Some of my friends had complained about the lack of money, while others had found the academic work so challenging that they almost considered giving up. I must admit I found the workload was much heavier than I'd expected. I seemed to have essays to write every week, and there certainly wasn't time for all the nights out that some of my friends had talked about. I doubt I'd have had enough money for that anyway!

D I didn't have any difficulty settling into university life. I'd spent quite a bit of time researching my course before I applied, so I had a good idea of what I was in for. I was slightly concerned that I might feel lonely, leaving my family and school friends behind, but I needn't have worried as my evenings were full in the first few weeks with countless 'meet and greet' get-togethers – all with discounts on the prices, which was a nice surprise. All in all, I soon realised that university life was definitely for me!

3 Read two extracts (E and F) about people who work in the world of fashion.
- **a** Find a mention of qualifications in each extract.
- **b** Find one mention of the fact that qualifications alone won't get you a job.

E Stefan Corelli is a fashion photographer for a leading fashion house in Milan. Although he says the work is hard and involves long hours, it also has quite a few plus sides, like visiting exotic locations to do shoots. Stefan says he had originally intended to be a wildlife photographer, which is why he studied for a degree in photography. However, his final year project involved some fashion photoshoots, and he decided this was the career for him and applied for a post as soon as he left college.

F Ruby Adams works as a fashion designer for a small fashion house in London. Although she admits she would prefer to work for a top-name company, she's very happy to be using her design skills. After graduating from college with a BA in fashion design, she expected to start work quite quickly. However, she soon found that a degree wasn't in itself enough to get her noticed by employers, and she needed to do a few seasons as a volunteer helper at fashion shows before a career opportunity came along.

SPEAKING BOOST

Discuss or answer.

1 Talk about a time when the weather spoiled your plans.
2 British people are known for talking about the weather. Is there an equivalent stereotype of people from your country?

Recognising attitude and opinion

Some questions ask you to identify the writer's attitude or opinion. Look out for words and expressions that express feelings or opinions.

5 Look at the extracts (A–F) and match them to the attitudes and opinions (1–6).

Which writer

1 expresses a regret? _____
2 gives a warning? _____
3 expresses an initial doubt? _____
4 makes a recommendation? _____
5 expresses a criticism? _____
6 expresses surprise? _____

A A few years ago, I was invited to trek across the Pyrenees with a couple of friends. Although I'm a very keen hiker, I was slightly cautious about taking on such a challenging walk. However, my friends soon won me round and I agreed.

B I had always got on well with all my colleagues, so I was shocked when my boss called me into her office one day and told me that someone had made a complaint about me.

C It was an amazing trip and I've got lots of wonderful memories, and photos to remind me of them. I spent far too much money, unfortunately, but that's the only thing I would change.

D The northwest of Scotland boasts some beautiful landscapes. If you've got some time on your hands, it's well worth taking the train up to Mallaig, as it's one of the best ways to enjoy the stunning scenery.

E I love watching live football, and there's nothing like the thrill of being part of a huge crowd. But I can't get over the behaviour of the fans. Five minutes into the game and people start shouting and screaming in ways they would never think of doing in other situations.

F The sales can be a great way to save money, as prices are often reduced by fifty percent or more. But make sure you know exactly what you want, or you're likely to end up spending a lot of money on things you never use.

You are going to read an article about people who have attended music festivals. For questions 1–10, choose from the sections (A–D). The sections may be chosen more than once.

Which writer

had not intended to attend the festival?	**1**
mentions a problem with unsuitable clothing?	**2**
is pleased to have chosen more expensive accommodation?	**3**
mentions a personal need for quiet time?	**4**
gives advice on how to prepare for the festival?	**5**
mentions enjoying the experience of being in a large crowd?	**6**
was surprised at the variety of music types?	**7**
regrets a lack of planning?	**8**
mentions a difficulty in choosing which acts to watch?	**9**
enjoyed spending relaxed time with friends?	**10**

FESTIVAL FEVER

It's that time of year again, when music fans are thinking about the festival season. Four people share their festival experiences with us.

A There's definitely something special about Glastonbury, which is why it continues to be so popular. As a first-timer, I found the worst thing was queuing up to get in, for over three hours, in the heat of the day. I was wearing jeans and heavy boots (just in case of rain!) and we had to walk over three kilometres to find our camping space! Seriously, Glastonbury is exhausting, so make sure you get plenty of sleep before you go. The stages are far apart and you'll find yourself on your feet most of the day. But somehow it's all worth it when you see the main headline acts. There's always a great selection. For me, the highlight was the Foo Fighters. The whole place was packed with people, which made for a totally crazy atmosphere – it was amazing to be in the middle of it, and they played brilliantly!

B I happened to be in Madrid this summer with some friends, so we decided at the last minute to check out the Mad Cool Festival. It's quite a new festival, so we didn't know much about it, but the list of big-name performers looked impressive. In fact, this turned out to be both a plus and a minus. Of course, it's amazing to see so many well-known bands, but it led to some tough choices when acts were scheduled at the same time. It also meant there wasn't much time for wandering around the smaller stages and coming across new favourite artists, or just chilling, away from the noise and all the fans. And because the numbers at this year's festival were so much higher than last year, there were long queues at the food and drink tents, which definitely didn't add to the fun!

C Coachella was my first festival experience and it was a real mixture of highs and lows. As well as the amazing music of every kind, the highs were meeting people from all over the world and chilling out with mates in beautiful surroundings – although it's in the desert, the campsite has green grass and palm trees. There are other sleeping options, too, if you're prepared to spend more! The lows were mainly the result of tiredness. Four days is a long time to go with very little sleep. And if you're camping, it's impossible to escape the music and crowds, which I found tough. Although I'd known for months that I wanted to go to Coachella, I wish I'd been more organised and bought my ticket in advance – buying on the day was really stressful. And I'll definitely pack more next time – four outfits is nowhere near enough!

D I'd always wanted to go the Isle of Wight Festival and now that I live closer to it, it seemed a shame not to try it. We decided to abandon camping and treat ourselves to a decent night's sleep in an eco-lodge at a nearby farm. Good decision! We also paid the extra for VIP tickets, which gave us access to better toilets and some of the nicer food and drink tents. I was expecting the acts to be mainly older, established bands, but in fact there was a bit of everything, from electronic to hard rock and rap, and some local talent, too. It's definitely a family-friendly festival, with so many rides that it was in danger of feeling more like a fairground than a festival. But the music was great, and I'd definitely go again.

ABOUT THE TASK

- Writing Part 1 is compulsory, so you have no choice in what you write about.
- The task asks you to write an essay for your teacher.
- You are given a question or statement and two ideas to write about. You have to discuss the question or statement using both of these ideas, and you have to add another new idea of your own.
- You have to agree/disagree with the question/statement, give opinions and reasons and reach a conclusion.

- It is important to include ideas that are relevant to the topic of the essay, to include the two ideas you are given and to add a new idea of your own.
- You should organise your essay into clear paragraphs and have an introduction and a conclusion.
- Your essay should be written in a formal or neutral style.
- You should try to use a variety of vocabulary and language structures.
- You need to write between 140 and 190 words.

Practice task

1 Read the essay task and write a first draft of your essay.

> In your English class you have been discussing the best way to learn a language. Now, your English teacher has asked you to write an essay.
>
> Write an essay using **all** the notes and giving reasons for your point of view.

> Many people think that the best way to learn a second language is in the classroom. Do you agree?
>
> **Notes**
> Write about:
>
> **1** travelling to the country
> **2** learning online
> **3** _____ (your own idea)

Write your **essay**.

How did you do?

2 Read your essay and answer the questions.

1 Does your draft include a clear introduction in the first paragraph?
2 Is the rest of your essay divided into clear paragraphs?
3 Does your draft include ideas about travelling?
4 Do you give your opinion about learning online?
5 Do you include your own idea?
6 Does your essay have a clear conclusion?
7 Do you use linkers to add ideas or contrast information?
8 Do you use any formal language?

3 Read the example essay below. How does it compare to your first draft?

The first paragraph is a general introduction which introduces the topic.

Linking words introduce contrasting ideas.

The writer uses formal language.

The writer adds a reason to support their opinion that classes are a good way to learn.

The final paragraph is the conclusion.

It is very important to learn different languages in the modern world. This essay will discuss the best ways to learn a new language.

It is clear that travelling to another country is an excellent way to improve your language skills. You have to speak the language every day, in order to communicate, and you can also make new friends. However, it is not always possible for people to do this, as it can be expensive.

Learning online has some advantages. There are lots of free lessons online and you can study when you want. But the disadvantage is that you are learning on your own and not speaking the language.

Another good way to learn a language is to go to a class in your own country. Classes are sociable and fun, and you get lots of practice of speaking.

All in all, I think travelling to live in a country is the best way to learn a language, but if this is not possible, a class is the next best option.

The second paragraph discusses the idea in the first note.

The next paragraph discusses the idea in the second note.

The next paragraph introduces your own idea.

In the conclusion, the writer expresses their own opinion.

172 words

Strategies and skills

Audience, structure and tone

It is important to structure your essay clearly. Use each paragraph to focus on just one idea. Only include ideas that are relevant, and remember to cover the two ideas in the task as well as your own idea.

> **TIP:** Your first paragraph should be an introduction and your final paragraph should be a conclusion.

1 Read the essay task and look at a student's notes. Match one idea to each paragraph in the paragraph plan.

In your English class you have been discussing the ways in which we use mobile phones. Now, your English teacher has asked you to write an essay.

Write an essay using **all** the notes and giving reasons for your point of view.

Some people think it is impossible to live in the modern world without a mobile phone. Do you agree?

Notes

Write about:

1 communicating with friends

2 work

3 _____ (your own idea)

---

1 People often need to check their emails when they are away from their office.

2 It would be difficult to make social arrangements without a phone.

3 A mobile phone could save your life if you have an accident.

4 Most people nowadays have a mobile phone.

Plan

Paragraph 1: Introduction _____

Paragraph 2: Communicating with friends _____

Paragraph 3: Work _____

Paragraph 4: My idea – staying safe _____

Paragraph 5: My opinion and conclusion

2 Read the example answer. Does it cover all the points in the essay task in Ex 1? What is the writer's conclusion?

Most people nowadays have a mobile phone, and it is difficult to imagine living without one. While in the past phones may have been a luxury, I believe they are now a necessity.

Firstly, phones allow people to communicate easily with each other and make social arrangements such as meeting friends. This is especially necessary nowadays because friends and family members do not live close to each other. Furthermore, sharing photos with friends is fun and enables people to build good relationships.

Another reason is that many people depend on their phones to do their jobs well. People are often required to check emails when they are away from their office, and being able to communicate in this way allows them to make important decisions more easily.

Lastly, phones can keep people safe. You can call for help if you are in danger, and your phone might even save your life if you have an accident as you can use it to call an ambulance.

In conclusion, I believe that mobile phones are necessary and it is not possible to live in the modern world without one.

3 Look at the example essay in Ex 2 again. Choose the correct words to complete the sentences about it.

1 The essay uses **formal / informal** language.

2 It **uses / doesn't use** contractions.

3 The tone is **serious / chatty**.

4 The essay is written for **a general / an academic** audience.

4 Match the informal words and phrases in bold in the sentences (1–6) with their more formal equivalents (a–f).

1 Doing exercises can help you **get better** from injuries.

2 Most children **get on well** with their siblings.

3 Watching nature programmes can **help** people to learn about the natural world.

4 It is difficult to **do well** without working hard.

5 Some people **find it hard** to make new friends.

6 When something becomes fashionable, the price **goes up**.

a have a good relationship

b struggle

c recover

d enable

e increases

f achieve success

Writing introductions and conclusions

5 **Choose two correct sentences (A–D) about introductions and two about conclusions in essays.**

1   An introduction should …
   A   start with a general statement about the topic.
   B   mention personal experiences.
   C   introduce the main ideas or opinions the writer will write about.
   D   give detailed information to support the ideas in the essay.

2   A conclusion should …
   A   introduce one or two new ideas.
   B   sum up the different arguments in the essay.
   C   mention personal experiences.
   D   express a personal opinion.

6 **Look at the essay question. Then choose the best introduction and the best conclusion (A–C). Why are they the best?**

> Some people believe it is better to watch films at the cinema, rather than at home. Do you agree?

1   **Introductions**
   A   I love going to the cinema with my friends. My favourite films are adventure films. But some of my friends prefer to watch films at home.
   B   Going to the cinema is quite expensive, and a lot of young people cannot afford it. On the other hand, anyone can watch a film at home.
   C   Going to a cinema and watching a film on the big screen is certainly enjoyable. However, in my opinion, there are also benefits to watching films at home, with friends.

2   **Conclusions**
   A   On balance, some people enjoy watching films at the cinema, and others like to stay at home and watch. There are many reasons for this, for example it is cheaper to watch films at home.
   B   In conclusion, watching films at home with a few friends is a relaxing and sociable experience. However, I believe it is worth going to the cinema to see films that have a lot of special effects, as these look much more impressive on the big screen.
   C   To sum up, I don't often go to the cinema because it is too far from my home. But I really enjoy watching movies at home with my friends.

Connecting ideas in a paragraph

Linkers help to structure your ideas by showing whether ideas support each other or give a contrast.

> **TIP:** Remember that different linkers are used in different ways in sentences. Learn how to use each one.

7 **Choose the correct linkers to add or contrast ideas in the sentences.**

1   **While / However / Despite** team sports are enjoyable for many people, others prefer to do sports on their own.

2   Parks provide a safe environment for children to play **also / too / as well as** giving older people a place where they can meet friends and relax.

3   Fashionable clothes are often extremely expensive. **As well, / Although / In addition to this,** fashions change quickly, so people have to replace their clothes regularly.

4   Tourism can bring a lot of benefits to a place. **Although, / However, / Even though,** it can also create problems.

5   **Despite / Instead / However** there being lots of interesting things to do in a city, there are also some disadvantages to living in an urban environment.

6   I believe that students benefit greatly from having a long summer holiday. **Furthermore, / Too, / As well,** teachers also need time to relax between terms.

Language for structuring your essay

Using phrases to help structure your essay helps to make your ideas clearer to read.

8 **Add the phrases for structuring an essay to the lists below. Then find the phrases that the writer uses in the essay in Ex 2.**

> All in all,   Another reason is   Finally,   Firstly,
> First of all,   In conclusion,   Lastly,
> Last but not least,   Next,   Secondly,
> The first reason is   To sum up,

Introducing the first point:

Introducing further points:

Introducing the last point:

Introducing your conclusion:

9 Choose the best words and phrases to structure part of an essay.

I think it is extremely important to do exercise every week. ¹**All in all, / First of all,** exercise keeps your body healthy because it makes your heart stronger. ²**Another reason is that / Last but not least,** it improves your mood, so can help you to feel confident and motivated. ³**Finally, / Next,** doing exercise can be a good way to meet new friends, especially if you join a gym.

⁴**Lastly, / To sum up,** I would say that there are many different advantages to doing exercise, and it should be a regular part of everyone's life.

Complex sentences

In formal writing, such as an essay, try to avoid simple sentences. Join simple sentences together into more complex sentences. Use linkers, relative clauses and conjunctions.

10 Join the simple sentences together to make complex sentences. Use the words in brackets.

1   I think that people should eat less meat. It is bad for the environment.
    I think that _____ bad for the environment. (**as**)

2   There are a lot of facilities in cities. There aren't many in villages.
    There are _____ in villages. (**more**)

3   It is possible to study at home. You don't need to go to a class.
    It is possible _____ to a class. (**rather than**)

4   Travel teaches you a lot. I think all young people should be encouraged to travel.
    Travel teaches _____ encouraged to travel. (**so**)

5   The book might be successful. Then you can write more.
    _____ write more. (**If**)

6   These animals might disappear forever. That would be terrible.
    These animals _____ terrible. (**which**)

Impersonal sentences

In an essay, we do not usually use *I* and *we*. We usually use impersonal sentences, and talk about people and topics in general.

> **TIP:** Using impersonal language will make your essay sound more formal.

11 Complete the less personal ways of expressing ideas with the phrases from the box.

> an extremely popular place   are known to cause stress
> fear of losing friendships   it can be difficult for people
> countries all over the world   people of all ages

1   The climate where I live is changing.
    _____ are experiencing changes in climate.

2   I love going to the beach for a day out.
    The beach is _____ for a day out.

3   My family doesn't have a car.
    There are now _____ who choose not to own a car.

4   I always get really worried about exams.
    Exams _____ to young people.

5   I find it hard to eat healthy food all the time.
    _____ to stick to a healthy diet all the time.

6   If I don't look at my phone, I'm scared that I'll lose my friends.
    _____ is a reason people often give for needing to check their phones regularly.

EXAM TASK

Read the task and write your essay. Write your answer in 140–190 words in an appropriate style.

In your English class you have been talking about sport. Now, your English teacher has asked you to write an essay.

Write your essay using **all** the notes and giving reasons for your point of view.

All sports facilities in towns and cities should be free. What is your opinion?

Notes

Write about:

1   fitness

2   making friends

3   _____ (your own idea)

Write your **essay**.

TEST

ABOUT THE TASK

- In Writing Part 2, you choose one question to answer from a choice of three. One of these may be an article.
- You are told who you are writing the article for; this will usually be for an English-language magazine, newspaper or website. You are given a topic for the article, and some ideas to write about or questions to discuss. You should include all these in your article.
- You should think of an interesting title for your article.

- It is important to write your article in an engaging and interesting way, so you should use informal and semi-formal vocabulary and a variety of language structures. You can also use devices such as rhetorical questions to interest the reader.
- You should organise your article into clear paragraphs, with an introduction and a conclusion.
- You should write between 140 and 190 words.

Practice task

1 Read the task and write a first draft of your article. Write 140–190 words.

> You see this announcement on an English-language website.

ARTICLES WANTED

Do people attach too much importance to giving gifts?

When do people give gifts in your country? What kind of gifts do they give? Is it always necessary to give gifts? Do we pay too much attention to giving gifts?

Write an article sharing your ideas. The best ones will be published on our website.

Write your **article**.

How did you do?

2 Read your article and answer the questions.

Have you:

1 given your article an interesting title?
2 answered all the questions?
3 included an introduction and a conclusion?
4 divided your article into clear paragraphs?
5 used linkers to connect your ideas?
6 used interesting language?

3 Complete the boxes in the example article with the correct numbers from the box.

> 1 Include a conclusion which is thought-provoking or amusing.
> 2 Give personal examples to interest the reader.
> 3 Use a rhetorical question to engage the reader from the start.
> 4 Give your own opinion about the topic.
> 5 Use questions to make the reader think.
> 6 Answer the questions in the task clearly.
> 7 Use linking words or phrases to connect your ideas.
> 8 Use interesting and varied vocabulary.

Gift giving — good or bad?

We all like giving gifts, don't we? ▢

In my country we give gifts on birthdays or anniversaries. For these occasions it's incredibly important to choose our gift carefully, and perhaps spend lots of money, because we want to show how much we love our friend or relative. We also take gifts when we visit someone in their home, but these are less important, and are usually flowers or chocolates. These gifts are a way of saying thank you for the invitation. ▢

Is it really necessary to give gifts at all, though? A gift tells you more about the giver than you think — for example, I was given some jazz music by a so-called friend who forgot I hate it! I think if you can't choose something appropriate, it's better not to give anything. ▢

The problem is some people expect gifts, and you don't want to offend them. But is that a good reason for you to give them a gift? They could just be making the gift too important. ▢

Perhaps we should stop giving gifts completely and donate the money to charity. Problem solved! ▢

188 words

Strategies and skills

Engaging the reader

An article should entertain as well as inform, so you should try to interest the reader from the start. Thinking of an eye-catching title is a good way to do this.

1 Look at the descriptions of articles taken from tasks (1–6). Choose the best title for each one (A or B).

1 Gifts that you like giving, and those you don't. What's the best gift you've ever given anyone?
   A The best and worst gifts ever!
   B Why I like giving gifts

2 An activity you enjoy doing, and why it's important for you to keep doing it.
   A Life would be poorer without it
   B I really enjoy playing tennis

3 What young people do to help others, and why they do it. How do they feel about it?
   A What I do to help others
   B How helping others helps me

4 Something you own that means a lot to you, and why.
   A My most important possession
   B The one thing I can't imagine being without

5 A journey you remember well, and what made it so memorable.
   A A nightmare that I can never forget
   B A very memorable journey

6 A great place to go on holiday, and what makes it so good.
   A The place I like to go on holiday
   B There's nowhere better to have a break

Rhetorical questions are another good device for engaging your reader, and you can use them at the start of your article or to introduce a new point.

2 Turn the sentences below into rhetorical questions.

For example:

0 I don't know whether there are many places to buy unusual gifts.
   Are there many places to buy unusual gifts?

1 Older people appreciate gifts more than younger people.

2 People think it is a good idea to stay active even if they hate it.

3 I don't know whether many young people try to help others.

4 It's actually important to own something special.

5 It's impossible for anyone to forget something like that.

6 It's a good question, and perhaps there isn't an answer.

As well as your title, the content of your article needs to keep your reader interested right from the start.

3 Look at the task below. There are two possible titles and introductions (A and B). Which one is more interesting? Why?

> You see this advertisement in an English-language magazine for young people.

Is there a good place for young people to hang out where you live?

Is there somewhere in your town where young people can meet? What can they do there? What makes it special? Is it important for young people to have somewhere to go?

Write us an article answering these questions. We will publish the best articles in next month's edition of the magazine.

Write your **article**.

A

It's the only place to meet!

Wouldn't it be great if there were one place where we young people can hang out and just enjoy time together? Well, there is, and I'll tell you about it!

B

A good place to meet friends

I like meeting friends as often as I can, and usually at weekends when we like to go to a little café in town. It's good because there's music and we can stay there all day talking.

Using descriptive language and a range of adjectives, verbs and phrases can also help to keep your reader engaged with what you are saying to them.

> **TIP:** Try not to repeat words or phrases too often.

4 Read the main part of the article written for the task in Ex 3. Choose words from the box to replace the highlighted words.

> chat   energetic   guess   I expect you were imagining
> incredibly   spectacular   take part in   trendy

You may be surprised to discover that it's actually the local leisure centre – **(1)** you thought _____
it would be a café or a shopping centre! But in our town we're encouraged to **(2)** do _____
all kinds of sport – tennis, football and lots of other **(3)** sporting _____ activities. There's a(n) **(4)** nice _____ swimming pool, too, where they hold competitions. It's a(n) **(5)** very _____
popular place, but not only for the sport.

You see, there's also a jazz club there that meets every weekend, and it's so cool. It means everyone can relax there after sport, listen to **(6)** nice _____
music, and **(7)** talk _____ to each other. What's not to like?

I **(8)** think _____ there are some things that could be better – like longer opening hours, but it's so good already that I wouldn't want to spoil it!

If you include amusing personal anecdotes (stories) and examples, your article will be more interesting for your reader.

5 Complete the sentences (1-6) with the anecdotes (a-f).

1 Choosing gifts can be hard –
2 I often go there to chat to friends because it's friendly and comfortable –
3 One year I chose a gift for a friend that was something she'd already got –
4 I once played tennis against the club champion –
5 My best friend took me to a jazz club for the evening –
6 The last time I went to the club I bumped into an old friend –

a what's not to like?
b I lost 6-0!
c it took me a week to find something for my best friend!
d how lucky was that?
e it was very embarrassing when I gave it to her!
f she loved it, but I hated every moment!

Make sure that you conclude your article in an amusing or interesting way, but it is important that your conclusion is also logical.

6 Look at the two conclusions (A and B) to the article written for the task in Ex 3. Which one is best?

A

> *Is it important for young people to have a welcoming place like this to meet friends? In my opinion it's necessary, otherwise they get bored. And no one wants to feel like that – I know I don't!*

B

> *It's important for young people to have somewhere to meet friends, and it's a good idea to have it in a leisure centre where they can do other things. I like that idea.*

EXAM TASK

Read the task and write your article.

Write your answer in 140–190 words in an appropriate style.

> You have seen this announcement on a travel website.

Your best holiday ever!

Do you think holidays are important? We want to know about your best holiday ever. Write us an article telling us about the holiday, why it was so special and how it has affected you.

We will publish the best articles on our website.

Write your **article**.

ABOUT THE TASK

- In Writing Part 2, you choose one question to answer from a choice of three. One of these may be an email or a letter. This may be formal or informal.

- You usually write the email or letter in response to one you have received, or to an advertisement you have seen. For example, your email or letter may be to a friend, colleague, potential employer, college principal or magazine editor.

- You may have to respond to questions from a friend, or give information in response to an advertisement (e.g. a job application). You should address all of the points required.

- It is important to write your email or letter in a style appropriate for the person you are writing to. If you know the person well, you should use an informal style. In other situations you should use a semi-formal or formal style.

- You should organise your writing into clear paragraphs, and use the appropriate conventions for opening and closing your email/letter.

- You should write between 140 and 190 words.

Practice task: informal email

1 Read the task and write a first draft of your email. Write 140–190 words.

> You have received this email from your English-speaking friend, Clare.

From: Clare
Subject: Advice on entertaining guests

Hi,

I need advice, please! Some students are visiting our town from Spain, and I have to suggest some things to organise for them during their stay. I also want ideas for something memorable they can do on their last evening.

What do you think of a barbecue? What activities could we do with them?

Thanks for your help!

All the best,

Clare

Write your **email**.

How did you do?

2 Read your email and answer the questions.

Have you:

1 used informal language?
2 answered all the questions?
3 included an appropriate introduction and a conclusion?
4 divided your email into clear paragraphs?
5 used linkers to connect your ideas?
6 used the conventions of opening and closing your email?

TIP: Remember that you should use paragraphs in an informal email task as well as in a formal email or letter.

3 Complete the boxes in the example email with the correct numbers from the box.

> 1 Refer to your friend's email.
> 2 End your email by referring to your reason for writing.
> 3 Include some personal information at the start.
> 4 Use appropriate phrases to begin and end your email.
> 5 Give reasons for your suggestions.
> 6 Answer the questions your friend has asked.
> 7 Make suggestions in a friendly way.
> 8 Use phrasal verbs and informal expressions.

Subject: Re: Advice on entertaining guests

Hi Clare, ☐

It was so good to hear from you. It's been a long time, and I've been very busy at college so I haven't got round to writing to you either! ☐ I'm happy to make suggestions for your visitors.

I'm sure they'd enjoy a barbecue because it's ☐ very sociable. It's easy to cook lots of different things, too, so everyone can enjoy the food and have a good time. The only problem I've got with the idea is the weather. What would you do if it rained? But I guess you've thought of that already! ☐ The alternative would be to go out to a restaurant, but that'd be expensive and probably difficult to arrange.

I've been thinking about activities you could do. ☐ What about English-language games? Or a sing-song; that'd be really good if you had the barbecue. You could even organise a walk around the town with a quiz sheet for them to fill in before you all eat. If you want something they'll remember, then how about some fireworks? ☐

I hope these ideas are useful. Get back to me if you want any more help! ☐

Best wishes, ☐

190 words

Strategies and skills

Common expressions – informal language

Using common expressions makes your writing sound more natural.

> **TIP:** Make a note of common expressions to use in your writing, and learn them so that you can use them appropriately.

1 Correct the mistakes in the common expressions used in emails.

1 Hi Emily – great hear from you!

_____

2 I can wait to see you!

_____

3 I hope that is helped you.

_____

4 How about go to the beach?

_____

5 Hope to hearing from you soon.

_____

6 Get you back to me soon!

_____

7 I'm free every time you need me.

_____

8 All best,

_____

Using contractions

Contractions are informal, so you should use them in an email to a friend.

2 Put the apostrophe in the right place in the contractions.

1 I havent finished.
2 Youll enjoy the party.
3 Dont forget to write.
4 I wont be able to see you.
5 I wouldnt enjoy it.
6 Itll be a good party.
7 Its a good idea.
8 Wouldnt you like to come?

3 Rewrite the sentences using two contractions in each one.

1 I am sure you will enjoy a barbecue.
2 You will find loads of things you would enjoy doing.
3 The only problem I have got is the weather – it is going to rain!
4 You are more likely to have a good time if the party is planned.
5 I am sorry that I have not got round to replying.
6 The weather cannot be ignored because it is very changeable.
7 Unfortunately, I will not be able to come but it will be fun anyway.
8 I am happy to accept whatever you would like to do.

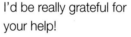

EXAM TASK

Read the task and write your email.

Write your answer in 140–190 words in an appropriate style.

> You have received this email from your English-speaking friend, Jack.

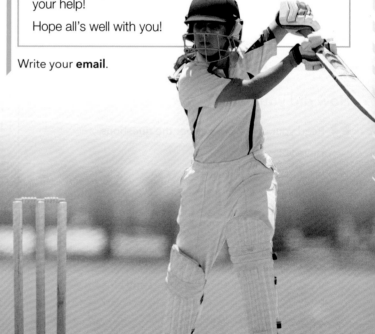

👤 **From:** Jack   **Subject:** I need information!

Hi! I've got to write an article on which sportspeople enjoy doing around the world – can you tell me about where you live? What are the most popular sports, and why do people do them? I also need to find out if a lot of professional sports are shown on television and which ones people like to watch.

I'd be really grateful for your help!

Hope all's well with you!

Write your **email**.

Practice task: formal letter

1 Read the task and write a first draft of your letter. Write 140–190 words.

> You see this advertisement in an English-language newspaper.

We need a part-time waiter/waitress in our international restaurant

Can you speak a foreign language? Are you good with people? Have you got experience of working in a restaurant? Can you work two evenings a week and start immediately?

Send us a letter with your details, telling us why you would be suitable for the job.

Mrs Margaret Jones, Euro-restaurant

Write your **letter**.

How did you do?

2 Read your letter and answer the questions.

Have you:

1 used formal language?
2 answered all the questions and provided all the required information?
3 included an appropriate introduction and a conclusion?
4 divided your letter into clear paragraphs?
5 used linkers to connect your ideas?
6 used the conventions of opening and closing the letter?

3 Complete the boxes in the example letter with the numbers from the box.

> **TIP:** You don't need to include an address in your letter, but don't forget to include the full name of the person you are writing to.

1 Say when and how you can be contacted.
2 End your letter appropriately.
3 Use linkers to connect your ideas.
4 Say why you are writing.
5 Link your points clearly to the given task.
6 Use the full name of the person you are writing to.
7 Answer the points in the task clearly.
8 Give reasons for why you would be suitable for the job.

Dear Mrs Jones, ☐

I have seen the advertisement in the local newspaper and would like to apply for the job of waitress in your restaurant. ☐

I am currently studying languages at the local college. My French is very good, and I also speak a little Italian. ☐

I am a very sociable person, and I'm good at dealing with people, as I run a social club at college at weekends. ☐

I am a team-player, and so I feel that I would be a good person to join your current staff. ☐

Although I have not worked in a restaurant before, I am very interested in cooking and food, and I would like to learn more about international cuisine. ☐

I am able to work two or three evenings every week, and this schedule would fit in very well with my study programme as my lectures take place during the day. I would be able to start next Monday. ☐

I would be grateful if you could contact me during the evenings from 5 p.m. to 8 p.m.. My telephone number is 077994466773. ☐

I look forward to hearing from you. ☐

Yours sincerely, ☐

189 words

Strategies and skills

Common expressions – formal language

You should use formal expressions in a formal letter.

1 Replace the bold informal words and phrases in the sentences (1–8) with formal words and phrases from the box.

> am looking forward to seeing   can I ask for your opinion of
> how are you   I'd like to request   increase   inform you of
> one possibility is to   put forward

1 I would like to **make** a suggestion. _____
2 **One thing we could do is** change the plan. _____
3 **What do you think about** the idea? _____
4 **Could you please send me** some information. _____
5 Holiday prices **go up** every year. _____
6 I'm writing to **tell you about** my plans. _____
7 I **can't wait to see** you. _____
8 **How are things going with you**? _____

Organising your letter

It is important to organise a formal letter clearly, so that it is easy to read and gives a good impression to the reader.

2 Look at part of the letter a student wrote in answer to the task below. It is badly organised. Put the paragraphs (A–D) in the correct order.

New course!

We are starting a new course in creative writing at the college, and welcome new students. The classes will be small, and teaching will focus on fiction through study of classic novelists.

Write us a letter telling us about yourself, why you are interested in the course and how you think it will benefit you.

Mr John Simmons, Principal

Write your **letter**.

Dear Mr Simmons,

A *This course would be really beneficial for me, as my writing is not very good at the moment. I don't find it easy to organise my thoughts, and often express myself badly.*

B *The course sounds very interesting, especially as it focuses on the creative side of writing. In my opinion, the study of classic novelists is a good way to learn good techniques, which is what I need.*

C *I have always wanted to be a novelist, ever since I was a child. I used to keep a diary and write everything down, so I am good at noticing and remembering details.*

D *Even if I don't achieve my ambition, I know that my writing will improve if I do this course. I hope that you will accept me on the course.*

EXAM TASK

Read the task and write your letter.

Write your answer in 140–190 words in an appropriate style.

> You have received this letter from the organisers of a photography competition.

> We are writing to inform you that you have won first prize in our photography competition. Your prize is a weekend in Paris or in Rome, and includes return flights, two nights' accommodation in a hotel or with a family, and all meals.
>
> Please contact us by letter addressed to Mr Rawlings, explaining which city you would prefer to visit and when. Could you also let us know of any special requirements, and any questions you may have?

Write your **letter**.

ABOUT THE TASK

- In Writing Part 2, you choose one question to answer from a choice of three. One of these may be a review.
- The purpose of a review is to make recommendations and give reasons for your opinion.
- You are told who you are writing the review for; this may be for an English-language magazine, newspaper or website.
- You are given a topic for the review, and some ideas to write about or questions to discuss. For example, you may be asked to write a review of a film, a game, a place, an event, a shop or restaurant.

- It is important to write your review in an engaging and interesting way. The reader needs to understand exactly what you are reviewing and what you think about it. Try to give examples and reasons to support your opinions.
- Your review should be organised into clear paragraphs, with an introduction and a conclusion. Explain or describe the subject in the introduction, and reasons why you would or would not recommend it in the conclusion.
- You should use informal and semi-formal vocabulary and a variety of language structures.
- You should write between 140 and 190 words.

Practice task

1 Read the task and write a first draft of your review. Write 140–190 words.

TIP: Think about how many questions you need to answer and how many paragraphs you will write.

You see this notice on a music website.

Reviews wanted

Have you seen a musical in the cinema or theatre that impressed you? Why do you remember it so well?

Write us a review telling us what you liked about it, and anything you didn't enjoy. Would you recommend this musical to other people?

Write your review. The best ones will be published on our website.

Write your **review**.

How did you do?

2 Read your review and answer the questions. Have you:

1 described the musical so that readers would understand what it's about?

2 answered all the questions in the task?

3 included an introduction and a conclusion?

4 divided your review into clear paragraphs?

5 used linkers to connect your ideas?

6 avoided repetition and used devices such as rhetorical questions?

7 given reasons or details to support your opinions?

8 included a clear recommendation to help readers decide whether to see the musical?

3 Complete the boxes in the example review with the correct numbers from the box.

> 1 Explain what the musical is about, but don't give too much detail.
> 2 Give the name of the show you're reviewing.
> 3 Try to engage the reader from the start, for example with a personal anecdote.
> 4 Use linking words or phrases to connect your ideas.
> 5 Answer all the questions in the task clearly.
> 6 Give your recommendation clearly, but not until the end.
> 7 Support your opinion with reasons and details.

I don't usually enjoy musicals, but I went to see 'Sing-along' at the Theatre Royal. It was amazing, and in fact I saw it twice! That's why I remember it so well.

The story was a romantic one of two teenagers who lost contact with one another when they went to college, and then met up again in London several years later. There were quite a few misunderstandings to be sorted out, but then there was a happy ending.

I enjoyed the quality of the music and the standard of the dancing. This was what I remember most, because it was so impressive. It looked really difficult! The two leading actors were totally believable, and it was easy to feel involved with their story.

If I had to pick something I didn't enjoy, it would be some of the scenes with the family in Paris. That's because they went on too long, and weren't part of the main story. However, the songs were still fun.

Would I recommend this musical? Definitely! I think even people who are not usually fans of the genre would have a good time.

188 words

TEACH

Strategies and skills
Developing ideas in a paragraph

A review should be clear and easy to follow, and each paragraph should have one main idea.

1 Look at the short paragraphs (1–6) and identify the main idea (A or B) in each one.

1 There were so many people in the theatre that every seat was taken. The event had been sold out for months, and tickets were hard to get and expensive.
   A The event was a success.
   B The theatre was a popular venue.

2 The critics all had the same opinion of the production of the new play. They only gave it one star.
   A The play was badly written.
   B The production of the play was poorly received.

3 The quality of the singing in the musical was superb. It was a pity that the acting let the production down, as there was much to admire otherwise.
   A The standard of the performers varied.
   B The acting was very bad.

4 The layout of the seats in the theatre was not well planned. I could only see half of the stage from where I was sitting, which spoiled the evening for me.
   A The stage was difficult to see.
   B The theatre was badly designed.

5 I tried and tried to enjoy the computer game, but I just couldn't get into it at all. The characters were so standard – there was nothing about them that could hold my attention.
   A The computer game was too difficult to play well.
   B The computer game was boring.

6 The course was enjoyable, and I learnt a lot. In fact, it has helped me to get my first job, because it was recognised by so many employers who knew how good it was.
   A The course was accepted as a good qualification by employers.
   B The course was useful because I learnt so much.

A paragraph may begin with a topic sentence. This introduces the main idea which is developed in the rest of the paragraph.

2 Look at the topic sentences in bold. Each is followed by another sentence which gives more information. Choose the type of information that develops the topic sentence.

1 **The review was rather negative.** Part of it not only criticised the singers, but also the music and the dancing. **(example / effect)**

2 **The concert venue felt quite different from any other I'd been to.** Although it was huge, it still had a cosy feel to it that I really liked. **(reason / effect)**

3 **This is a film about loyalty.** At the end, it is only true friends who survive, which is very appropriate. **(example / reason)**

4 **The event was very badly organised.** As a result, many people complained to the manager as they left. **(example / effect)**

5 **The location of the event was excellent.** This was due to the fact that it was right in the middle of the town. **(example / reason)**

6 **It was very difficult to hear the speakers on the stage.** This was caused by a failure in the loudspeaker system. **(effect / reason)**

7 **The range of music was spectacular.** It ranged from pop to rock and all types of fringe genres, including bands I had never heard of, and it really opened my eyes and ears to new musical experiences. **(effect / reason)**

8 **Tickets were beyond the reach of most ordinary people.** In fact, they were so expensive that I had to do hours of overtime to afford one, and that was for a seat right at the back of the auditorium. **(reason / example)**

3 Read the paragraphs (1–6) below. Match the topic sentence A–G to each one. There's one you don't need to use.

A I often play computer games with friends.
B There's a new café in the town.
C I don't really enjoy thrillers.
D The book is extremely well written.
E The new sports centre in town is great.
F It's really important to do different things.
G The fashion show was more successful than many events of its type.

1 _____ I find them disturbing to watch, and I often can't sleep afterwards. Last week I lay awake for hours after seeing one on television! That means I rarely go to see them at the cinema.

2 _____ The characters are well developed and it's easy to empathise with them. I really liked Jane, and was pleased that she had a happy life. I went out and bought a copy of another one by the same author as soon as I finished it.

3 _____ What we do is go online and play against each other, so it's easy to do it without having to go to one another's flats. My favourite one is called 'Enterprise' as it involves quite a lot of strategy. I'm good at that, so I often win!

4 _____ There are so many different activities to take part in, and it's not expensive. I often play badminton with friends, which is not only fun but keeps me fit.

5 _____ It only opened last month, but it already has a great reputation for fresh sandwiches and cakes. I go there regularly, and have never been disappointed.

6 _____ Some designers produce very unusual designs for shows which would never be bought by ordinary people, and this makes them rather disappointing. They are just for a niche market. This time, though, the models were wearing clothes that looked like those on the high street, so people were more interested in them.

Using functions and making recommendations

In a review, you use different functions. You describe, explain, give examples and opinions and then, finally, recommend.

4 Look at the words and phrases (1–10) and match them to a function in the box. The functions can be used more than once.

> describing   explaining   giving example(s)
> giving opinion(s)   recommending

1 That's why … _____

2 What happens first is … _____

3 What I mean is … _____

4 It seems to me that _____

5 It's a fast-moving film with lots of special effects. _____

6 I loved everything, but it was particularly the speed of the game … _____

7 I suggest that you give it a go. _____

8 It's something not to be missed. _____

9 That's largely due to … _____

10 What I like best about the game was the first section. _____

It is important that you include a recommendation in your review that is clear and shows exactly what you think.

5 Choose the best word to complete the recommendations below.

1 I **might / would** recommend this film to anyone who likes science fiction.

2 I **strongly / hardly** advise you to listen to this recording.

3 You should **definitely / thoroughly** give this game a try.

4 I **thoroughly / completely** recommend this restaurant.

5 I **completely / seriously** consider this to be one of the best films I've ever seen.

6 You won't **regret / miss** seeing this play as it will certainly make you think.

6a Look at the exam task in Ex 6b and the student answer. Which function from Ex 4 does the writer use in each paragraph (2–6)?

Para 2 _____   Para 5 _____

Para 3 _____   Para 6 _____

Para 4 _____

6b Does the writer recommend the game or not?

> You see this advertisement on a computer games website.

Reviews wanted

Is there a computer game that you really like playing? How often do you play? Where do you play?

Write a review describing the game, and explaining what you like or don't like about it. Would you recommend it to other people of your age?

We will publish the best reviews on our website.

Write your **review**.

1 I've been playing 'Smart Move' for a few months and it's awesome. I play it every evening with my mates online, and the only problem I have is stopping!

2 It's a kind of strategy game, which means you have to think a lot and plan ahead – that makes it different from a lot of other games. The story is quite complex, too, which is really challenging, and there are interesting characters to interact with.

3 What I like about it is the variety you find at each level, plus the fact that it's so competitive when I play against my friends.

4 There's one part in particular where it gets tricky and that's good fun. The soundtrack is great, too, and it holds your attention all through the game.

5 If I have a criticism, it is that it's rather expensive, and some people get annoyed that it takes so long to move through the different levels. I think it's good value for money, though.

6 So what's my overall opinion? I'd strongly recommend it to people who love gaming, but for anyone who doesn't, I'd say spend your money elsewhere.

Using adjectives that indicate opinion

Using a variety of value adjectives makes a review more interesting to read, and it is easier for the reader to understand exactly what you think.

7 Complete the table with the adjectives from the box.

> acceptable   brilliant   competent   convenient
> entertaining   horrible   impressive   memorable   odd
> outstanding   remarkable   ridiculous   satisfactory
> stunning   upsetting   useful   worthwhile

strongly positive	positive	neutral	strongly negative

8 Look at the lists of quantifiers and some adjectives (1–10). Cross out the quantifier that does <u>not</u> collocate with the adjective.

0	incredibly	~~slightly~~	totally	brilliant
1	totally	partly	completely	outstanding
2	quite	absolutely	more or less	acceptable
3	slightly	absolutely	definitely	remarkable
4	very	completely	incredibly	ridiculous
5	really	very	a bit	worthwhile
6	rather	truly	very	satisfactory
7	fairly	rather	completely	convenient
8	rather	greatly	slightly	odd
9	mildly	thoroughly	terribly	entertaining
10	reasonably	completely	rather	useful

9 Choose the best word to complete the recommendations from reviews.

1 The gallery has some **stunning / ridiculous** exhibits, particularly the paintings of landscapes and the amazing sculptures. However, what seemed rather **acceptable / odd** to me was the unusual way in which the rooms were organised – it was extremely difficult to find a link between them. However, overall it was still a really **worthwhile / competent** experience.

2 I enjoyed my visit to the restaurant, although I'd describe the standard of the cooking as only **competent / memorable**. What made the experience special was the service, which was totally **satisfactory / brilliant**. I'd recommend giving it a try, if only for the **convenient / impressive** decoration, which has to be seen to be believed.

3 The show was mildly **entertaining / amazing** although I wouldn't go so far as to describe it as completely **outstanding / competent**. I passed a pleasant couple of hours in the theatre, but was glad I hadn't spent a lot of money on my ticket. It was a(n) **remarkable / acceptable** experience, but nothing more.

4 The design of the hotel was **impressive / useful**, even though this was more in appearance than convenience. It was an old building which looked **stunning / useful** from the outside. However, inside it wasn't really very **convenient / acceptable** as there was no lift. Carrying bags up to the fifth floor wasn't easy, and not recommended for anyone with mobility problems.

5 The shop was new to me, and my expectations weren't great from the outside. However, once I got inside I found the range of hand-made jewellery was definitely **remarkable / horrible**. There were rings, necklaces and bracelets in beautiful designs that were original and truly **outstanding / satisfactory**. If you want to buy a present for someone special, I recommend this shop – I'm sure that you will find a(n) **memorable / acceptable** gift.

6 This website is easy to use, and all the links are clear. I found it slightly **remarkable / odd** that you had to go back to the home page every time you wanted to search for a new product, but once you get used to it then everything is arranged in a **satisfactory / worthwhile** way. You don't need to be a technical expert to use it, so I'd recommend the site as it's a **useful / horrible** way of shopping from home.

Read the task and write your review. Write 140–190 words.

> You have seen this announcement in a leisure magazine.

Reviews wanted

What was the last outdoor event you went to? Was it a sports tournament, a traditional festival or a local market?

Write us a review, telling us what happened, and what was good or bad about it. Would you recommend this event to other people?

We will publish the best reviews in our next edition.

Write your **review**.

- In Writing Part 2, you choose one question to answer from a choice of three. One of these may be a report.

- A report is usually written for a manager, a teacher or a member of a club or similar group, so it is usually formal. You are given a situation which you have to make suggestions or recommendations about, giving your reasons.

- The main purpose of a report is to present facts and ideas in a clear, logical way, so it is important to organise your report into clear sections. It is a good idea to use a heading for each section, but you don't have to.

- You should end with some recommendations and a clear conclusion.

- You should write between 140 and 190 words.

Practice task

1 Read the task and write a first draft of your report.

> Your local science museum recently put on a special evening event to raise money for local charities. The director of the museum has asked you to write a report to assess how successful the event was. The report should:
>
> - outline which parts of the event visitors most enjoyed.
> - comment on the success of the event in raising money.
> - say whether you would recommend future events like this.

Write your **report**.

How did you do?

2 Read your report and answer the questions.

Have you:

1 organised your report into clear sections or paragraphs?

2 started with a general introduction?

3 said which parts of the event visitors enjoyed?

4 analysed whether the event was successful at raising money?

5 written a clear conclusion?

6 made recommendations about future events?

7 used formal language?

3 Complete the boxes in the example report with the correct number from the box.

> 1 Answer the second point in the task.
> 2 End with a recommendation.
> 3 Start with a general introduction, giving the aim of the report.
> 4 Include a clear conclusion in the final section.
> 5 Answer the first point in the task.
> 6 Use formal language.
> 7 Organise the report into clear sections, each with a heading, such as 'Introduction'.

Introduction

The aim of this report is to provide feedback on the recent charity event at the science museum and make recommendations on future events. I spoke to 80 people there and collected their opinions.

Highlights

The majority of people were very positive. They particularly enjoyed the tour of the parts of the museum where visitors are not usually allowed. The quiz about space travel was also extremely popular.

Success at raising money

The event raised nearly £500 for local charities. Although this is a significant sum, it is not as much as the organisers hoped. Some people felt that the tickets were too expensive, and this put some off coming. Others commented that there could be more items for sale at the event, which would increase the amount raised.

Conclusions and recommendations

It is clear that people enjoyed this event, and it was successful in raising money for charity. To raise more from future events, I suggest that the ticket price should be lower, to attract more people, and there should be more opportunities for people to spend money once they are there, for example on souvenirs or refreshments.

190 words

TEACH

Strategies and skills

Organising ideas in a report

It is important to divide a report into clear sections. Adding a heading for each section helps make it clear what each one is about.

1 Read the exam task and the two main sections of a report. Choose the best heading (A–F) for each section. There are four headings you don't need.

> Your office wants to improve the range of food and drink that is available for staff.
>
> You have been asked to write a report for the facilities manager. Your report should:
> * assess the food that is currently available to staff.
> * suggest ways it could be improved.

Write your **report**.

(1) _____

In general, staff are happy with the range of hot food available in the cafeteria. The dishes are considered to be tasty and healthy, and there is a good variety each day. The majority of staff are happy with the coffee bar, and feel that it offers good-quality drinks at reasonable prices.

(2) _____

The most common complaint was that the cafeteria does not always offer a salad option. This is felt to be a problem especially in the summer, when many staff do not want to eat a hot meal. The other main complaint was that the coffee bar is too small with not enough seats. In addition to this, it only sells unhealthy snacks like crisps and chocolate bars.

A Advantages and disadvantages of the cafeteria and coffee bar
B Problems with current facilities
C Positive aspects of current facilities
D How facilities could be improved
E The cafeteria
F Why staff aren't happy

2 Find three points about the coffee bar in paragraph 2 in Ex 1 that could be given in a bulleted list.

3 Look at the task and sections of the report in Ex 1 again. Then choose the best introduction and the best conclusion for the report (A–C). Why are they the best?

> **TIP:** It's a good idea to end your report with some recommendations as part of your conclusion.

1 **Introduction**
   A In this report, I'm going to recommend some changes we could make to improve food at the office.
   B This report describes some problems with the food in the office cafeteria and discusses why staff are not keen to eat there.
   C This report aims to look at the current food facilities in the office and suggest how they could be improved.

2 **Conclusion**
   A In conclusion, the cafeteria and coffee bar are both popular with staff. I recommend that the cafeteria should offer a greater selection of salad dishes. I also suggest that the coffee bar be increased in size and offer more healthy snacks such as fresh fruit.
   B To sum up, the food in the office cafeteria is not bad, and the hot dishes are often amazing. But it would be great to have a bigger coffee bar with more healthy snacks.
   C On balance, there are many positive things about the food currently available at the office, for example the hot food in the cafeteria. However, there are also some clear problems and these should be addressed as soon as possible.

4 Complete the sentences from reports with the correct words/phrases from the box. Then decide if each sentence could be used in an introduction (I) or a conclusion (C).

> conclusion   intended   looks at   overall
> purpose of   sum up

1 The _____ this report is to assess the public transport in the city centre.

2 To _____ , the majority of people are happy with the current train services.

3 This report is _____ to show the strengths and weaknesses of the current public transport system.

4 _____ , people are not satisfied with the current provision of buses.

5 In _____ , the current public transport system is not adequate.

6 This report _____ the current public transport system and suggests some ways it could be improved.

Referring to research

Referring to research findings can make your report sound more accurate and authentic. You can imagine that you have done some research and invent the details of what you found.

5 Match the beginning of each sentence (1–5) with its ending (a–e) to make sentences you can use to refer to your research.

1 I carried out
2 I interviewed
3 According to most
4 A survey of
5 The majority

a of the people I questioned, there are several problems with the current theatre.
b a survey of 30 students.
c over 20 young people who live in the city.
d shoppers in the city centre showed a high level of satisfaction.
e of young people would like more access to sports facilities.

If you include numbers of people when you refer to research you have done, it can help to make your report sound more authentic.

6 Complete the second sentence with one word, so it has a similar meaning to the first.

1 Most people would like a swimming pool.
The _____ of people would like a swimming pool.

2 A few people complained about the prices.
A small _____ of people complained about the prices.

3 No one I interviewed was happy with the bus service.
_____ of those I interviewed was happy with the bus service.

4 Everyone was enthusiastic about the idea of a music festival.
_____ those I surveyed were enthusiastic about the idea of a music festival.

5 Fifteen out of the twenty people I questioned would like better access to the library.
Three _____ of the people I questioned would like better access to the library.

6 Eight of the fifteen people in my survey complained about the entrance fee.
Just over _____ the people in my survey complained about the entrance fee.

Formal language

We use formal language in a report.

7 Complete each second, formal, sentence with a suitable phrase from the box so it has a similar meaning to the first, informal, sentence.

> cause of dissatisfaction   concerned about   enthusiastic about
> fortunate to have   insufficient space   popular with

1 Luckily, we've got a really good cinema in the town.
We are _____ a very good cinema in the town.

2 Students love this café.
This café is extremely _____ students.

3 There wouldn't be enough room for a car park.
There would be _____ for a car park.

4 Everyone loved the idea of a film club.
Everyone was _____ the idea of a film club.

5 Some people are scared that prices might increase.
Some people are _____ possible price increases.

6 One thing everyone complained about was the long queues.
One _____ was the long queues.

We often use passive sentences in a report as they are more formal than active sentences.

8 Complete the passive sentences.

1 People consider this restaurant to be the best in the town.
This restaurant _____ the best in the town.

2 Some people have suggested that there should be a new sports centre.
It _____ there should be a new sports centre.

3 We expect that over 50 people will attend the event.
Over 50 people _____ attend the event.

4 Everyone criticised the theme park for being too expensive.
The theme park _____ for being too expensive.

5 People thought a cookery class was a good idea.
A cookery class _____ a good idea.

6 Most students think the library is excellent.
The library _____ by most students.

EXAM TASK

Read the task and write your report. Write your answer in 140–190 words in an appropriate style.

> Your local council wants to improve public transport in your area. You have been asked to write a report for the council to provide information on how people feel about public transport where they live, what things are working well and what could be improved.

Write your **report**.

TEST

ABOUT THE TASK

- In Writing Part 2, you choose one question to answer. In the B2 First for Schools exam, you may choose to write a story.

- A story is usually written for an English-language magazine or a website for teenagers. You are given the first line of a story, which you have to continue, and two prompts with ideas that you must include in your story. Your story should follow on clearly and smoothly from this first line, use the two prompts successfully and have a good ending.

- The main purpose of a story is to entertain the reader, and to engage and keep their interest. There should be a clear storyline or narrative that's easy to follow, and the language should be interesting.

- You should write between 140 and 190 words.

Practice task

1 **Read the task and write a first draft of your story. Write 140–190 words.**

> We are looking for stories for our website. Your story must **begin** with this sentence:
> *Sam picked up his wallet and headed into town.*
> Your story must include:
> - a meeting
> - a meal

Write your **story**.

How did you do?

2 **Read your story and answer the questions.**

Have you:

1 started with the sentence in the task?

2 made sure the rest of the story follows on clearly from the first sentence?

3 included a meeting?

4 included a meal?

5 used narrative tenses (past simple, past continuous and past perfect) to describe the events of the story?

6 used time words and expressions to make it clear when things happen?

7 included adjectives and adverbs to describe things in an interesting way?

8 given your story a clear ending?

3 **Complete the boxes in the example story with the correct numbers from the box.**

> 1 Use time expressions to show when events happened.
> 2 Use adverbs to describe actions.
> 3 Explain the situation around the first sentence.
> 4 Use a range of different narrative tenses to describe the events of the story.
> 5 Give the story a clear ending.
> 6 Include the first prompt (a meeting).
> 7 Begin with the sentence in the task.
> 8 Include the second prompt (a meal).
> 9 Use adjectives to describe things in an interesting way.

Sam picked up his wallet and headed into town.

He had finally saved up enough money to buy the new computer game that he wanted, and he was looking forward to playing it with his friends.

The bus ride into town felt long and boring, but after 30 minutes the bus arrived at the shopping centre, and Sam hurried excitedly to the games shop. Just as he was going into the shop, he heard someone calling his name. He turned around quickly and saw his old best friend, Stefan. Stefan had moved away from the town a few years ago, so Sam was very surprised to see him. 'Hi,' he said. Stefan came towards him, smiling cheerfully. 'Hi,' he replied. 'We've moved back into the town. Fancy a pizza?' Sam looked at the shop and thought about his new game, but then made his decision. 'Sure, a pizza would be great,' he said.

As they ate, they chatted and made plans about all the exciting things they could do together. And Sam didn't mind at all that he didn't have his new game!

184 words

Strategies and skills

Sequencing events

It is important to use time words and expressions so that the order of the different events is clear. Make sure you know how to use a wide range of time words and expressions.

1 Choose the correct time words and expressions to complete the extracts from stories (1–8).

1

Poppy got onto the train and sat down, and **then / already** took out the letter to read.

2

Just then / While we were waiting for the others, we checked the directions to the stadium.

3

At first / Later, I felt a bit nervous, but I soon relaxed.

4

Before long / By the time we got home, it was nearly dark.

5

No one spoke **while / during** the journey home.

6

As soon as / Later I saw the old wooden chest, I knew it was the one we were looking for.

7

We waited outside **until / meanwhile** we were sure the room was empty.

8

Later / After a few minutes, Jack looked up and smiled.

Narrative tenses

Use a range of narrative tenses in a story: the past simple for the main events, the past continuous to describe longer actions and the past perfect to describe actions that happened earlier.

2 Read part of a student's story. Complete it with the correct form of the verbs in brackets. Use the past simple, past continuous or past perfect.

Abbie was excited, so she quickly **(1)** _____ (**run**) downstairs. Her parents and her brother **(2)** _____ (**stand**) by the front door, with all the bags. It **(3)** _____ (**be**) the first day of their mystery holiday, and the taxi **(4)** _____ (**wait**) outside, to take them to the airport. Abbie **(5)** _____ (**know**) that the holiday was abroad somewhere, but her parents **(6)** _____ (**not tell**) her exactly where. But they **(7)** _____ (**say**) that she should pack summer clothes. Abbie **(8)** _____ (**hope**) that she **(9)** _____ (**not forget**) anything!

Adjectives and adverbs

Using a range of different adjectives will help you describe the people and places in your story in an interesting way.

> **TIP:** Thinking about adjectives can help you think of ideas for your story. Ask yourself questions about the events and the characters, for example, *Where were the people? What was the weather like? How did the main character feel?*

3 Complete the table with the adjectives from the box. Then add at least three more adjectives to each column.

crowded   delighted   elegant   enthusiastic   icy
nervous   noisy   peaceful   slim   stormy   sunny   tall

appearance	feelings	places	weather

4 Choose the correct word to complete each sentence.

1 I don't know why Tom looks so **miserable / miserably**.
2 Laura was sleeping **peaceful / peacefully** on the sofa.
3 Don't panic! Try to stay **calm / calmly**!
4 Dan opened the letter **nervous / nervously**.
5 Tasha walked **confident / confidently** onto the stage.
6 That was really **kind / kindly** of you – thank you!

Direct speech

You can use direct speech in a story if the characters speak to each other. Learn the correct punctuation to use, and learn a range of verbs you can use with direct speech.

5 Rewrite the reported speech sentences as direct speech.

1 Molly explained that her bus had been late.

   _____

2 The man shouted at us to leave him alone.

   _____

3 Lily asked me where I was going.

   _____

4 The woman told us that the zoo was closed.

   _____

EXAM TASK

Read the task and write your story. Write your answer in 140–190 words in an appropriate style.

> We are looking for stories for our magazine. Your story must **begin** with this sentence:
> *Amy picked up the map and set off on her bike.*
> Your story must include:
> - a secret
> - a phone call

Write your **story**.

TEST

ABOUT THE TASK

- In Listening Part 1, you listen to eight unrelated short extracts.
- Each extract is a monologue or a dialogue, and there will be a range of different speakers and contexts.
- There is one multiple-choice question for each extract, with three options. You choose the correct option, based on what you hear.

- The questions can be about what the speaker thinks or feels, why they are speaking, what they are doing when they speak, a detail about the point the speaker is making or whether two speakers agree with each other.
- You will have time to read the questions before you hear the recording, and you will hear each extract twice.
- Each question is worth one mark.

Practice task

1 🎧 **L01** You will hear people talking in three different situations. For questions 1–3, choose the best answer (A, B or C). You will hear each situation twice.

1 You hear two people talking about a film they've seen.
   What do they agree about it?
   A The story was quite upsetting.
   B Some parts were all right.
   C It was as enjoyable as expected.

2 You hear part of a talk about a coral reef.
   What is the presenter doing?
   A describing the factors that threaten it
   B identifying species of wildlife that live in it
   C emphasising the importance of preserving it

3 You hear a man talking to a friend about his course at college.
   What does he think about it?
   A It's more time-consuming than he'd imagined.
   B It's less interesting than he'd thought.
   C It's more difficult than he'd expected.

How did you do?

2 Check your answers.

3a Look at the audioscript for Ex 1 question 1. All three options (A–C) are mentioned by one or other speaker, but only one is mentioned by both. Match sentences 1–4 to A–C in Ex 1 question 1.

Man:	I'm glad that's over – I can't believe I actually paid to see it!
Woman:	¹I'd read the reviews, so I knew what was coming – even though the last film that director made won awards. ²But there were some good things – like the music – oh, and the special effects were stunning!
Man:	If you say so, though I honestly didn't notice. ³The plot made me so sad.
Woman:	The script wasn't particularly good, so the actors didn't have a chance to show how good they were. ⁴It did make me cry, though, especially the ending.
Man:	Well, I go to the cinema to be cheered up!

3b Which parts give you the correct answer?

4a Look at the highlighted parts of the audioscript for Ex 1 question 2. Match each highlighted part with the topic in one of the options (A–C) in question 2.

Today I'm talking about the coral reef off the Australian coast. It's huge, and although people probably assume it's one reef, it's actually more like thousands of individual reefs. The area's stunning, with colours ranging from blue and pink to purple and green. But the coral is under threat and ¹so many creatures that live there are losing their habitat. So, for them its survival is crucial. Conservationists are trying to clean the water in the area, partly because ²certain predators search for food in polluted water. ³This attracts them to the reef and makes them yet another hazard for already endangered reef dwellers.

4b Which highlighted part of the audioscript gives you the answer? Why are the other options wrong? To help you, think about these questions (1–3).

1 The speaker mentions preserving the reef and the habitat it provides, but is she **emphasising** this?

2 The speaker mentions different types of wildlife, but is she **identifying** them?

3 The speaker says that the reef is in danger, but is she **describing** all the factors that threaten it?

5a Look at the audioscript for Ex 1 question 3. Highlight the part that refers to each of the options (A–C) in question 3.

Kira:	Hi Sam – how's the course going?
Sam:	Well, I've got through the first part but I'm not sure how! I knew it would be demanding, though – I've never done anything like it before.
Kira:	But you're enjoying it?
Sam:	The coursework, yes, though some of the lectures aren't as fascinating as they looked in the prospectus! Maybe I'm just not used to sitting and listening to someone talk for hours on end.
Kira:	But you'll keep going?
Sam:	Definitely – though, inevitably, it's kind of taken over my life: I knew I'd miss going out in the evenings with you guys.
Kira:	It'll be better next term, I'm sure.

5b Which option gives you the right answer? Why are the other options wrong?

Strategies and skills

Listening for agreement

You won't hear speakers agree using specific phrases such as 'I agree with you'. You must identify the general points each one makes, and decide whether they are saying the same thing.

> **TIP:** You will hear each situation twice. Use the second time you listen to check your ideas.

1 🎧 **L02 Listen to six short conversations. Do the speakers both think the same thing (S), or something different (D)? You will hear each conversation twice.**

1 _____   3 _____   5 _____

2 _____   4 _____   6 _____

SPEAKING BOOST

Discuss or answer.

1 Do you like surprises? Give examples.

2 What's the best surprise you could get or give to someone else this year?

Identifying a speaker's purpose

Questions will often ask about the purpose of a speaker. The function verbs in the options will not appear in the recording so you need to think about what you learn from the speaker's actual words to identify their purpose.

2 Look at what some speakers say and decide what they are doing. Choose their purpose.

1 It's probably better to go on Tuesday because the town gets busy on Fridays. **(encouraging / advising / describing)**

2 Can we meet at seven instead of six? That would give me more time to get there.
   (offering / requesting / demanding)

3 I have never had such a badly cooked meal!
   (requesting / complaining / identifying)

4 Once we've arrived, it might be a good idea to check into the hotel before doing anything else.
   (warning / suggesting / emphasising)

5 I've heard that the weather will get worse, and if that happens, we could find driving conditions very difficult.
   (suggesting / warning / advising)

6 The first part of the story takes place in an old warehouse, where the main characters meet for the first time.
   (justifying / highlighting / outlining)

7 I'm sure it'll be successful even if you're worried about it now.
   (encouraging / advising / warning)

8 If you'd spent more time on your homework, you'd have done it better; but you never do.
   (criticising / describing / identifying)

Identifying attitude and opinion

Options will paraphrase (use different words to say the same thing) and summarise what a speaker says. You need to listen carefully to how a speaker expresses their views in order to identify the correct option.

> **TIP:** In the exam, you have some time before each conversation to look at the options for each question. Use this time to familiarise yourself with the options and prepare yourself for what you are likely to hear.

3 🎧 **L03 Listen to some speakers (1–6). What do they think? Choose the correct option (A or B). You will hear each speaker twice.**

1 A The course is going on too long.
   B The work is taking up too much time.

2 A It's not a good idea to go then.
   B I think we could possibly go then.

3 A I don't trust what you've suggested.
   B I'm grateful for what you've said.

4 A I didn't enjoy the programme very much.
   B I wasted my time, but I don't mind much.

5 A Being interviewed was not enjoyable.
   B Being interviewed is part of the prize.

6 A I don't like being on stage because I make mistakes.
   B I'm nervous in front of an audience.

Identifying feelings

For questions that ask about how a speaker feels, you won't hear the speaker use the exact words that you read in the options. You must think about what they mean and decide how they really feel about something in order to choose the best option.

4 🎧 **L04 Listen to some speakers (1–6). How do they feel? Choose the correct option (A, B or C). You will hear each speaker twice.**

1 A jealous   4 A relieved
   B offended   B angry
   C sorry   C anxious

2 A tired   5 A confident
   B annoyed   B worried
   C sad   C hopeful

3 A excited   6 A pleased
   B bored   B unwilling
   C tired   C angry

L05 **You will hear people talking in eight different situations. For questions 1–8, choose the best answer (A, B or C). You will hear each situation twice.**

1   You hear two friends discussing a science experiment on living on another planet.
    What do they both think about it?
    A   The conditions must have been unpleasant.
    B   The isolation must have been difficult to deal with.
    C   The scientists must have worked very hard.

2   You hear two friends talking about a tennis match they watched.
    What do they agree about?
    A   The result was unexpected.
    B   The atmosphere was amazing.
    C   The standard of play was exceptionally high.

3   You hear a woman telling a friend about a community eco campaign.
    How does she feel about it?
    A   She's keen to get more people involved.
    B   She's pleased with the way it's been organised.
    C   She's surprised about how little impact it's had.

4   You hear a man leaving a voicemail message for a friend.
    Why is he leaving the message?
    A   to suggest a place to eat
    B   to apologise for being late
    C   to ask her for a favour

5   You hear a young singer talking about her career so far.
    What does she think about it?
    A   It's crucial to have support from other people.
    B   It's important to choose the best opportunities.
    C   It's necessary to compromise on the music she plays.

6   You hear two friends talking about a video posted on the internet.
    What do they both think about it?
    A   It's quite amusing to watch.
    B   It's an unusual topic.
    C   It's irresponsible to post it.

7   You hear part of an interview with the presenter of a TV documentary.
    What is the focus of the documentary?
    A   The place of unusual architecture.
    B   The need for better housing.
    C   The importance of interior design.

8   You hear two friends talking about a team quiz they took part in.
    How does the girl feel about it?
    A   disappointed with her own performance
    B   upset about the final result
    C   irritated by the behaviour of some of the contestants

ABOUT THE TASK

- In Listening Part 2, you hear one long monologue. The speaker is usually giving a presentation or talk on a particular subject.

- There are ten sentences, each one with a gap. You listen and complete these gaps in the sentences with a word or a short phrase.

- The sentences provide a kind of summary of what the speaker says, and are in the same order as the information you hear. You won't hear the actual sentences on the recording as they paraphrase the information given by the speaker.

- Most answers are concrete pieces of information, such as nouns, although the sentence may tell you about the speaker's opinion or attitude towards their topic.

- You must complete the gap with the exact word or words you hear, not a paraphrase, and the words you write should fit the sentence grammatically.

- You'll have time to read the questions before you hear the recording, and you'll hear the recording twice.

- Each question is worth one mark.

Practice task

1 🎧 **L06** You will hear a young woman called Shelly Jonson talking about her job making and selling unusual ice cream. For questions 1-5, listen and complete the sentences with a word or short phrase. You will hear the speaker twice.

A SUCCESSFUL YOUNG
ICE CREAM SELLER

Shelly decided to study **(1)** _____ at university because she first considered being a teacher.

Shelly's early ice cream was popular in the **(2)** _____ , especially with children.

Shelly thinks her ice cream maker looks like a **(3)** _____ because of its size and colour.

Shelly uses the word **(4)** _____ to describe how she feels about her ice cream.

Shelly gives the example of **(5)** _____ as a popular flavour when the weather's hot.

How did you do?

2 Check your answers.

3 🎧 **L07** A student wrote the wrong answers for Ex 1. Look at their answers, then listen again. Choose the best option to complete the reason they made the mistake. The correct answer is highlighted.

Shelly decided to study **(1)** _____technology_____ at university because she first considered being a teacher.

It was Shelly's **friend / teacher** who suggested that she should study technology, but Shelly decided to study chemistry instead.

Shelly's early ice cream was popular in the **(2)** _____local cinema_____ , especially with children.

Shelly did sell ice cream in the local cinema, but she sold it **most successfully / sometimes** in the weekly market, where all the young ones loved it.

Shelly thinks her ice cream maker looks like a **(3)** _____magic box_____ because of its size and colour.

Shelly's **mother / partner** thinks it looks like a magic box, but Shelly thinks it's more like a washing machine because it's big and white.

Shelly uses the word **(4)** _____worry_____ to describe how she feels about her ice cream.

Shelly actually says that she **does / doesn't** worry, but instead she is proud of her product.

Shelly gives the example of **(5)** _____pumpkin pie_____ as a popular summer flavour.

Shelly mentions different flavours – pumpkin pie, pickled mango or pear and blue cheese – but says she **can / can't** make these. She can, however, make rose, which is a popular summer flavour.

Strategies and skills
Listening for cues

The answer is indicated (or cued) by a key word or phrase that could come before or after the word(s) you need to write. Cues will often indicate how a person feels about something, how they describe something or how something is done.

> **TIP:** Look for words that indicate feelings such as **surprised** or **interested**. This will help you to identify the right place in the recording to find the answer.

1 Look at the sentences from a task. Highlight the key words and phrases that cue the answer and show what you are listening for.

LOOKING FOR TIGERS

Jason was surprised that people didn't like (1) _____ more than tigers.

Jason uses the word (2) _____ to explain what he thinks the hair on tigers' faces looks like.

Jason was very interested in the theory that (3) _____ might be areas where tigers now live.

According to Jason, the biologist considered the way he tried to photograph tigers as his (4) _____ .

Jason was thrilled to see images of a (5) _____ because they are very rare.

You won't hear the key words from the sentences in the recording – you will hear a paraphrase of them which will cue the answer.

2 The words and phrases below have a similar meaning to the words you highlighted in the sentences in Ex 1. Match them to the words you highlighted in Ex 1. There is one you don't need to use.

1 what he thought of as … _____
2 I couldn't believe that … _____
3 Apart from that, I enjoyed _____
4 what I'd describe as … _____
5 I found this a fascinating idea … _____
6 It was a delight … _____

3 🎧 **L08** Now listen for the cues you have identified in Ex 1. You will hear a young man called Jason Elliot telling a group of students about endangered tigers and where they live. Listen and complete the sentences in Ex 1 with a word or short phrase. You will hear the speaker twice.

> **TIP:** You should always try to spell the word you write correctly.

SPEAKING BOOST

Discuss or answer.

1 Think of your favourite wild animal, electronic device or food. Explain why it's your favourite.
2 Do different foods go in and out of fashion? Give examples.

Listening for specific details

Knowing the kind of word you need to listen for helps you to identify it.

4 Look at four sentences (1–4) from four different tasks. Choose the kind of word you need to complete each one.

1 Joe uses the word _____ to describe what he likes most about the job. **(verb / adjective)**

2 Chloe decided to go to Amsterdam after a _____ suggested it. **(person / thing)**

3 According to Darren, _____ is the key to any successful expedition. **(person / thing)**

4 Kath is upset that _____ are the biggest danger to bears in the wild. **(singular noun / plural noun)**

5 Read the audioscript for Ex 4 sentence 1. Look at the highlighted adjectives. Which one does Joe use to express what he likes best about the job? You don't need to write the word 'job' as it is already in the sentence.

I'm an actor, but you won't see me in ordinary films or on stage. What I do is appear in commercials, and it's actually a pretty good way to earn a living – quite well-paid, in fact. That was attractive initially, but everyone told me it'd be fun as well. You tend to meet the same people on set, so I'd say it's actually a very social job – that's what I really enjoy about it, although it's creative work, too!

6 🎧 **L09** Listen to the speaker for Ex 4 sentence 2.

a Which of the people in the list below are mentioned? Tick them.

sister	☐	cousin	☐
uncle	☐	friend	☐
mother	☐	brother	☐

b Which one of the people on the list has actually made a suggestion? How do you know?

7 Read the audioscript for Ex 4 sentence 3. Look at the highlighted word. What does the word refer to? How does the word give you the answer?

So, I've taken part in successful cycling expeditions all over the world, in remote mountainous areas and in deserts. Although all similar challenges are very different in terms of the equipment you need and the difficulties you face, they have one thing in common if they're to get the best results. It may seem obvious, but it's not physical fitness nor is it determination – it's preparation. Without that, any expedition you attempt will end in failure.

8 Read the audioscript for Ex 4 sentence 4. The highlighted word tells you how Kath is feeling. Look back in the script to see what caused her to feel that way. Why is 'because' important?

Bears in this area are endangered, not so much because they're hunted by other animals like predators, or through changes in weather patterns, but because their habitat is being destroyed by – you've guessed it – humans! That's what makes me so sad.

Identifying feelings

To complete a sentence correctly, you may need to identify the speaker's feelings about something. You will need to listen carefully to what they say in order to work out how they feel.

9 Look at what some speakers say (1–6). Choose the word that might appear in the sentence in the task to express how they are feeling.

> **TIP:** Remember that a word such as 'thrilled' can have a slightly different meaning in a different context. As you listen, make sure that you think about the context and not just about the word itself.

1 'I often find the way animals are treated upsetting.'
   She is **unhappy / annoyed** about the way animals are treated.

2 'I had no idea that the work would be so hard.'
   He didn't **like / expect** the work to be so hard.

3 'I was confused about whether it was a good idea.'
   She was **convinced / unsure** that it was a good idea.

4 'It's history that really attracts me as a subject, far more than maths.'
   She's **better at / more interested in** history than maths.

5 'I'm up for any kind of sport really, whatever the weather.'
   He's **passionate about / keen to do** any kind of sport in any weather.

6 'Watching animals playing often makes me laugh.'
   He is **amused by / keen on** animals playing.

Identifying and eliminating distractors

You will hear words that could be the answer, but they actually don't answer the question. These words are distractors.

10 Read the sentences and the audioscript for a short exam task. The words that correctly complete the sentences are highlighted in the script. Look for and highlight the distractors.

> You will hear a woman called Sue Thomas talking to a group of students about her job as a prompter in a theatre. For questions **1-5**, complete the sentences with a word or short phrase.

Being a prompter in a theatre

Sue uses the word **(1)** _____ to describe how she feels about being a prompter.

According to Sue, one disadvantage of her job is that her **(2)** _____ are unimportant.

Sue says that **(3)** _____ is what she needs most to do her job.

Sue thinks of her relationship with the performers as **(4)** _____ .

Sue really appreciated a **(5)** _____ she received from one singer.

I work as a prompter in a theatre – not a job that many people know much about! I specialise in opera, and I have to follow the performance on stage and whisper the words if one of the singers forgets them. It sounds boring, and it can be demanding, but I find it very ¹rewarding, even though there are some downsides – as with any job, I suppose.

I have to sit in a small space just below the stage for several hours – it's pretty cramped and can be uncomfortable. I get used to that, and do exercises for my legs and back to keep flexible. It doesn't matter what ²clothes I wear because no one can see me, though unfortunately that does make me a bit lazy with my appearance!

So what do I need to do my job? I must be musical, which I am, so it's difficult to stop myself singing along with the people on stage! I also have to have a lot of patience, but I guess it's ³concentration that tops the list.

The singers have to be able to trust me, so they can be relaxed on stage. This feeling of trust between us develops over time, and I regard it as ⁴special. I love being able to contribute to a great performance.

I don't do it for thanks, but it's always nice when the singers acknowledge what I do. Sometimes they turn and give me applause at the end of a performance, and sometimes they give me flowers. The nicest thing was a ⁵letter from a singer who had retired, telling me how much he had valued me during his time on stage!

11 🎧 **L10** Now listen to the task and think about why the answers are right.

🎧 **L11** You will hear a woman called Annie talking to a group of gardeners about her hobby of keeping bees.

For questions 1-10, complete the sentences with a word or a short phrase.

You will hear the speaker twice.

KEEPING BEES

It was a **(1)** _____ that caused Annie to become fascinated by bees.

Annie uses the word **(2)** _____ to describe how she likes to imagine bees living together.

Annie is convinced most people don't know that some **(3)** _____ need bees for their food.

Annie finds it strange that **(4)** _____ is the colour that bees can't see.

Annie describes the destruction of the bees' habitat as **(5)** _____ for her.

Annie is amused when people refer to bumblebee shelters in their gardens as **(6)** _____ .

Annie feels helpless when **(7)** _____ increase unexpectedly and bees aren't ready to collect pollen.

Annie is unhappy when people prefer to support **(8)** _____ rather than bees.

When dealing with her own bees, Annie always makes sure she has her **(9)** _____ with her.

Annie's advice to people is not to use **(10)** _____ when they're near bees.

- In Listening Part 3, you hear five short monologues on the same topic.
- There are five different speakers.
- You are given a list of eight different options. As you listen, you match the correct option to each speaker. You use each option only once, and there are three extra options that you do not need to use.

- The options test your understanding of attitude and opinion, and you need to listen to the general meaning (or gist) of what each speaker is saying.
- You'll have time to read the options before you hear the recording, and you'll hear the recording twice.
- Each question is worth one mark.

Practice task

1 🔊 **L12** You will hear three short extracts in which people are talking about visiting a city for the first time. For questions 1–3, choose from the list (A–E) how each speaker feels about their first visit to the city. There are two extra letters which you do not need to use. You will hear the speakers twice.

A disappointed by the amount of green space
B impressed by the architecture
C frustrated by the transport system
D fed up with the number of tourists
E surprised about the pollution

Speaker 1		1
Speaker 2		2
Speaker 3		3

How did you do?

2 Check your answers.

3a Read the audioscript for Ex 1 speaker 1. Look at the highlighted phrases (1–3). Which topic in the options (A–E) does each refer to?

> **TIP:** You may hear the topic or idea of more than one option mentioned, but the way the person feels about them will not be the same as in the option. You need to listen for both the feeling and the topic.

I'd been really looking forward to my first visit to the city, and in many ways it lived up to my expectations. There were loads of different things to do, places to see, great restaurants. I would have liked there to be ¹more parks – having open areas was something I felt was missing. Even so, the whole place had a buzz about it, and the ²huge groups of visitors everywhere only added to that. I didn't find it easy to get round, but I think that was my fault really – I hadn't done any research into ³buses and trams. On my second visit, I found they were actually very efficient.

3b Now, highlight the words in the audioscript that tell you how the speaker thinks and feels about the topic in each option you have identified. Why is only option A correct?

4 Look at the highlighted words in the audioscript for Ex 1 speaker 2. What feelings are they expressing? Which one tells you that the speaker is surprised? What was he surprised about?

We had a great weekend away in the city – it was difficult to take in how the designs of the buildings have changed over the centuries, not always for the better in my opinion! They didn't always blend in well. Any city that's very old tends to have narrow streets in its centre, and the air quality, caused by the buses and cars, was particularly poor – I didn't expect that. And like any place with history, there were lots of people enjoying the sights, so it was crowded, though not where we wanted to spend our time.

5a The highlighted words in the script for Ex 1 speaker 3 tell you how the speaker is feeling. Look forward in the script to see what caused her to feel that way.

> **TIP:** The right option (the answer) may come after the feeling itself.

I loved the atmosphere of the city – especially at night, when theatres and restaurants were crowded. I couldn't believe how difficult it was to get from one place to another, though – the maps were so difficult to understand and the buses were a nightmare! You waited for half an hour and then three came at once! We walked a lot because of that, particularly through the beautiful parks and gardens – we had a view of the whole city from one of them, which was amazing. We talked to people in our hotel about our reactions and we all felt we'd be back, particularly to see more of the old buildings and museums.

5b Are there any other feelings expressed in this audioscript? How does the speaker feel, and about what?

Strategies and skills

Identifying attitude

To identify how a speaker is feeling, you may need to listen for phrases you can link to an option.

> **TIP:** Make sure you listen carefully for the way the speaker explains his or her feelings, and don't just listen for the ideas in the options themselves.

1 Look at the options from a task (1–6) and two versions (A and B) of what a speaker says for each one. Both versions refer to the option, but only one matches the feeling as well. Choose the version (A or B) that matches the option best. Highlight the phrase that helped you.

How did each speaker feel about the course?

1   pleased with the method of teaching
    A   The lessons are taught by different people every day.
    B   The way the lessons are organised is really helpful.

2   encouraged by the attitude of the teachers
    A   The teachers make us feel really good about what we can achieve.
    B   The teachers are quite helpful in general, though we don't see them often.

3   happy with the others on the course
    A   The other students are good fun and very supportive, and that makes it easier.
    B   There are a lot of students studying the same thing, which is fine.

4   challenged in a good way by the course content
    A   The topics are hard, but we have lots of time to read up on them.
    B   What we study is really difficult, but that makes us work even harder.

5   surprised by how interesting the course was
    A   I'd already been told that I would find it boring.
    B   I couldn't believe that anything could be as engaging as this.

6   motivated to try a similar course in future
    A   It's really made me realise how much more I want to learn.
    B   I've learnt so much that I feel like an expert now.

SPEAKING BOOST

Discuss or answer.

1   In what ways can a plan or project failing have a positive outcome?

2   How do you respond when things go wrong? Give examples.

Listening for gist

Sometimes you may not be able to link an option directly to a single word or phrase used by the speaker. Then you need to think about the general meaning (or gist) of what the speaker is saying.

> **TIP:** In the exam, you hear the speakers twice. The first time you listen, just put a pencil mark against the option you think is correct. The second time, check all the options again, and confirm your answer.

2a Look at the extracts (1–5), where speakers are talking about holidays. What does each speaker think about them? Match the opinions (A–F) to the extracts. There is one letter which you do not need to use.

A   I have mixed feelings about it.

B   I don't mind doing something I'm not keen on.

C   I prefer old things to new ones.

D   I think carefully before choosing somewhere to go.

E   I was disappointed with the experience I'd chosen.

F   I felt I had to complain about a particular aspect of it.

1   The lodges in the resort we chose to stay in had been converted from really historic houses. They had so much more character and interest than boring modern purpose-built resorts. I enjoyed imagining who had lived in them in the past.

2   I often go to the beach for a holiday with my family, which can be good and bad. Beach resorts are often crowded and noisy, but they have loads of facilities so you don't get bored. Having a break in a resort in my country can be hit and miss with the weather, though.

3   I don't usually go for self-catering accommodation, especially as I then have to do the cooking, so I don't get a break. On the other hand, it's more convenient for the whole family which makes everything more enjoyable in the long run, so it's actually fine with me!

4   The hotel we stayed in was very luxurious, and I couldn't fault the facilities. I can't say the same about the staff, though, and in fact I mentioned this to the manager at the end of our stay. If a hotel wants people to return, then they need to employ friendly and helpful staff.

5   The safari we went on was very well organised, but our aim was to see animals and there weren't that many around. I don't really understand why – maybe we were just unlucky, or maybe we picked the wrong time of year.

2b 🎧 **L13** **Now listen and think about your answers. Are they correct?**

Interpreting opinion

A speaker may not always give his or her opinion directly and you need to think about what they really mean.

3 🎧 **L14** Listen to some speakers (1–6) and choose the opinion (A or B) each speaker expresses. You will hear the speakers twice.

> **TIP:** Don't be distracted if you hear a word and also see it in an option – think about what the speaker is actually saying.

1 A It's always better to tell the truth.
  B Telling a lie is sometimes acceptable.

2 A Photos in black and white are more impact than those in colour.
  B Colour photos are better than black and white ones.

3 A It's possible to find more interesting things in independent shops.
  B You have more choice in a shopping mall than in independent shops.

4 A Sport is overrated as an enjoyable pastime.
  B Sport is good for everyone to enjoy.

5 A I'm fed up with the traffic management in town.
  B I'm glad that there's discussion of how to manage traffic in town.

6 A It's always better to save money than spend it.
  B It's a good idea to save money, but it's also important to enjoy yourself.

EXAM TASK

🎧 **L15** You will hear five short extracts in which people are talking about leading happy and satisfying lives. For questions 1–5, choose from the list (A–H) what each person says is most important for a happy and satisfying life. Use the letters only once. There are three extra letters which you do not need to use. You will hear the speakers twice.

A having new challenges
B earning a lot of money
C having a status and position in society
D maintaining long-lasting relationships
E keeping relaxed and stress-free
F being able to help other people
G getting a good work/life balance
H being open and honest

Speaker 1		1
Speaker 2		2
Speaker 3		3
Speaker 4		4
Speaker 5		5

TEST

ABOUT THE TASK

- In Listening Part 4, you hear one long text which lasts around 3-4 minutes. This is usually an interview. There are two speakers, an interviewer and an interviewee, and seven questions, each with three options to choose from.

- Each question relates to a specific part of the recording, and is introduced by the interviewer.

- The questions on the page follow the order you hear them on the recording. The answers come from what the interviewee says, not the interviewer.

- The questions test your understanding of the speaker's attitude, opinion or feeling. You may also be tested on detail or specific information, or on a particular point the speaker makes.

- Some questions might focus on a specific phrase or sentence in the recording, and others might ask you to understand the main idea of what the speaker is saying.

- You will have a minute to read through the questions before you hear the recording, and you will hear the recording twice.

- Each question is worth one mark.

Practice task

1 🎧 **L16** You will hear part of a radio interview with a bookseller called Paula Adams, who is talking about selling children's books. For questions 1-3, choose the best answer (A, B or C). You will hear the interview twice.

1 Paula suggests that gender-specific books
 A look more attractive to shoppers.
 B are more straightforward to sell.
 C make more money than other genres.

2 What is Paula's attitude towards consumers?
 A She dislikes the way they prefer to shop.
 B She regrets the type of book they often choose.
 C She understands that they need advice about purchases.

3 What is Paula's opinion about providing separate books for boys and girls?
 A It's the only way to please them both.
 B It's difficult to change people's perceptions.
 C It's possible to write popular books about all subjects.

How did you do?

2 Check your answers.

3a Look again at Ex 1 question 1 and the highlighted part of the audioscript, which gives you the answer. What is the question testing? Choose A, B or C.
 A opinion   B feeling   C detail

I: Today on our programme about current social issues around gender, I'm talking to Paula Adams, a bookseller who specialises in children's books. Paula, how do you feel about the way children's books are often marketed?

P: Well, my livelihood depends on marketing and selling books, and I want people to buy as many as possible. If a book is labelled as being for girls or boys, it makes it clearer for me to categorise and put onto shelves with similar books. That means it's much easier for shoppers to find and buy when they're browsing. In fact, if books have also got covers that are coloured blue or pink, so much the better from my point of view!

3b Does the speaker say that gender-specific books are
 A more attractive?   B easier to find?

3c The speaker mentions her livelihood, but does she mention the money she actually makes?
Yes / No

4 Look again at Ex 1 question 2 and the highlighted parts of the audioscript (1-3). All the topics in the options are mentioned, but look at the feelings mentioned in the question. Which highlighted section indicates that Paula understands a situation, instead of disliking or regretting it?

I: Don't you think consumers can make their own minds up about what books they buy?

P: Many of my books are bought as gifts, often by people who don't have much contact with kids directly,[1] so they may not make the right choice. [2] When these people shop for a book, they don't browse through all those on offer – they go straight for the target market of the book they want – that is, boys or girls. [3] So, if that's what they want, I know I have to give them the support they obviously require. If they look online, they'll certainly search with those words, not by title or author.

5 Look again at Ex 1 question 3. It is testing Paula's opinion, and you need to understand the gist of what she is saying. Does she talk about pleasing people, changing perceptions or writing books? Highlight the part of the audioscript where you can find the answer.

I: But what about the argument that you're cutting children off from learning about the whole world by doing this?

P: Well, I agree that not all boys like the kinds of things we think they do – football, cars and so on – and not all girls want to read about princesses, but you have to understand that, as a sweeping generalisation, the opposite tends to be true. I don't want to perpetuate a stereotype, and seem to be promoting traditional gender roles, but I have to accept what I see as a fact, which is there's no other possibility to keep everyone happy. People may try to pretend that boys and girls share the same interests, but they really don't.

Strategies and skills

Identifying the main idea

Questions often test your understanding of the speaker's main point.

1 🎧 **L17 Listen to six different people talking about consumerism. What is the main point each person is making? Choose the correct answer (A or B). You will hear each speaker twice.**

1 A Buying books without thinking too much can be a good thing.
   B Buying books because they look good is not sensible.

2 A Parents don't have to think carefully about the toys they buy their children.
   B People don't understand how strong the influence of toys on children can be.

3 A We spend too much money on buying new things.
   B We should look after our possessions more carefully.

4 A We all own too many things.
   B It's difficult to know what to throw away.

5 A What people spend money on has changed.
   B Fashions in home design are different nowadays.

6 A There are too many advertisements in everyday life.
   B Advertising has become too effective and difficult to resist.

2 **Complete the sentences with a phrase from the box that highlights the main point the speaker (1–6) is making. The purpose of their main point is in brackets.**

> in fact   one thing is   the fact is   the key
> the main one is   what often happens is

1 People often intend to go to the gym regularly, but _____ that they lose motivation and give up. **(give the common result)**

2 I love flying to other countries, but _____ that air travel is bad for the environment. **(state the issue in general)**

3 I try to find ways of improving my study habits. _____ to set aside specific time in the evening to do it. **(give an example)**

4 There are lots of reasons why people should save money but _____ to avoid getting into debt. **(give the most important reason)**

5 There are lots of important environmental issues nowadays, but in my opinion _____ underlying one is climate change. **(state the most important issue)**

6 Many people think that it's all right to use plastic, but _____ it's doing a lot of damage to the environment. **(state the truth)**

Speakers often use phrases to introduce a reason or an example for their main idea.

3 **Choose the best word or phrase to complete each sentence.**

1 Advertising should be controlled **for example / because** it causes people to spend too much.

2 It's good that we all know about environmental issues, **which leads to / thanks to** television documentaries.

3 I have lots of hobbies, **for instance / as** birdwatching.

4 I'd love to play in an orchestra, but the main **reason / problem** is that I don't have the ability.

5 There's a great film on at the cinema, and **that's why / that's because** I'm going on Saturday.

6 I stayed up too late last night, and **the result of that / the reason for that** is that I'm tired today.

Discuss or answer.

1 What toys, games and activities did you like when you were young? Why do you think you liked these things?

2 What do you wish you had tried when you were young?

Understanding opinions

It is important to understand what a speaker thinks about something, even though they may not state it clearly.

> **TIP:** Remember, it's important to listen for the gist (general meaning) of what a speaker says and not to get distracted by individual words that also occur in the options.

4 🎧 **L18 Listen to some speakers (1–6) and choose their opinion (A or B). You will hear each speaker twice.**

1 A I prefer to have fewer friends.
   B I like to know a lot of people.

2 A I like it when people don't say what they think.
   B I think that there is more involved when people don't say what they think.

3 A I don't think the problem is serious.
   B I don't like the personalities of the people involved.

4 A The problem is easier to solve than I expected.
   B The problem is completely unimportant.

5 A I don't find psychology interesting for any one reason.
   B There are different aspects of psychology that I like.

6 A It's good that history is interesting.
   B The most important aspect of history is learning from it.

Dealing with paraphrase

You won't hear the same ways of expressing things as you read in the options. The information will be expressed in a different way, or paraphrased.

5 Complete the second sentence with a word or phrase from the box.

> argue   deafening   follow my dreams
> inconvenient   in the spotlight   simplicity

1 It's difficult for me to get the bus into town – it's always scheduled at the wrong time.

The bus times are _____ for me.

2 The siblings got on very well most of the time, and rarely fell out.

It was unusual for the siblings to _____ .

3 The noise from the jet engine made it difficult to hear anything.

The sound of the jet engine was _____ .

4 I'm really ambitious, and will do anything to achieve my aims.

I'm determined to _____ , whatever it takes.

5 I love the idea that the trip will be so straightforward.

It's the _____ of the trip that appeals to me.

6 Famous people must hate having no privacy – they're always on view.

It must be hard for famous people to be _____ all the time.

🎧 **L19** You will hear part of a radio interview with a man called Alan Winters, who is a professional musician playing the clarinet in a theatre orchestra. For questions 1–7, choose the best answer (A, B or C). You will hear the interview twice.

1 Alan decided to take up the clarinet because he wanted to
   A play in an orchestra.
   B satisfy a family member.
   C fulfil a long-held ambition.

2 What does Alan think about the practice he has to do?
   A It has a psychological impact on him.
   B It can be difficult to fit enough into his schedule.
   C It is more important than he'd realised before he started work.

3 According to Alan, when he's playing in the pit in theatres he
   A finds it an interesting space to work in.
   B feels frustrated that there isn't more room.
   C is comfortable with the feeling he gets there.

4 According to Alan, people don't realise that a pit player
   A should develop specialist musical skills.
   B needs to work closely with other musicians.
   C has to accept a lot of time-wasting.

5 How does Alan feel if he can't play a particular performance?
   A He appreciates the fact that other people can take over.
   B He is glad to be able to do something different.
   C He feels guilty about letting people down.

6 In Alan's opinion, the conductor of a pit orchestra
   A must have a good relationship with all the musicians.
   B has more responsibilities than a regular conductor.
   C needs to understand both vocal and instrumental music.

7 What advice would Alan pass on to other aspiring pit musicians?
   A get your name well known
   B develop a variety of interests
   C make friends with other musicians

ABOUT THE TASK

- In Speaking Part 1, the examiner asks you some questions about yourself.

- The first question is always the same, and the examiner asks you where you are from. The following questions are on everyday topics, such as what you enjoy doing with friends, holidays, interests and so on.

- If you don't understand a question, ask the examiner to repeat it.

- The examiner asks you and your partner questions individually. You should not talk to your partner in this part, so don't interrupt them, agree or disagree with what they've said or add any information to their answer.

- The examiner will ask you and your partner different questions, but you should still listen to what your partner says even though you won't be asked to comment.

- You should try to give interesting answers, but don't speak for too long.

- The examiner will not respond to what you say, but will move on to the next question once you've finished speaking. You may be asked three or four questions, and the part takes about two minutes.

- Use this first part of the test to relax, and to settle into the exam situation.

Practice task

1 **S01** Read these Speaking Part 1 questions. Now listen to the questions and answer them.

1 Where are you from?
2 Do you have a favourite colour? (What is it?) (Why?)
3 Can you tell us about your family?
4 What do you enjoy doing at the weekends? (Why?)
5 Are you interested in any sports? (Why? / Why not?)
6 Can you speak any other languages apart from English? (What are they?)

How did you do?

2a Look at the questions from Ex 1 again and some answers to them (A, B and C). Choose the best answer for each question.

1 Where are you from?
   A Milan is a city in the north of Italy. There's a river and a cathedral and lots of good places to go shopping. There are lots of tourists there.
   B It's Barcelona in Spain.
   C I come from Paris, and I've lived there all my life.

2 Do you have a favourite colour? (What is it?) (Why?)
   A Oh, definitely blue – I often wear clothes in that colour and it matches my eyes.
   B I don't have one – I don't think about it.
   C My football team wears red and black.

3 Can you tell us about your family?
   A I have a brother and a sister.
   B I have two brothers who are older than me, and a sister who's younger.
   C My mum is a doctor. I want to do the same as her.

4 What do you enjoy doing at the weekends? (Why?)
   A I go shopping with my friends.
   B I watch television after school and I like comedy programmes best.
   C I love going to the cinema, although, if the weather is good, I prefer doing something outside like playing tennis.

5 Are you interested in any sports? (Why? / Why not?)
   A I like to listen to music and watch television.
   B I don't like sport. I like music.
   C I used to play hockey, but now I only run because I don't have as much time.

6 Can you speak any other languages apart from English? (What are they?)
   A I love speaking other languages, and I'm learning Spanish and French now.
   B No, not really. I don't like it.
   C I really enjoy learning English, because I like the pronunciation of the language.

2b Check your answers.

3a Think about what is wrong with the other answers in Ex 2 and choose the best option (1 or 2) for each one.

1 It doesn't answer the question, and has irrelevant information.

2 It uses very simple language.

> **TIP:** You should try to give interesting answers and use a range of complex language from the start of the Speaking test. Make sure that you really do answer the question you've been asked and don't include too much irrelevant information.

3b **S02** Improve the incorrect answers in Ex 2a. Then listen to some answers given by students to compare your ideas.

4a Think about your own answers to the questions in Ex 1. Did you:
- answer the questions? ☐
- give interesting answers, not simple ones? ☐
- only give relevant information? ☐

4b Try the task in Ex 1 again, using the checklist above.

TEACH

Strategies and skills

Extending your answers with appropriate detail and examples

Answers to Speaking Part 1 questions should include some relevant details, such as reasons or examples.

TIP: If you practise adding **because** or a similar phrase to your answer to give a reason, this will encourage you to say more.

1 All the words or phrases in the box can be used instead of 'because' to extend your answers by giving a reason, except one. Which is the odd word out?

> as   due to the fact that   otherwise
> owing to   since   the reason is

2 Rewrite the sentences using the word in brackets instead of 'because'.

1 The reason I like films is the escapism they provide. (since)

   I like _____ escapism.

2 The reason I haven't been abroad is I hate flying. (as)

   I haven't _____ flying.

3 I need to practise my English more, but the reason I haven't is the lack of time. (owing to)

   I can't practise _____ time.

4 It's difficult for me to get to college – the reason is that the bus route has been changed. (due to the fact that)

   It's difficult for me _____ the bus route has been changed.

3 Choose the correct word to complete the answers. What do all the correct words do?

1 I often go out in the evenings – **for example / when** I go for a walk in the countryside if the weather's nice.

2 I listen to a lot of different kinds of music, **such as / as well as** jazz.

3 I'm good at lots of sports, **for instance / as** tennis and hockey.

4 My favourite kind of film is science fiction, **like / so as** *Star Wars*.

5 I'm hopeless at choosing colours that suit me – **such / for example** my jacket clashes with my skirt now!

6 I'd love to eat at a Chinese restaurant tonight – **since / like** that one in the centre of town.

4 Look at the questions below. What extra information could you add to the answers already given? Complete the sentences with your own ideas.

TIP: You can prepare ideas for the kinds of topics that you may be asked about, but don't learn answers by heart.

Everyday life

1 How do you travel to college every day? (Why?)

   I go to college by bus because _____ .

2 Do you like to do the same things every evening, or something different? (Why?)

   I like to do something different due to the fact that _____ .

3 How much free time do you have during the week? (Why?)

   I don't have much free time. The reason is that I spend most of my time working, so I'm glad when _____ .

4 Do you like to have a routine in your life? (Why / Why not?)

   Oh, absolutely! If I don't, then I _____ , like I _____ .

Entertainment

1 Do you prefer to watch films at home or at the cinema? (Why?)

   I prefer _____ since _____ .

2 What's your favourite kind of television programme? (Why?)

   I really like _____ , for example _____ .

3 Do you ever go to the theatre? (Why? / Why not?)

   I'd love to, but it's difficult where I live owing to _____ – like _____ .

4 Do you usually like the same kind of entertainment as your friends? (Why? / Why not?)

   We do share a lot of interests, but actually _____ , for instance _____ .

Asking for repetition

If you have not heard or understood a question correctly, you can ask the examiner to repeat it.

> **TIP:** Remember that the examiner can only repeat the question to help you, not rephrase it.

5 Match 1–6 to a–f to make phrases you can use to ask the examiner to repeat the question.

1	I'm sorry, but could	**a**	did you say?
2	Would you mind	**b**	you say it again, please?
3	I'm not sure what	**c**	I'm afraid I didn't catch what you said.
4	I didn't hear	**d**	repeating the question, please?
5	Sorry, but what	**e**	what you said.
6	Pardon?	**f**	you said, I'm sorry.

Using a range of language

It is important not to repeat words too much, and to use a range of language.

6 Choose a word or phrase from the box to replace the highlighted words in the sentences.

> boring   comfortable   decided on   drove
> enjoy   prefer   relaxing   sunny   visited

1 I went _____ to the beach last weekend. After that I went to see _____ my aunt.

2 I went on holiday to the coast last year, and stayed in a nice _____ hotel.

3 It took me ages to choose a present for my sister. Eventually I chose _____ a book.

4 The weather wasn't very nice _____ so I stayed at home at the weekend. It was nice _____ though, because I just took it easy.

5 I like playing football and I also like _____ watching it on television too, though I like _____ playing it more.

6 It's not interesting _____ just sitting on a beach – it's more interesting to visit new places.

🎧 **S03** Listen to the questions. Answer them so that they are true for you.

Where are you from?

First we'd like to know something about you.

Future plans

What are you going to do this coming weekend? (Why?)

Where would you like to go for your next holiday? (Why?)

Do you have any plans for your career in the future? (What are they?) (Why?)

Education

What was your favourite subject at your first school? (Why?)

Tell us about a favourite teacher from school or college. (Why did you like them?)

Do you often see your friends from school or college? (Why? / Why not?)

Technology

Do you use the internet much for shopping? (Why? / Why not?)

Do you ever switch off your mobile phone? (Why? / Why not?)

Do you find out about the news on the internet, or another way? (Why?)

- In Speaking Part 2, you have to speak alone for about a minute. You should not help your partner or interrupt them in this part.

- The examiner gives you two photographs, and tells you what they show. The examiner then reads out a task related to the photographs for you to do.

- This task has two parts – first you compare your two photographs and then answer a question about them. You have about a minute for this and should try to spend about half the minute on each part.

- The question is written on the paper above the photographs. You should always answer this question based on what you can see in the photographs.

- When you have finished speaking, the examiner will ask your partner a follow-up question about your photographs. This question is not written down, is about your partner's personal preferences and only requires a short answer (about thirty seconds).

- Your partner is given two different photographs and a task to complete. When they have finished speaking, the examiner will ask you a follow-up question about your partner's photographs.

Practice task

1 🎧 **S04** Look at the photographs and listen to the instructions. Complete the task.

Your photographs show people choosing fruit in different situations. I'd like you to compare the photographs and say why you think the people are choosing fruit in these situations.

> **Why are the people choosing fruit in these situations?**

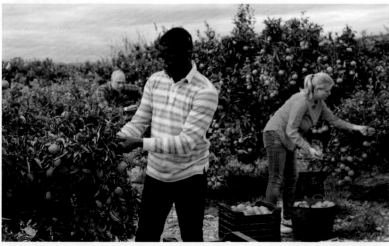

How did you do?

2a 🎧 **S05** Listen to two students (A and B) doing the task in Ex 1 and put ticks in the correct boxes.

Which student:	Student A	Student B
describes the photographs?	☐	☐
compares the photographs?	☐	☐
answers the question fully while talking about both photographs?	☐	☐
talks only about the people in the photographs (not about themself)?	☐	☐

2b Which student gave the best answer? Why?

3a Think about your own answer to the task in Ex 1. Did you:

- compare the photographs? ☐
- answer the question? ☐
- talk about the people in the photographs? ☐
- talk for about minute? ☐

3b Try the task in Ex 1 again, using the checklist above.

Strategies and skills
Comparing different but related situations

In the Speaking Part 2 task, you have to compare two photographs which show different situations but which have some things in common. You need to identify things that are the same or similar and things that are different.

> **TIP:** Examples of things that might be the same or different include whether it is inside/outside, in the city/countryside, sunny/raining, etc.

1 **Read the exam task and look at the photographs. Think about how they are similar and different.**

Your photographs show friends having a snack together in different places. Compare the photographs and say what you think the friends are enjoying about having a snack together in these places.

> **What are the friends enjoying about having a snack together in these places?**

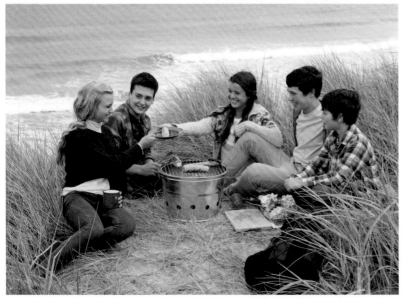

2 **Complete the sentences (1–5) comparing the photographs.**

> **TIP:** You need to talk about both photographs, so don't describe too much detail in one of them.

1 Both photographs show _____ .

2 What's the same in both photographs is _____ .

3 The first photograph shows _____ while the second one shows _____ .

4 Another thing that's different is _____ .

5 The women are _____ whereas the group of friends are _____ .

3 **Look at the question above the photographs. Complete the sentences (1–7) about them, answering the question.**

> **TIP:** Remember to compare the two photographs before you move on to answering the question.

The first photograph:

1 In the first photograph the women are enjoying _____ .

2 They look _____ .

3 The women seem to be _____ .

The second photograph:

4 In the second photograph the friends are enjoying _____ .

5 The friends look _____ .

6 The whole group seem to be _____ .

Both photographs:

7 In both photographs the people are enjoying _____ .

4 🎧 **S06 Listen to a student doing the whole task. Did they have the same ideas as you?**

Making speculations

The question gives you the opportunity to use complex language, and to speculate about the people in the photographs. This means you can say what you think they are doing or feeling.

> **TIP:** Remember to talk about the people in the photographs, not yourself.

5 Look at the photograph below. It shows people studying outside. What can you say in answer to each of the questions (1–3)? Make sentences using these phrases.

- They might be …
- It's possible that …
- They could have …
- I think they are …

1 What are the people enjoying about studying outside?

2 What are the people finding difficult about studying outside?

3 Why have the people decided to study outside?

6 🎧 **S07** Listen to three students answering the questions in Ex 5. Did they have the same ideas as you?

Organising a long turn

You should connect your ideas using linking words to make your answer sound well thought-out and organised.

7 Look at the task and choose the best words to complete the student's answer so that it makes a well-organised talk.

Your photographs show people waiting in different situations. Compare the photographs and say what you think the people are finding difficult about waiting in these situations.

> **What are the people finding difficult about waiting in these situations?**

¹To begin with, / At the beginning, both pictures show people waiting, but they're in different situations. **²To compare them, / In comparison**, in the first picture the people are inside an airport, and they're waiting in a queue to check in their bags. I can see a lot of luggage, and the people are wearing light clothes. **³Also, / On the other hand**, the people in the second photograph are waiting for a bus, but they're standing outside in a – I'm not sure about it, but I think it's called a bus shelter – and they're wearing warm clothes. **⁴Because / As for** what they're finding difficult, the people in the airport may be going on holiday. **⁵For that reason, / Since** they're looking forward to their journey, so they are finding it difficult to be patient. The reason the people might find it difficult waiting for the bus is that they're very cold **⁶as / so** I can see snow on the ground. **⁷To that end, / To finish**, I must say that I think the people outside are in the more difficult situation!

Answering the follow-up question to your partner's long turn

When your partner has finished talking about their photographs, you will be asked a follow-up question about them. This question is about you and your opinion and preferences.

> **TIP:** You can extend your answers by giving an example, but don't speak for too long.

8 Look at the follow-up questions (1–4) and the student answers (A and B). Which answer is best? Why?

1 Which of these things would you prefer to do?
   A I'd rather go to the beach, because I love swimming and being in the fresh air.
   B The people are enjoying swimming, which is nice.

2 Do you enjoy doing sport?
   A I don't. I'm not good at it.
   B I don't enjoy it very much, although I do it because I need to keep fit.

3 Would you like to go on these holidays?
   A I'd rather go to the beach, like the people in the first photograph.
   B I always go on holiday to the mountains.

4 Do you often travel by bus?
   A I love going by bus, and I go to school by bus every day. I meet my friends on the bus and we talk about lots of things. When I go shopping I use the bus, too, and one year I even went on holiday with my family and we took a bus tour around the lakes. We did windsurfing and sailing even though it rained a lot. It was great.
   B I don't usually go by bus, because the service in my town is not very good. I prefer to walk or drive.

Dealing with unfamiliar vocabulary

You may have to talk about something you don't know the words for, or you may have forgotten them. There are some phrases you can learn to help you in these situations.

9 Complete the sentences with the words from the box. They form phrases you can use if you are not sure of a word.

> call it   can't remember   gone blank
> not sure   should know   what's

1 I _____ the word for this, but I just can't think of it at the moment.

2 I'm sorry, but my mind's _____ .

3 That's a … what do you _____ ?
   … a bench.

4 I want to talk about that thing in the corner – _____ the word for it? Um – it's something you can sit on.

5 I'm _____ about it, but I think it's called a bench.

6 I know it's something you use for writing with, but I _____ the name.

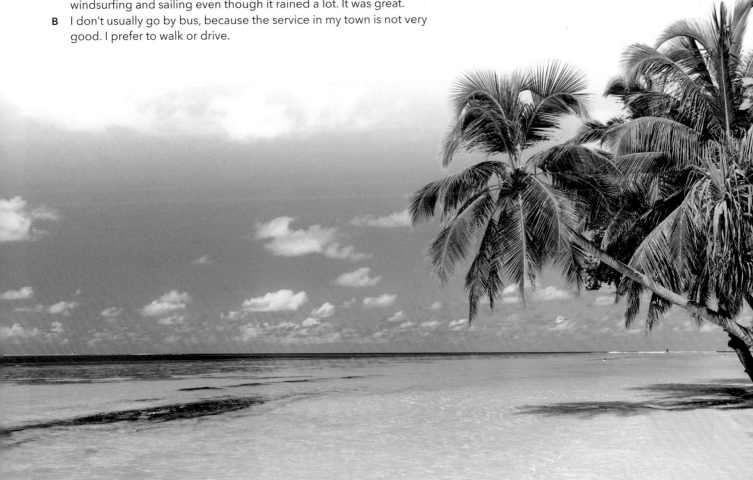

🎧 **S08** **Listen and complete the exam task.**

Candidate A, your photographs show people enjoying painting in different situations.

I'd like you to compare the photographs and say what you think the people are enjoying about painting in these situations.

What are the people enjoying about painting in these situations?

Candidate B, do you enjoy painting?

Candidate B, your photographs show people feeling tired in different situations.

I'd like you to compare the photographs and say why you think the people are feeling tired in these situations.

Why are the people feeling tired in these situations?

Candidate A, have you ever been cycling in the mountains?

ABOUT THE TASK

- In Speaking Part 3, you have to talk to your partner.
- The examiner reads out a situation and then gives you both a question to discuss. This question is presented as a diagram on a piece of paper, with five written prompts which give you ideas for your discussion.
- You have a short time to look at the task before you need to start speaking.
- You have about two minutes for your discussion.
- You do not have to speak about all of the prompts, and you can add ideas of your own.

- The examiner stops you after about two minutes, and asks you a second question which is related to the topic you have been discussing. This question is not written down, and you are asked to reach a decision with your partner.
- You have about a minute for this. It doesn't matter if you and your partner are unable to agree on a final decision - it's your discussion that is important, and there is no right answer.

Practice task

1 🎧 **S09** Look at the diagram, and listen to the examiner giving students the task. Think about what you would say about each of the prompts in the diagram.

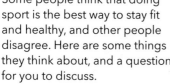

> Some people think that doing sport is the best way to stay fit and healthy, and other people disagree. Here are some things they think about, and a question for you to discuss.
> First you have some time to look at the task.
>
> Now, talk to each other about **whether doing a sport is the best way to stay fit and healthy**.

| eating the right food | enjoying competition | benefiting mentally |

Is doing some kind of sport the best way to stay fit and healthy?

| not having sporting ability | getting injured |

> Now you have about a minute to decide **what the best reason is for choosing only to do sport to stay fit and healthy**.

2 🎧 **S10** Listen to a student talking about the first part of the task and respond to their comments. Mention the following things in your response when you hear numbers 1–3.

1 enjoying competition
2 not having sporting ability
3 getting injured

How did you do?

3 🎧 **S11** Listen to two students doing the first part of the task in Ex 1. Do they have the same ideas as you, or do they mention different ones? Tick the points they make in their discussion.

- doing sport with friends is fun ☐
- it's important to eat well and do sport ☐
- it's OK to eat chocolate sometimes ☐
- it's easy to lose motivation ☐
- watching sport on television is useful ☐
- it's possible to avoid injuries when doing sport ☐

4 🎧 **S12** Listen again to the students doing the first part of the task in Ex 1.

1 Do they ask one another what they think? **Yes / No**

2 Do they give their own opinions? **Yes / No**

3 Do they give examples and reasons to support their opinions? **Yes / No**

5a 🎧 **S13** Listen to the students doing the second part of the task in Ex 1. Do they reach a decision? If so, what is it?

5b 🎧 **S14** Listen to the second part of the task again. Tick the two phrases that the students use to reach their decision.

- Is that all right with you? ☐
- I'll go along with that. ☐
- I agree with the decision. ☐

6a Think about your own answer to the first part of the task (Ex 2).

Did you:
- give your own opinion? ☐
- ask for your partner's opinion? ☐
- use expressions for agreeing/disagreeing? ☐

6b Try the task again, using the checklist above.

Strategies and skills

Asking for and giving opinions

In the Speaking Part 3 discussion, you should ask your partner for their opinions as well as giving your own.

1 Complete the table with expressions for asking for and giving opinions from the box. Add question marks where necessary.

> Any ideas about this one
> Don't you think that
> From my point of view
> It seems to me that
> My thinking is
> My view on this is
> The point I'm making is
> What do you think
> What do you think about that
> What's your opinion on this

asking for opinion	giving an opinion

You should try to give a reason for your opinion, as this leads to a better discussion. It also helps your partner by giving them ideas, and something to respond and react to.

2 Look at the task and the prompts below. Using the phrases (1–8), make sentences about each prompt, thinking of a good reason for your idea.

> Some people think it's important to take photographs of special events, and other people disagree. Here are some things they think about, and a question for you to discuss.
>
> | having lasting memories | enjoying events at the time | sharing experiences with friends |
> | --- | --- | --- |
>
> **Is it important to take photographs of special events?**
>
> | deciding what to photograph | having the technical skills |
> | --- | --- |

1   **For me,** it's important to take photographs **because** …

2   **My opinion on** taking photographs **is** that it's not a good thing **as** …

3   **My point of view is** … **since** …

4   **I see it like this.** …

5   **What I'm saying is,** taking photographs all the time is bad, **owing to** …

6   **I would say that** taking photographs is hard, **due to** …

7   **Let me explain. The reason I think** taking photos at special events is bad **is** …

8   **It seems to me that** everyone takes photos nowadays **because** …

3 🎧 **S15** Listen to two students discussing the task in Ex 2 and answer these questions (1 and 2). You will hear the discussion twice.

1   Do they ask for each other's opinion? Tick the phrases they use from Ex 1.

2   Do they give reasons for their own opinion? What are they?

4 🎧 **S16** Listen again and compare their reasons with your ideas.

Showing how far you agree or disagree

You can agree or disagree with your partner very simply or show your opinion more strongly.

5 Look at the dialogues. Read the opinions (1–6) then choose the strongest form of agreement or disagreement (A or B).

1   I think that everyone should do some kind of exercise.
    A   I partly agree, but it's not easy to do it.
    B   I totally agree – they definitely should.

2   In my opinion, it's nice to have a short break occasionally.
    A   Good point – it's important to do that.
    B   I guess you're probably right, though it's expensive.

3   In my view, people watch too much television.
    A   Possibly, but don't you think that they do other things as well?
    B   I think exactly the same – it's a waste of time.

4   In my view, shopping is a great leisure activity!
    A   I have a slightly different idea of leisure activity to be honest.
    B   I can't go along with that – it's really not a good use of time.

5   There's no point in having a holiday if you don't go abroad.
    A   How can you say that?
    B   I agree up to a point, but they say that people travel too much nowadays.

6   My thinking on choosing a career is that it's best done when you're really young.
    A   I think the same – it's key to making the right decision.
    B   I guess you're probably right.

Before you agree or disagree with your partner, you can summarise what they have said. This is a useful way of checking you have understood their point of view.

> **TIP:** You should explore each point fully with your partner before moving on to the next.

6 Complete the table with the phrases for summarising and checking from the box.

> Did you mean … ?   Do you mean that … ?
> I guess what you mean is …
> I understood what you meant was …
> Is that right?
> Just to make sure I've understood, …
> Thinking about what you said about …
> When you said that …
> You said that …

summarising	checking

7a 🎧 **S17** Listen to six dialogues and complete the sentences (1–6) with the phrases from Ex 6 the second speaker uses to summarise or check their partner's opinion. You will hear each dialogue twice.

1   _____ sportspeople are paid too much, and I think the same. **(agree / strongly agree)**

2   _____ everyone should be able to drive a car, I wasn't sure about it. **(disagree / strongly disagree)**

3   _____ music being a great way to relax, I definitely find that myself. **(agree / strongly agree)**

4   Sorry, but _____ by damage to the environment _____ that it's actually harmful to the places people visit. I can't go along with that. **(disagree / strongly disagree)**

5   So, _____ , you think that adverts are boring, _____ ? I completely agree with you! **(agree / strongly agree)**

6   _____ that we should work less and holiday more! That sounds really good to me! **(agree / strongly agree)**

7b Does the second speaker in Ex 7a agree, strongly agree, disagree or strongly disagree with their partner's opinion? Choose the correct option.

Negotiating towards a decision

It's important that you discuss your decision in detail and don't decide too quickly.

> **TIP:** It doesn't matter if you don't manage to reach a final decision in the time given. It's the language you use that counts, and there's no right answer!

8 Match the beginning of the sentences (1–6) in each section about decisions with the correct phrase (a–f) to complete them.

Negotiating towards a decision

1	How do you	a	our final decision then?
2	Do you think	b	what we both think?
3	Shall we make	c	feel about it?
4	Is that all	d	agree on that?
5	So is that	e	right with you?
6	Shall we	f	the same?

Reaching agreement on a decision

1	We both feel that's	a	agreement on that.
2	I'll go	b	final decision.
3	I think we've come	c	along with that.
4	So we've definitely reached	d	on this one.
5	We've both decided	e	to a decision.
6	That's our	f	the best choice.

Expressing inability to reach a decision

1	I'm sorry, we can't agree	a	agree to disagree.
2	We both have a	b	an easy decision to make.
3	We're never going	c	we'll never agree on this.
4	It's not	d	different opinion on what's best.
5	We'll just have to	e	on a decision.
6	I think	f	to agree on this.

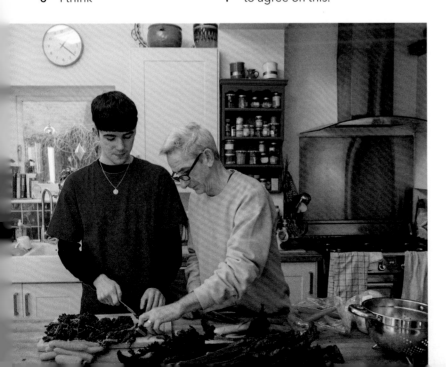

9 🎧 **S18** Complete the dialogues using appropriate phrases from Ex 8. Then listen to check your answers.

1 **A:** So we've talked about all the options and we have to make a decision. I'd like to choose this one – is that _____ ?
  B: Absolutely – I'll _____ .
  A: Great – then that's decided.

2 **A:** You said that you thought this was the best one. Shall we _____ ?
  B: Yes, I think we've definitely reached _____ .
  A: OK.

3 **A:** Any idea which one to choose? How do you _____ ?
  B: Well, we both _____ .
  A: We'll never make a decision, then.

4 **A:** I'd go for this one. Do you feel the same?
  B: It's not _____ – I'm not sure that's the right choice.
  A: Well then, I'm sorry, we'll just have to _____ .

10 Look at the questions and the options (A–C) for each one. Which one would you choose?

1 What's the most important reason for planning things in advance?
  A taking away pressure
  B looking forward to something
  C knowing what's happening

2 What's the best reason for cycling in a town?
  A cost
  B environmental concerns
  C time

3 What's the best reason for working abroad for a short time?
  A understanding the culture
  B making new friends
  C new experiences

4 What's the main reason for taking young people to the theatre?
  A relaxation
  B learning new things
  C having fun

5 What's the most important reason for learning to cook?
  A being independent
  B staying healthy
  C enjoying food

11 🎧 **S19** Listen to students discussing the options. Which one do they choose? Do they all make a final decision?

S20 Listen and complete the exam task.

Some people think it's a good idea to have advertisements during television programmes, and other people disagree. Here are some things they think about, and a question for you to discuss. First you have some time to look at the task.

Now, talk to each other about **whether it's a good idea to have advertisements during television programmes**.

need for information	pressure to buy	interrupting programmes

Is it a good idea to have advertisements during television programmes?

influencing children	paying for good programmes

Now you have about a minute to decide **what the best reason is for not having advertisements during television programmes**.

ABOUT THE TASK

- In Speaking Part 4, the examiner asks you questions that are related to the topic you discussed in Part 3. These questions develop the topic in different ways, and you should give your opinion on what you are asked.

- There is no specific number of questions you may be asked, because it depends on how much you want to say about each one. Part 4 usually lasts for about four minutes in total.

- The examiner may ask you and your partner individual questions, or ask you to discuss a question together. Even if your partner has been asked an individual question, you can still add your own opinion and develop a discussion.

- It's a good idea to refer to what your partner has said if you are adding to their answer.

- You should try to use complex language, and justify your opinions by adding reasons or personal examples.

- There is no right answer to any of the questions, so you should just say what you think. Try to give full answers if you can.

Practice task

1 🎧 **S21** In Speaking Part 3, you have been discussing the advantages and disadvantages of having a positive outlook on life. Now the examiner will ask you some further questions about the topic.

Listen to the questions. Make notes on what you would say in answer to each one.

1 Some people say that doing exercise helps people feel positive. What do you think?

2 In your opinion, does using social media help people have a positive attitude to life? (Why? / Why not?)

3 How important is it for people to show their feelings? (Why?)

How did you do?

2 🎧 **S22** Listen to students giving their own answers to the questions in Ex 1. Were their ideas similar to yours?

3 🎧 **S23** Listen to the answer to Ex 1 question 1 again.

1 Do the students give a personal example to support their idea?

2 Do they agree or disagree with each other?

4 Look at the students' answer to Ex 1 question 2.

1 Highlight the phrases they use to refer to what their partner has said.

2 Highlight the phrases they use to agree.

Examiner:	In your opinion, does using social media help people have a positive attitude to life?
Man:	Social media can create problems. If people post photos of themselves having a good time, it can make you feel a bit jealous.
Woman:	You say it can make you feel jealous, but actually those photos are often not the whole truth. People try to pretend they're having a better life than they really are.
Man:	You're right about that.

5 Look at the students' answer to Ex 1 question 3.

1 What example does the woman give for why it's good to share feelings?

2 Does the man agree or disagree with her?

Examiner:	How important do you think it is for people to show their feelings?
Woman:	It's really important, and I think women are better at it than men. If you can share your feelings with friends, it stops you thinking too much and getting depressed.
Man:	You said that women are better at showing their feelings, and I guess that used to be true, but maybe it's changing. I talk to my friends about lots of things – certainly more than just sport!
Woman:	OK – I accept what you say.

6 Look at your notes for Ex 1. Did you include examples to make your answers fuller and more interesting?

Strategies and skills
Giving full answers with examples and justifications

Try to add details to your answer. This gives you more to say and makes your answer more interesting.

1 Choose the correct word or phrase (A, B or C) to complete the added detail in the sentences.

1 I think it's important to feel positive about your work, because you work harder – _____ then you enjoy what you do more.
   A top of that   B plus   C as well

2 Obviously it's good if you can cook, because you eat better and _____ that you save money.
   A also   B on top of   C as well as this

3 It's important to have a holiday every year, because you relax and there's also _____ you can spend time with your family.
   A the point that B true that   C plus

4 I love sport because it keeps me fit, and _____ I have fun, too.
   A as well   B the point that C it's also true that

If you can, give a general example to support your opinion. This helps your partner by giving them something to respond to.

2 Complete the examples in the sentences with the words from the box.

> common   example   like   look   most   such

1 People are trying to do something about their carbon footprint – for _____ , they're walking more and using the car less.

2 People should do more exercise because it's _____ knowledge that we all lead sedentary lifestyles.

3 People buy too many things they don't need – just _____ at the number of shoppers in the shopping malls at the weekend.

4 I collect different kinds of pens, _____ as really old ones that used ink.

5 Tourists can cause problems in small towns – _____ in my town, it's very difficult to park when there are lots of visitors.

6 I hate seeing litter on the ground – _____ people are good, though, and do pick it up when they can.

Giving personal examples to support your opinion makes your answer more interesting.

> **TIP:** The information you give about yourself does not have to be true!

3 🎧 **S24** Listen to three students talking. Tick the phrases they use to give personal examples.

Speaking for myself ☐
I had a friend who ☐
Once, when I went to ☐
My sister enjoyed it, though I ☐
I really like it when ☐
What happened to me was ☐

You should also try to give a reason to justify your opinion. This gives you more opportunity to use complex language.

4 Match the sentences (1–6) to the reasons (a–f).

1 In my opinion, eating well is easier than doing exercise. That's because

2 I feel that we don't recycle enough. The reason I say that is

3 There's something to be said for getting a good qualification, even though it's hard. On balance, it shows that

4 I feel strongly about staying in nice hotels when I travel. As far as I'm concerned,

5 My family often go camping on holiday. The main reason is

6 The world temperatures are increasing. Surely that means that

a global warming is a fact.
b there are so many plastic bags just dumped in litter bins.
c you take your career seriously.
d comfort is everything.
e having nice meals is fun and exercise isn't.
f they like the outdoor life.

Adding ideas and developing a discussion

It's important to pick up on and extend what your partner has said when they answer a question.

5 Complete the phrases that you can use to develop a discussion with the words from the box.

> add   come in   example   interesting point
> the same   wouldn't

1   If I could _____ something to that …

2   Is it OK if I _____ here …?

3   That's a really _____ you've made, and I'd just like to say …

4   Really? It's not _____ in my country. We …

5   I agree completely with you. It _____ be a good idea to do that.

6   I've got an _____ of that to add to what you've said.

6 Look at the questions. What could you say in answer to them? Make notes on some ideas for each one.

1   Do you agree that social media is essential for keeping up with friends?

2   Do you think the time people spend using social media could be better spent doing other things?

3   How important is the internet for finding out about the news?

7 Look at the ideas students thought of to develop their answers to the questions in Ex 6. Match their ideas to the appropriate question. Were their ideas the same as yours?

- enjoying things like sport instead
- making arrangements easily
- convenience of communication
- importance of knowing what's happening in the world
- having time to read newspapers
- wasting time online

8 **S25** Listen to two students answering the questions from Ex 6. Tick the ideas they mention from Ex 7.

9 **S26** Listen again and tick the phrases from Ex 5 they use to develop the discussion.

Responding to a difficult question

If you think a question is difficult, you can respond to the examiner in different ways. For example, you can ask them to repeat the question or admit that you don't know how to answer it.

> **TIP:** It's better to say you haven't got an answer than to give irrelevant information.

10 The phrases below (1-6) give some ways of responding to the examiner if you find a question difficult. There are mistakes in four of them. Find the mistakes and correct them.

1   Oh, I've never thought about that.

2   I'm sorry but I don't have no ideas about that.

3   That's a good question – but I don't know how the answer is!

4   Sorry, I'm honestly not sure about that.

5   Could you repeat again the question, please? I didn't quite catch it.

6   Let me to think about it.

EXAM TASK

S27 In Speaking Part 3, you have been discussing whether it's important to be competitive in life. Now the examiner will ask you some further questions about the topic. Listen and answer the questions.

1   Do you enjoy taking part in competitions? (Why? / Why not?)

2   Do you think that being competitive is a natural quality, or can it be taught? (Why?)

3   Some people say that young children should be encouraged to be competitive at school. What do you think?

4   Do you think it's necessary to be competitive to be successful in life? (Why? / Why not?)

5   Is it possible to be too competitive? (Why? / Why not?)

6   In your opinion, what does success really mean? (Why?)

TEST

Questions 1-8

For questions 1-8, read the text below and decide which answer (A, B, C or D) best fits each gap.
There is an example at the beginning (0).

High heels

High heels are a familiar **(0)** _____B_____ around the world. Coming in all shapes, sizes and heights, they are widely **(1)** _____ to be an essential part of any elegant outfit for women. **(2)** _____ , the first high heels were in fact worn by men. They became fashionable among wealthy European men in the sixteenth century, as a **(3)** _____ of their status. The idea was that **(4)** _____ someone very rich, who didn't have to work, could wear such impractical footwear! Women began to wear them in the nineteenth century as part of their battle to take **(5)** _____ traditional male power and authority. In **(6)** _____ years, they have again become part of the **(7)** _____ for women's rights – this time for the right NOT to wear them. Women who work in jobs where they are **(8)** _____ to wear high heels are calling for the right to wear flatter, more comfortable footwear. I can understand why!

0	A	view	B	sight	C	scene	D	glance
1	A	considered	B	suggested	C	approved	D	regarded
2	A	Although	B	Despite	C	However	D	Therefore
3	A	notice	B	symbol	C	display	D	logo
4	A	except	B	instead of	C	otherwise	D	only
5	A	up	B	out	C	on	D	in
6	A	modern	B	recent	C	latest	D	current
7	A	quarrel	B	fight	C	dispute	D	conflict
8	A	expected	B	demanded	C	insisted	D	proposed

Questions 9–16

For questions 9–16, read the text below and think of the word which best fits each gap.
Use only <u>one</u> word in each gap. There is an example at the beginning (0).

How Italian food took over the world

Studies over the last few years have shown repeatedly that Italian food is the
(0) _____MOST_____ popular in the world. This is true not **(9)** _____ in
Europe, but also in countries as diverse **(10)** _____ Brazil and South
Africa. So why **(11)** _____ pizza and pasta become such universal
favourites? One big advantage of both is that they are cheap and can easily
(12) _____ adapted to different tastes. It is possible to conjure up a
tasty pasta sauce using a wide range **(13)** _____ different ingredients,
and there is **(14)** _____ limit to what you can put on a pizza, from
pineapple to eggs, and even bananas! Another reason for their popularity may
have less to do with flavour and **(15)** _____ to do with industrial food
production. Both foods are easy and cheap to mass-produce and transport, and
it may be **(16)** _____ characteristic which has led to their spread to all
corners of the globe.

Questions 17–24

For questions 17–24, read the text below. Use the word given in capitals at the end of some of the lines to form a word that fits in the gap in the same line. There is an example at the beginning (0).

Singing for their supper

Gorillas are well known for beating their chests when they are

(0) _____ANGRY_____ , but it seems they also have a gentler   **ANGER**

and more (17) _____ side to their character. A new   **CREATE**

study has shown that gorillas 'sing' (18) _____   **QUIET**

while they are eating. A group of (19) _____ who   **RESEARCH**

studied the animals in the wild found that they make a range

of different (20) _____ sounds, especially when   **MUSIC**

eating their favourite foods. And different gorillas have their

own favourite 'tunes'. The sounds may show their

(21) _____ in what they are eating, but they may   **PLEASE**

also be used as a form of (22) _____ . The larger,   **COMMUNICATE**

male gorillas are the ones who make all the

(23) _____ for the group. The 'singing' may be   **DECIDE**

their way of saying that it is time to sit down and eat. This is

perhaps the most (24) _____ discovery, as it   **FASCINATE**

might shed light on how human language evolved.

Questions 25-30

For questions 25-30, complete the second sentence so that it has a similar meaning to the first sentence, using the word given. <u>Do not change the word given.</u> You must use between <u>two</u> and <u>five</u> words, including the word given. Here is an example (0).

Example:

0 It is said that eating a vegetarian diet is good for your health.

SUPPOSED

Eating a vegetarian diet _____IS SUPPOSED TO BE_____ good for your health.

25 'You shouldn't go out,' the doctor told me.

ADVISED

The doctor _____ out.

26 My hair needs cutting this weekend.

HAVE

I need to _____ this weekend.

27 I haven't seen David for three years.

SINCE

It's _____ I last saw David.

28 I broke the teapot by accident.

MEAN

I _____ the teapot.

29 The exam wasn't as easy as I'd expected.

MORE

The exam was _____ I'd expected.

30 It was a mistake not to accept her offer.

TURNED

I shouldn't _____ her offer.

Questions 31–36

You are going to read an article about diving. For questions 31–36, choose the answer (A, B, C or D) which you think best fits according to the text.

Exploring the oceans

I guess the sea has always been a part of my life. I grew up on the coast and spent hours as a kid playing on the beach, although I was never that keen on being in the water. I had friends who were into surfing, and who urged me to join them, but somehow, I never shared their fascination with the sea. But everything changed when my uncle came to stay one summer, when I was about 15. Hearing him talking with passion about the joys of diving and the amazing things he had seen underwater awakened something in me. I started watching old TV documentaries and fell in love with the mystery of the oceans.

The basic training for your first dive is fairly straightforward. After an afternoon in a swimming pool learning how to use the breathing equipment, you head for the sea for your first real-life experience. That first moment of feeling the water close over your head, leaving you with just a little tube of air to keep you alive, is slightly alarming, and I thought at first that I might panic. Although we were in quite shallow water, it was still easy to feel disoriented and lose track of which way was up and which was down, but luckily the instructor stayed right beside us to make sure we were OK.

15 After building up some experience in my local area and getting more qualifications **under my belt**, I was completely hooked on the thrill of diving and keen to explore some of the more challenging and exciting diving locations around the world. I booked onto an organised trip and headed to Indonesia, home to tropical seas, amazing underwater scenery and exotic fish. From there, I've gone on to explore the oceans all over the world, from the Caribbean to Australia and the Pacific Islands.

When you spend time under water, you can't help but be amazed by the whole other world that exists below the waves, invisible to us most of the time. From huge, elegant creatures that move slowly and effortlessly through the water, to tiny fish that you notice only as brief flashes of colour as they turn with lightning speed and head off in different directions. And what really fascinates me is their attitude to you as you travel through their world, seeing you not as a threat but almost as one of them, to be quickly inspected and then rejected as of no further interest.

I have only once had a moment of fear, when I suddenly came face to face with an enormous shark while diving in the Caribbean. I recognised it at once and knew that this species could be dangerous. My first instinct was to ignore it, in the hope that it might not notice me and swim off in search of a more suitable food source. But the oxygen tank on my back obviously caught its eye and it moved in to investigate, swimming backwards and forwards above me until two other divers swam towards me and it decided it was time to leave.

After 15 years of diving, I have seen some wonderful and inspiring sights. But, in recent years, I have also seen first-hand the growing problem of damage to the oceans from pollution. More and more divers now give their time to help clean up the oceans that they love. I spent last summer working on a series of conservation projects in Portugal, working with a team of divers to remove all kinds
36 of unwanted objects from the sea bed, including thousands of small pieces of plastic. **These** cause problems with the underwater ecosystem and are particularly dangerous as fish and other creatures can eat them and then, feeling that their stomachs are full, starve to death. Let's hope the world takes action in time and manages to preserve these magical environments.

31 **What first led to the writer's interest in diving?**
    A living by the sea as a child
    B watching TV programmes
    C listening to a family member's experiences
    D taking up a challenge from friends

32 **During the training, the writer felt**
    A relieved that the teacher was close to him.
    B confident about using the breathing equipment.
    C excited at thought of doing a real dive.
    D disappointed that they didn't go very deep.

33 **What does 'under my belt' in line 15 mean?**
    A planned
    B achieved
    C discovered
    D created

34 **What does the writer find most surprising about sea creatures?**
    A their amazing colours
    B the speed with which they move
    C their lack of fear of humans
    D the way they interact with each other

35 **When the shark saw the writer, it**
    A took no interest in him.
    B became aggressive.
    C showed that it was frightened.
    D was curious about his equipment.

36 **The word 'these' in line 36 refers to**
    A small pieces of plastic.
    B divers.
    C unwanted objects.
    D conservation projects.

Questions 37–42

You are going to read an article about wood. Six sentences have been removed from the article. Choose from the sentences A–G the one which fits each gap (37–42). There is one extra sentence which you do not need to use.

From old-fashioned to high-tech

Wood has been recognised as a valuable resource for thousands of years. It has been used as a fuel and for making all kinds of things from buildings and furniture to paper and children's toys. It is easy to produce, has many different uses and is sustainable. And now it seems it may become the super-material of the 21st century.

In the past, people chose to use wood because it was the strongest material available. However, in its natural form wood is far from perfect. **37** ☐ These qualities meant it went out of fashion in the 20th century. Instead, architects chose concrete for buildings, which is cheap and lasts a long time. For smaller items, manufacturers preferred plastic as a lighter, cheaper alternative.

However, concrete and plastic both rely on using products made from oil, and making them produces large amounts of the gases which cause climate change. This is not sustainable, and scientists are now looking for greener alternatives, which is why they are turning back to wood. But this is not wood as we traditionally think of it. The new 'modern' wood is processed into an improved material by gluing together thin sheets of wood into large, flat pieces. **38** ☐ It also has the advantage that it doesn't burn.

As a result of these developments in wood technology, wooden buildings are now being put up all over the world and there is a race to build the world's tallest wooden skyscraper. Candidates include the Mjøsa Tower in Brumunddal, Norway. It is 85 metres high, with 18 storeys, and includes a hotel, private homes and offices. **39** ☐

In the future, wood could also be used instead of glass. Scientists in Sweden have found a way to remove the natural colour from wood. This process produces a strong, thin material, like glass, which you can see through. But it is a more sustainable material than glass, and is also good at keeping warmth inside buildings. **40** ☐

Even more exciting is the idea that wood might one day replace plastic. Sulapac, a company in Finland, is working on breaking wood down into the basic plant materials it is made of. They then mix this with glue that is made from other plants, to produce a material that looks very much like plastic. The company is hoping to start selling its environmentally friendly drinking straws soon. **41** ☐ But, as they are made of wood, they will break down and disappear if they end up in the oceans. Similar wood-based materials could be used to make clothes, cars and even aeroplanes.

42 ☐ This is due to a material processed from wood that can be made into very thin sheets which are extremely strong and allow electricity to pass through them. This makes it ideal to use in electronic devices. Some companies, including the American computer firm IBM, are already using this material in their computers and electronic products, and scientists believe its use will increase over the next few years. It seems the future might indeed be made of wood!

A This means less energy is needed for heating, which is good for the environment.

B They will look and feel like the ones we are used to.

C This 'hi-tech' material is stronger than steel, yet also light and easy to work with.

D It seems that wood has a lot more uses than we realised.

E And wood could even move into the digital world.

F It does not last very long, becomes weak when it gets wet and burns easily.

G It is made mainly of wood, although there are some concrete parts to give increased stability.

Questions 43-52

You are going to read an article about young businesspeople. For questions 43-52, choose from the sections (A-D). The sections may be chosen more than once.

Which writer

made a decision about how to run their business while at college?	43
mentions an initial difficulty with funding?	44
experienced a health benefit from setting up the business?	45
was surprised at the speed of their success?	46
mentions experience with a similar business in the past?	47
feels grateful for help from a family member?	48
was concerned about a loss of financial security?	49
felt angry about a rule?	50
warns about the amount of work involved in starting a new business?	51
runs a business which helps with people's education?	52

Social enterprise

Are businesses just about making money? It seems not, as more and more people are choosing to set up businesses that also bring social benefits. Four young businesspeople tell us about their work.

A

Melissa Evans

I worked in a supermarket and I was horrified at the amount of food that was thrown away every day – literally dumped into rubbish bins! Then, one day, a guy asked if he could have some of the food. He was obviously poor. My colleague refused, saying we weren't allowed to sell or give the food away. That really annoyed me – it was such a waste! I had some money saved up, so I set up the Social Food Store. I persuaded local supermarkets to give us food they were throwing away. This food goes into our store, then customers can come and shop for free. I couldn't believe how quickly we built up our customer numbers. People like it because it feels like a normal shop, not a charity. All the staff are volunteers, and we get funding from the local government. It's great to feel I'm helping people.

B

Dan Rudofsky

I'd always wanted to set up my own company, but when I went to business school, I was alarmed that what we learnt was all about profit. It was as if nothing else mattered. That was when I made up my mind that I would do things differently. I did some research and came up with the idea of Light Up. It's an online lighting store, selling lights and lamps. For every item we sell, we donate a solar-powered lamp to a charity, for children in developing countries with no electricity at home. Light is incredibly important because it allows kids to study and improve their lives. The business is doing well. I've worked incredibly hard, but I know it wouldn't have been possible without the support and generous start-up loan my dad gave me. Hopefully, I'll earn enough to pay him back one day!

C

Helen Sousa

Homelessness is a huge problem in my city, and when I lost my job two years ago, I decided to do something about it. I had managed restaurants before, so I set up the Street Café. We're a normal café during the day, and we use the profits from this to offer free meals to homeless people in the evenings. All our staff have been homeless themselves. They often have mental health problems or a low level of education, which make it difficult for them to find other work, but I think everyone deserves a chance. We struggled to get people to invest in the business at first, but it soon became clear that it was a sound business idea. I would encourage more people to set up companies like this, although they should be aware of the long hours they'll need to put in at first!

D

James Walker

I definitely believe in breaking the rules and doing something different. Three years ago, I had a high-paid job in banking. But I started suffering from anxiety because of the stress, so I quit my job and went back to college for a year. I then set up my own business, Planet Beauty, an online store selling cosmetics and beauty products. I must admit I was nervous about giving up a regular salary, and my experience wasn't really relevant to the cosmetics industry, but I was determined to make a success of it and help the planet, too. Everything we sell is plastic free and safe for the environment, and we donate 40 percent of our profits to environmental charities. I enjoy much more job satisfaction now than I ever did in my old job, and I feel much better in myself, too!

1 You must answer this question. Write your answer in 140–190 words in an appropriate style.

> In your English class you have been discussing online shopping.
> Now, your English teacher has asked you to write an essay.
> Write an essay using **all** the notes and giving reasons for your point of view.

Is it better to shop online or go to shopping centres?

Notes

Write about:

1 prices

2 choice

3 _____ (your own idea)

Write an answer to <u>one</u> of the questions 2–4 in this part. Write your answer in 140–190 words in an appropriate style.

2   A sports centre in the town has just been improved. The local council has asked a small group of regular users to write a report on the improvements.

The council want to know:

- whether the facilities are better than before, and if there are any problems.
- suggestions for further improvement.

Write your **report**.

3   You see this announcement on an English-language education website.

> ### Reviews wanted
>
> ### Interesting courses
>
> Have you done a course recently? Tell us what kind of course it was. What were the classes like? What was good or bad about it? Would you recommend this course to other people?
>
> We will publish the best reviews on our website.

Write your **review**.

4   You have received an email from your English-speaking friend Tara.

> **From:** Tara   **Subject:** Your visit
>
> Hi! I'm so looking forward to your visit next month! I'm planning everything, so let me know what you want to do. I've already organised a trip along the river, but I don't know what else you'd enjoy. We could go to museums, or do some sport. I've just passed my driving test, so we can get around easily. Oh, and by the way, I can't remember what kind of food you like.

Write your **email**.

Questions 1–8

🎧 **PE01** You will hear people talking in eight different situations. For questions 1–8, choose the best answer (A, B or C).

1 **You hear two people talking about a film they've just seen.**

   What do they agree about it?
   A The acting was poor.
   B The dialogue was realistic.
   C The story was easy to follow.

2 **You hear two friends talking about an arrangement they've made.**

   How does the man feel about it?
   A unhappy about the timing of it
   B unwilling to make any changes to it
   C unsure whether it has been confirmed

3 **You hear a man telling a friend about a graphic design course he's doing in his free time.**

   Why is he taking the course?
   A to improve his career prospects
   B to learn about some new software
   C to please his current employer

4 **You hear a girl telling a friend about going away to college.**

   How does she feel about it?
   A nervous about meeting new people
   B concerned about the level of study
   C worried about leaving her family

5 **You hear an announcement about a concert.**

   What is the purpose of the announcement?
   A to promote a future event
   B to outline changes in the evening's programme
   C to explain how to buy refreshments

6 **You hear a boy telling a friend about his tennis lessons.**

   What does he say about them?
   A He thinks they are too long.
   B He finds them tiring.
   C He disagrees with their focus.

7 **You hear a girl telling a friend about a holiday in a national park.**

   What was she surprised about?
   A The amount of wildlife she saw.
   B The variety of activities available.
   C The type of accommodation she stayed in.

8 **You hear a man telling a friend about an advertisement he saw on television.**

   He thinks that the advertisement
   A provided misleading information.
   B contained some unpleasant images.
   C was extremely irritating.

Questions 9-18

🎧 **PE02** You will hear a woman called Jane Wilson talking to a group of drama students about her work as an actress in television commercials.

For questions 9-18, complete the sentences with a word or short phrase.

My work as an actress in television commercials

Jane feels that getting more **(9)** _____ is the most valuable part of working as an actress on television commercials.

Jane regrets that she can't develop a **(10)** _____ while working on a commercial.

Jane admits she should have practised more **(11)** _____ which would have helped her with her acting.

Jane advises people hoping to act in commercials to have lots of **(12)** _____ to show potential employers.

Jane says her biggest mistake was trying to get a job selling **(13)** _____ , because of her appearance.

Jane explains the reason she wasn't asked to audition for commercials for **(14)** _____ was that she had once worked for a competitor.

In Jane's opinion it is **(15)** _____ to accept all invitations to auditions.

Jane uses the word **(16)** _____ to describe the quality she sees as most important in her job.

Jane describes the experience of filming commercials as **(17)** _____ .

Jane was surprised when an advertiser changed the appearance of **(18)** _____ so that it would look better.

Questions 19-23

🎧 PE03 **You will hear five short extracts in which people are talking about their new jobs. For questions 19-23, choose from the list (A-H) the reason each person gives for deciding to do this new job. There are three extra letters which you do not need to use.**

A   I was ready to be given more responsibility.

B   I wished to prove other people wrong.

C   I aimed to earn more money.   Speaker 1 [   ] 19

D   I realised it would provide greater challenges.   Speaker 2 [   ] 20

E   Someone recommended I apply for the job.   Speaker 3 [   ] 21

                                                                              Speaker 4 [   ] 22

F   I had always wanted to do this kind of work.

                                                                              Speaker 5 [   ] 23

G   I wanted to have more free time.

H   My family were keen for me to stay near them.

Questions 24–30

🎧 **PE04** You will hear part of a radio interview with a woman called Lina Beecham, who works as an animator in cartoon films. For questions 24–30, choose the best answer (A, B or C).

24 When talking about her childhood ambitions Lina says that
  A she had no doubts about her plans.
  B she was influenced by her family.
  C she wanted to do the same as her friends.

25 How does Lina feel now about the book she illustrated as a child?
  A grateful for having been given the opportunity
  B embarrassed by the pictures she drew
  C surprised that it is still for sale

26 Lina feels that her natural talent for drawing
  A made it easy for her to improve her technique.
  B was enough to enable her to succeed at college.
  C had always been something she was proud of.

27 In Lina's opinion, animators
  A are particularly selfish.
  B need to be very imaginative.
  C must work as part of a team.

28 How does Lina feel about her job?
  A She isn't happy about the time it takes to do it well.
  B She would prefer to be able to work more flexibly.
  C She sometimes finds it difficult to stay motivated.

29 What is Lina's attitude towards creating her characters on film?
  A She accepts that she has to put herself into them.
  B She wishes she could have more help with them.
  C She gets ideas from watching actors prepare for a role.

30 What is Lina's opinion about directing a film rather than animating it?
  A The amount of work is less.
  B The degree of responsibility is higher.
  C The level of artistic input is more satisfying.

PE05

> Where are you from?
> And you?
> First we'd like to know something about you.

The examiner will ask you a few questions about yourself and what you think about different things. For example, the examiner might ask you about:

The past

What did you do last weekend? (Why?)

Have you been to any special celebrations recently?

Tell us about a film you've seen recently that you really liked.

Have you ever been to a live music concert? (Why? / Why not?)

Sport and exercise

Do you like doing exercise in a gym? (Why? / Why not?)

What's your favourite sport at the moment? (Why?)

How often do you watch sport with your friends?

If you could be really good at one sport, what would it be? (Why?)

Daily life

How do you generally travel to work or college? (Why?)

What do you like doing in the evenings? (Why?)

Is it important to you to have a regular morning routine? (Why? / Why not?)

Where do you usually meet your friends? (Why?)

PE06

In this part of the test, I'm going to give each of you two photographs. I'd like you to talk about your photographs on your own for about a minute, and also to answer a question about your partner's photographs.

(Candidate A), it's your turn first. Look at the photographs on page 110. They show people **having a meal together in different places.**

I'd like you to compare the photographs, and say **what you think the people are enjoying about having a meal together in these places.**

All right?

[Candidate A speaks for 1 minute.] _____

Thank you.

(Candidate B), **which of these places would you prefer to have a meal in? (Why?)**

[Candidate B speaks for about 30 seconds.] _____

Thank you.

Now, *(Candidate B)*, look at your photographs on page 110, which show **people doing different things on holiday in a city.**

I'd like you to compare the photographs and say **why you think the people have decided to do these things on holiday in a city.**

All right?

[Candidate B speaks for 1 minute.] _____

Thank you.

(Candidate A), **which of these things would you prefer to do in a city? (Why?)**

[Candidate A speaks for about 30 seconds.] _____

Thank you.

Candidate A

What are the people enjoying about having a meal together in these places?

Candidate B

Why have the people decided to do these things on holiday in a city?

PE07

> Now I'd like you to talk about something together for about two minutes. Look at page 112.
>
> **Some people think it's necessary for young people to plan their life and career when they're at school, and other people disagree. Here are some things they think about**, and a question for you to discuss. First you have some time to look at the task.
>
> Now talk to each other about **whether it's really necessary for young people to plan their life and career when they're at school.**
>
> *(Candidates talk for 2 minutes.)*
>
> Thank you.
>
> Now you have about a minute to decide **which is the most important reason for young people to plan their life and career when they're at school.**
>
> *(Candidates talk for 1 minute.)*
>
> Thank you.

 PE08

Use the following questions, in order, as appropriate.

- How easy is it for young people to plan a career nowadays? (Why?)
- Can friends influence the choices young people make about life and work? (Why? / Why not?)
- Do you think young people get the best advice about life or work from parents or teachers? (Why? / Why not?)
- Is it better for people to plan a career based on salary, or the satisfaction they would get from doing the job? (Why?)
- In your opinion, what's the most important decision people have to make in life? (Why?)
- Some people say it's often better to avoid planning anything at all, and just be spontaneous. What do you think? (Why?)

> *Select any of the following prompts, as appropriate:*
> - What do you think?
> - Do you agree?

Thank you. That is the end of the test.

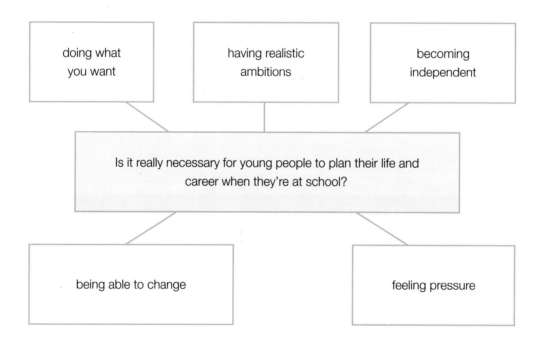

doing what you want

having realistic ambitions

becoming independent

Is it really necessary for young people to plan their life and career when they're at school?

being able to change

feeling pressure

Write an answer to <u>one</u> of the questions 2–4 in this part. Write your answer in 140–190 words in an appropriate style.

2 You see this announcement on an English-language website.

Articles wanted

My favourite gadget or technical device

What's your favourite gadget or technical device? What do you do with it? Why do you love it so much? Could you live without it?

Write us an article answering these questions.

We will publish the best articles on our website.

Write your **article**.

3 You see this advertisement in an English-language newspaper.

We need a part-time assistant in our tourist information office

Do you speak good English? Are you keen on history? Do you enjoy helping people?

Send us a letter giving us your details, explaining why you would be suitable for the job and what hours you could work.

Mr David Evans, Manager

Write your **letter**.

4 You have seen this announcement in a new English-language magazine for young people.

Story competition

Can you write a story for teenage readers? Your story must **begin** with this sentence:

When Tom set off for school, he expected it to be just a normal day.

Your story must include:

- a famous person
- a party

Write your **story**.

LISTENING
Part 1
Practice task | Ex 1

 L01

One. You hear two people talking about a film they've seen.

M: I'm glad that's over – I can't believe I actually paid to see it!

F: I'd read the reviews, so I knew what was coming – even though the last film that director made won awards. But there were some good things – like the music – oh, and the special effects were stunning!

M: If you say so, though I honestly didn't notice. The plot made me so sad.

F: The script wasn't particularly good, so the actors didn't have a chance to show how good they were. It did make me cry, though, especially the ending.

M: Well, I go to the cinema to be cheered up!

Two. You hear part of a talk about a coral reef.

Today I'm talking about a coral reef off the Australian coast. It's huge, and although people probably assume it's one reef, it's actually more like thousands of individual reefs. The area's stunning, with colours ranging from blue and pink to purple and green. But the coral is under threat and so many creatures that live there are losing their habitat. So for them its survival is crucial. Conservationists are trying to clean the water in the area, partly because certain predators search for food in polluted water. This attracts them to the reef and makes them yet another hazard for already endangered reef dwellers.

Three. You hear a man talking to a friend about his course at college.

Kira: Hi Sam – how's the course going?

Sam: Well, I've got through the first part, but I'm not sure how! I knew it would be demanding, though – I've never done anything like it before.

Kira: But you're enjoying it?

Sam: The coursework, yes, though some of the lectures aren't as fascinating as they looked in the prospectus! Maybe I'm just not used to sitting and listening to someone talk for hours on end.

Kira: But you'll keep going?

Sam: Definitely – though, inevitably, it's kind of taken over my life: I knew I'd miss going out in the evenings with you guys.

Kira: It'll be better next term, I'm sure.

Strategies and skills:
Listening for agreement | Ex 1

 L02

One

F: It's never OK to use text instead of calling – it's rude in my opinion.

M: You have to get with it – no one uses a phone for calling now – it's only there for social media.

Two

M: I can't keep up with all the updates on my phone – it's just change for change's sake.

F: If they don't keep software up-to-date, then hackers can get in. You have to make the effort.

Three

M: I can't believe they cancelled the show an hour before the start time. I know dancers get injured, but I've been looking forward to it for ages.

F: That's the same for all of us – it took me hours to get here, and it was just a waste of time and effort.

Four

F: I'm meeting an old friend for coffee tomorrow, but I'm worried. She contacted me on Facebook and I haven't seen her for years – we'll both have changed so much.

M: I find that when I get together with an old friend, it's easy to carry on as if we'd never been apart – we're just the same deep down.

Five

M: Did you see that man who won millions on the lottery? He was on television saying it won't change him, but honestly that's impossible.

F: It's hard to deal with stuff like that – his whole life'll be different and so will he.

Six

F: That film was certainly thrilling – I couldn't take my eyes off the screen.

M: There seemed to be so many characters and I found them distracting, to be honest.

Strategies and skills:
Identifying attitude and opinion | Ex 3

 L03

One

I wish I hadn't started the course – I'm spending hours finishing every assignment!

Two

The weather's never good at that time of year – do you really think we should go there then?

Three

Thank you for your advice, but I'm going to get a second opinion.

Four

The programme wasn't really worth watching – I could have done with something more useful.

Five

It was nice to win the competition but I would have preferred not to be interviewed afterwards!

Six

I'm worried about getting it wrong on stage – there are so many people watching!

Strategies and skills: Identifying feelings | Ex 4

 L04

One

I can't believe you said that – it's unacceptable!

Two

It's so hard to work when there's such a lot of noise in the house!

Three

I really can't wait to start my new job.

Four

It's a good thing I booked ahead – the hotel's completely full now.

Five

It will be a tough thing to do, but I guess it's not impossible if I really try hard.

Six

It's raining, so do I really have to go to the shops right now?

EXAM TASK

 L05

One. You hear two friends discussing a science experiment on living on another planet.

F: That experiment was a clever concept – the way scientists lived in this building in the desert miles away from anywhere so they could do research on what the problems might be.

M: But it looked horrible – so cramped and basic.

F: Well, that's probably just what it'd be like in space! I guess there was loads for the scientists to do, so maybe they were able to ignore all that.

M: I'd find it tough being cut off from the rest of the world. Like they deliberately delayed messages in and out as if they were really on another planet. I'd hate that!

F: It might be nice to get away from social media for once!

Two. You hear two friends talking about a tennis match they watched.

M: I'm exhausted after watching that match!

F: You could really feel the tension and excitement in the crowd, even watching it on television – that was awesome.

M: Imagine if we'd actually been there and experienced that!

F: For me, though, there'd been so much anticipation that the game was a bit of a let-down. They weren't at their best.

M: They both played some unbelievable shots – at times it could have gone either way.

F: It would've been a surprise if Sam had actually won, though – he was the clear underdog and nobody expected him to.

M: Well, I reckon he deserved to win.

F: He'll get another chance next year.

Three. You hear a woman telling a friend about a community eco campaign.

F: The new local eco project is such a good initiative – I'm really into getting people to recycle more. I particularly like the 'cut down on plastic' campaign – it's already having an effect in the local supermarket. They only give out paper bags now! Mind you, they could have done that sooner!

M: Well, I'm doing my bit – I always switch my phone charger off. I had no idea how wasteful they were.

F: Probably no one does! It's a shame not everyone's taking part in the campaign – we need to have better publicity about it really.

M: My local school's started doing stuff like clearing up litter – that's a start.

Four. You hear a man leaving a voicemail message for a friend.

Dina, it's Joe. You know we're supposed to be meeting at six before the show tonight? Well, I'm really looking forward to it, but something's come up and I can't leave the office before 5.30. That won't give us enough time for a meal before it starts, so why don't you go ahead without me and get yourself something – I don't want you to be hungry. The thing is, I'd booked a table at that little bistro round the corner and it doesn't open until five – would you mind giving them a call then to cancel it? Sorry about this, but we can go there next time!

Five. You hear a young singer talking about her career so far.

My parents say I could sing before I could talk! I didn't enjoy formal music lessons – they were boring, and the teacher got fed up with me. She recognised that I had talent, though, and suggested I went in for a talent competition. Unfortunately, I didn't win, but I made some great contacts and I got asked to be the front person in a start-up band. Now I have to sing what will sell commercially, which isn't my scene, but it's a start and I can't expect to have it my own way. Once I've got to the top I'll have the chance to sing my own stuff.

Six. You hear two friends talking about a video posted on the internet.

M: Did you see that internet video about the dog skateboarding round the streets? So funny!

F: Well, when you think about it, it's silly – what about if it tripped up an elderly person? And actually people are always posting loads of stuff like that on the net. I saw one about a cat that kept trying to climb up a door and falling off – but it could have got hurt. I don't think people should post stuff like that.

M: It brightened up my day, anyway – you shouldn't be so miserable about it.

F: I admit I did smile – and I guess we all need cheering up sometimes.

Seven. You hear part of an interview with the presenter of a TV documentary.

As I was doing my initial research for the documentary – which was originally supposed to be how the design of new-build housing is changing – it became apparent that what's inside is more important than the exterior, and that the colours you use in different rooms have more importance than you might think. I was quite taken aback by what I found, and felt that it would be more useful to explore that, so my original concept changed. You see, they're not just decorative – there's more psychology in them than that. Like having bright colours in a bedroom can be a bad thing, and how colours like blue can be calming.

Eight. You hear two friends talking about a team quiz they took part in.

M: Well, that was a really good quiz!

F: It was certainly closer than anyone thought it would be. At least it was done in a pretty good spirit – no one disagreed with the quizmaster or argued among themselves. I hate it when that happens!

M: Me too! It was a pity we didn't win.

F: But we did better than anyone expected – we got loads of answers right! I let the team down a bit though – I didn't do so well personally ... I had no idea about some of the questions.

M: Still, at least it's always nice to do something fun like that with friends.

LISTENING
Part 2
Practice task | Ex 1 and Ex 3

 L06 and L07

Shelly: Hi, I'm Shelly and I make unusual ice cream for a living! It wasn't a long-held ambition of mine, although ice cream's always been one of my favourite treats! At school I loved maths and my friend suggested I should study technology at university, but I chose to do chemistry, thinking I would teach it as that's what both my parents did. Then one hot evening I was out with friends and we stopped to buy an ice cream, and I was disappointed by the range of flavours on offer. That's when it hit me – why not make and sell my own?

I started really small, in my parents' kitchen at home, but it didn't take long for word to spread. I sold my ice cream to friends, in the local cinema and most successfully in the weekly market where all the young ones loved it. After a while I opened my own shop.

We store our ice cream in two huge refrigerators. At the start we mixed everything by hand, but now we have a special machine to do it. My mum calls it a magic box, though I think it's more like a washing machine when you see it as it's big and white and very efficient. It's also rather noisy!

Unlike many big ice cream manufacturers, our menu is constantly changing. That doesn't worry me, and I'm proud that my product is natural and organic, so no one needs to feel guilty when they eat it! I get all the ingredients locally, so flavours depend on what's available in any particular season. At the moment it's honey and lavender.

I want my customers to have new experiences, so I enjoy experimenting with unusual mixtures. I've heard of companies making flavours such as pumpkin pie, pickled mango or pear and blue cheese, but, because of my philosophy of keeping things local, I can't do that. I can produce flavours like rose, though, and people always enjoy that in the summer. I don't mind if some of my experiments don't work – it's good to try!

Strategies and skills:
Listening for cues | Ex 3

 L08

Jason: Hi everyone – I'm Jason, and I'm going to talk to you about tigers and where they live. One small interesting piece of information before I start: Did you know they've been declared everyone's favourite animal? I couldn't believe that people preferred them to dogs – though I'd guessed some other animals that were popular, like cats and koalas!

It's no problem identifying tigers for several reasons – first, their coats, which are almost orange. Then they've got what I'd describe as a beard on their face, and brown, black or grey stripes.

Tigers generally live in forests where there is dense vegetation and tall grass. However, because of deforestation, their habitats are disappearing and it's now thought that some could also be living in mountains. I found this a fascinating idea, but I wasn't sure how much evidence there was to support it.

Then I read an article about a biologist who wanted to prove it. What he did was climb as high as 4,000 metres, and set cameras at various locations. This created what he thought of as his opportunity because they would take a picture of any animal movements near them.

He left them there for several months. When he returned he was disappointed to find many pictures of rather predictable wildlife, such as foxes, leopards and bears. Not even the picture of a rarely seen red panda could cheer him up, although it was a delight to me. Then, suddenly, to his great joy, he found pictures of two tigers, a male and a female!

Strategies and skills:
Listening for specific details | Ex 6

 L09

Chloe: I loved my first visit to Amsterdam. It wasn't somewhere I'd been longing to go, and in fact I had turned down the opportunity when my sister went a couple of years ago with our mother. It was a visit to a London art gallery with my cousin that initially sparked my interest in Dutch painting, and then when a friend came up with the idea of going there together, I thought that the time had come.

Strategies and skills:
Identifying and eliminating distractors | Ex 11

 L10

Sue: I work as a prompter in a theatre – not a job that many people know much about! I specialise in opera, and I have to follow the performance on stage and whisper the words if one of the singers forgets them. It sounds boring, and it can be demanding, but I find it very rewarding, even though there are some downsides – as with any job, I suppose.

I have to sit in a small space just below the stage for several hours – it's pretty cramped and can be uncomfortable. I get used to that, and do exercises for my legs and back to keep flexible. It doesn't matter what clothes I wear because no one can see me, though unfortunately that does make me a bit lazy with my appearance!

So what do I need to do my job? I must be musical, which I am, so it's difficult to stop myself singing along with the people on stage! I also have to have a lot of patience, but I guess it's concentration that tops the list.

The singers have to be able to trust me, so they can be relaxed on stage. This feeling of trust between us develops over time, and I regard it as special. I love being able to contribute to a great performance.

I don't do it for thanks, but it's always nice when the singers acknowledge what I do. Sometimes they turn and give me applause at the end of a performance, and sometimes they give me flowers. The nicest thing was a letter from a singer who had retired, telling me how much he had valued me during his time on stage!

EXAM TASK

 L11

Annie: Hi everyone – I'm Annie, and I'm here to talk to you about bees and why I love them.

I first found out about them at school, when we had a nature lesson. I looked stuff up online after that, but then, a bit later, I saw a documentary which showed how they live and what they do. From then on, I was hooked.

Did you know there are three main types of bee? The most common of these is the bumblebee; there are also bees called solitary bees which are, as their name suggests, less common. The ones I keep are honeybees. They're really social insects, and live together in what are called 'colonies' though I prefer to think of them as communities because they all work for each other! Beekeepers make wooden structures known as hives for them to live in, although in the natural world bees create their own nests. I have five hives, with around 50,000 bees in each.

Bees collect pollen on hairs on their body and transfer it to other plants. This is known as pollination and it's crucial for maintaining our natural ecosystems. I knew that, but not that bees are the world's most important pollinator of food crops. According to scientists, one third of all the food that we eat regularly relies on pollination by bees – actually, some of our favourite food wouldn't even exist without them. You may know that some crops like blueberries and almonds depend almost fully on bees for pollination, but I'm very sure you hadn't thought about farm animals. Much of their food, like clover, also needs bees to pollinate it.

How do bees find crops or flowers? They can see colours really well, which surprised me. They're mostly attracted by blue, purple, violet, white and yellow. It seems odd to me that they can't see red, because it's so strong – but if there are bees around anything of that colour, it's probably because the centre of the flower is actually yellow. It's great that we can have pretty gardens that are also good for bees!

That's important, because their numbers are declining. That's mainly because of farming, forestry, the increasing use of pesticides and large housing developments which destroy their natural environment. Conservationists are concerned and say it's worrying, but I actually find it upsetting. The bees have to travel too far to find food, and then there might not be enough numbers left to breed.

What can we as individuals do about this? I realise not everyone wants to do what I do and keep hives in their garden, but you can plant wild flowers and avoid pesticides. My personal suggestion is to create a shelter for bumblebees – just a pot or a box. Some people call them hotels, which makes me smile.

Changes in weather and climate are problematic, too – like, bees find increased rainfall hard to adapt to. When I started beekeeping, I quickly discovered that if average temperatures go up, flowers come out earlier. This creates a mismatch between the time when the flowers produce pollen and when the bees are ready to collect it. Unfortunately, I can't do anything about that!

If bees are so important, why don't we take more care of them? It's probably perception. Just like spiders or snakes, some people find the appearance of bees frightening, because they're not cute and cuddly, and would rather give bears their support instead. I find this sad. And the bonus of keeping honey bees is having unlimited honey for breakfast!

Of course, bees can sting and should be treated with respect – you've all seen beekeepers wearing protective clothing including a thick suit and a large hood to protect their face. My gloves are what make me feel safest when I'm dealing with my bees, and I never forget them.

In most cases, though, a bee sting isn't serious. I've never totally understood why some people are more likely to get stung than others, but wearing strong or sweet-smelling products like sunscreen or body lotion might come into it. Personally, I'd say definitely avoid hairspray – you don't want bees around your head.

So – I'd love to answer your questions, and convince you about the importance of bees!

LISTENING

Part 3

Practice task | Ex 1

 L12

Speaker 1

I'd been really looking forward to my first visit to the city, and in many ways it lived up to my expectations. There were loads of different things to do, places to see, great restaurants. I would have liked there to be more parks – having open areas was something I felt was missing. Even so, the whole place had a buzz about it, and the huge groups of visitors everywhere only added to that. I didn't find it easy to get round, but I think that was my fault really – I hadn't done any research into buses and trams. On my second visit, I found they were actually very efficient.

Speaker 2

We had a great weekend away in the city – it was difficult to take in how the designs of the buildings have changed over the centuries, not always for the better, in my opinion! They didn't always blend in well. Any city that's very old tends to have narrow streets in its centre, and the air quality, caused by the buses and cars, was particularly poor – I didn't expect that. And like any place with history, there were lots of people enjoying the sights, so it was crowded, though not where we wanted to spend our time.

Speaker 3

I loved the atmosphere of the city – especially at night, when theatres and restaurants were crowded. I couldn't believe how difficult it was to get from one place to another, though – the maps were so difficult to understand and the buses were a nightmare! You waited for half an hour and then three came at once! We walked a lot because of that, particularly through the beautiful parks and gardens – we had a view of the whole city from one of them, which was amazing. We talked to people in our hotel about our reactions and we all felt we'd be back, particularly to see more of the old buildings and museums.

Strategies and skills: Listening for gist | Ex 2b

 L13

Speaker 1

The lodges in the resort we chose to stay in had been converted from really historic houses. They had so much more character and interest than boring modern purpose-built resorts. I enjoyed imagining who had lived in them in the past.

Speaker 2

I often go to the beach for a holiday with my family, which can be good and bad. Beach resorts are often crowded and noisy, but they have loads of facilities so you don't get bored. Having a break in a resort in my country can be hit and miss with the weather, though.

Speaker 3

I don't usually go for self-catering accommodation, especially as I then have to do the cooking, so I don't get a break. On the other hand, it's more convenient for the whole family which makes everything more enjoyable in the long run, so it's actually fine with me!

Speaker 4

The hotel we stayed in was very luxurious, and I couldn't fault the facilities. I can't say the same about the staff, though, and in fact I mentioned this to the manager at the end of our stay. If a hotel wants people to return, then they need to employ friendly and helpful staff.

Speaker 5

The safari we went on was very well organised, but our aim was to see animals and there weren't that many around. I don't really understand why – maybe we were just unlucky, or maybe we picked the wrong time of year.

Strategies and skills: Interpreting opinion | Ex 3

 L14

Speaker 1

I know there's a saying that honesty is the best policy, and most of the time it's right, but aren't there occasions when bending it a little does no harm?

Speaker 2

When I got married I wanted something different for the photos, so I went for black and white ones, thinking that they'd be more vivid than the usual colour ones. I regret that decision now!

Speaker 3

I love shopping, but my friends don't understand why I always avoid the huge centres with their chain stores. You find the same things in them all, which is less satisfying than the unusual stuff you can pick up in the smaller independent shops.

Speaker 4

My family are all sports mad – it doesn't matter what it is, if there's a ball involved, they love it. If they're not playing, they're watching it on TV – particularly football. I don't get it at all, even though I know it's popular.

Speaker 5

So, where I live in town there's always a huge traffic jam at peak times. There's been talk of improving the flow, but that's all – we're still waiting for any sign of it.

Speaker 6

I try to put some money in the bank every month if I can – I think that's important. That doesn't mean I put it all away, though – I want to have some fun as well!

EXAM TASK

 L15

Speaker 1

Most people want to have happy lives, and I'm no different. Getting there is another thing, though – what with all the pressures of modern life. It's all made even worse by the way we have to pretend that our lives are wonderful, that we're doing well and having a great time. We post pictures online of ourselves having fun when maybe we're not. It's all about image, but it's very unbalanced. That's not healthy, and if we can just tell the truth and not try to hide things, then those pressures fall away.

Speaker 2

I think that to have a happy life it helps if you can be financially secure – not necessarily rich, but enough to take away the pressure of having to work 24/7. Not that that's the key thing, it just makes life more pleasant and gives you options. Maybe I'm just not ambitious enough, but what works for me is just being with people who I value and love – I'd rather invest in that and know that I'll always have friends and family around me. I know people who have no other aim than to be the top dog so that everyone looks up to them, and in a way I can see the attraction of that, but it doesn't do it for me.

Speaker 3

I think that in these high-tech times social media has a lot to answer for. It gives people false expectations of what a happy life actually is, and creates a great deal of unhappiness. I think that being happy makes the ups and downs of life much easier to deal with – that means not getting stressed about things around you. Dealing with pressure is such a difficult thing, and learning how to maintain that calmness is really the answer to everything. Not that I would turn down a huge salary if it was offered to me, of course, but I don't think it would honestly make my life happier!

Speaker 4

I know people will say all the right things about being happy – like, it's friends and family, it's having lots of free time – well, those may work for them but not for me. Whenever I've achieved something, I have to set myself another target, something different to aim for. If I don't have anything to work towards, then I get frustrated, and that's not a happy feeling. If I get rich or famous along the way – well, that's OK, but I'm not looking for that. My friends support me, though they don't really understand what motivates me!

Speaker 5

I always thought that the way to be happy was to be successful at work – to have a high position and to be respected. And of course that's satisfying, but not necessarily a recipe for happiness. Now that I've achieved my long-held ambition of becoming a doctor, I do have both those things – plus a pretty good income. But I've discovered that what I really value is making people's lives better – I want to make a difference to them. I don't have a lot of free time, but that's fine – I can still see friends and so on, but my life is happy because of what I do.

LISTENING

Part 4

Practice task | Ex 1

 L16

M: Today on our programme about current social issues around gender, I'm talking to Paula Adams, a bookseller who specialises in children's books. Paula, how do you feel about the way children's books are often marketed?

F: Well, my livelihood depends on marketing and selling books, and I want people to buy as many as possible. If a book is labelled as being for girls or boys, it makes it clearer for me to categorise and put onto shelves with similar books. That means it's much easier for shoppers to find and buy when they're browsing. In fact, if books have also got covers that are coloured blue or pink, so much the better from my point of view!

M: Don't you think consumers can make their own minds up about what books they buy?

F: Many of my books are bought as gifts, often by people who don't have much contact with kids directly so they may not make the right choice. When these people shop for a book, they don't browse through all those on offer – they go straight for the target market of the book they want – that is, boys or girls. So, if that's what they want, I know I have to give them the support they obviously require. If they look online, they'll certainly search with those words, not by title or author.

M: But what about the argument that you're cutting children off from learning about the whole world by doing this?

F: Well, I agree that not all boys like the kinds of things we think they do – football, cars and so on – and not all girls want to read about princesses, but you have to understand that, as a sweeping generalisation, the opposite tends to be true. I don't want to perpetuate a stereotype, and seem to be promoting traditional gender roles, but I have to accept what I see as a fact, which is there's no other possibility to keep everyone happy. People may try to pretend that boys and girls share the same interests, but they really don't.

M: Thanks, Paula, there's a lot to think about there …

Strategies and skills: Identifying the main idea | Ex 1

 L17

One

I tend to buy books spontaneously – I don't waste time trying to decide which one – I guess that's because I'm attracted to the cover, or more likely by the reputation of the author or the blurb on the back. Does that mean I make bad decisions when I buy a book? Probably not, even though there's a saying that you shouldn't judge a book by its cover! That means that things are not always what they seem, but in the case of books you can often understand what you're buying quite easily. I rarely regret my choice.

Two

Parents have a strong influence on their children, and what their young ones want to get out of life. If we buy particular toys for young children, we may be shaping their expectations of what life has to offer them. What I mean is, buying engineering books for boys and dolls for girls may be storing up trouble for the future. Do we want girls to think that engineering isn't for them? Don't we want equality for all?

Three

We all buy too much stuff. I don't know whether that's because we're more interested in owning things than we used to be, or whether the retail industry has become better at persuading us that we need things. Whatever the truth, it's a fact that we buy and throw things away without much thought, and maybe we don't value the things we have as much as we should. When I was younger I used to save up to buy something new and I kept it for a long time. Was that better, or just different?

Four

We live in a consumer world, and one of the most popular leisure activities nowadays is shopping. But what that means is that our homes become full of stuff we've bought impulsively, without thinking, and now don't know what to do with. Decluttering and throwing away things we don't need should become a priority but it's not an easy thing to do. It's too easy to think – oh, I'll keep that because it might come in useful one day – but that day never comes!

Five

It's interesting that many young people are turning away from filling their homes with things and going for the minimalist look. Unlike their parents, they often have nothing at all on show – not even pictures on the walls! This could be because they can't afford to buy things, but that's unlikely. It's more that their priorities have changed. Young people choose to buy experiences rather than material goods.

Six

Marketing has a lot to answer for. We're surrounded by advertisements everywhere – on television, on buildings, in the cinema, on our computers. Almost every site we visit online has adverts, and they're targeted towards our own particular interests. It's hard to filter them out, to ignore the tempting goods they offer. So when we give in and buy something, we're just adding to the amount of stuff we've bought that we never really needed in the first place.

Strategies and skills:
Understanding opinions | Ex 4

 L18

One

Having lots of good friends is impossible – then they are just acquaintances, and you don't know them very well.

Two

I find it very interesting that people won't always say what they think.

Three

I'd say that the argument is more about a difference in personality than an actual problem.

Four

What I've come to realise is that it's less of an issue than I had thought.

Five

There are various reasons why psychology interests me.

Six

The really interesting thing about history is what you can learn from it.

EXAM TASK

 L19

F: This week I'm talking to Alan Winters, a professional clarinettist with a theatre orchestra. Alan, tell us why you took up the clarinet.

M: People are often surprised that I was ten before I picked up any musical instrument. I'd imagined myself as a guitarist in a band, but my mum was keen on the clarinet as she'd played it as a child. It was nice to make her feel good! I joined a local orchestra, and got into the social side of playing with other people, which I enjoyed. I did go to music college after that, though.

F: Now you're a professional, I suppose it's still necessary to keep practising?

M: Absolutely! There are more hopeful musicians than jobs, so obviously if you want to earn a living, you must be the best. That means practising constantly, however long it takes or however boring it is, just like an athlete keeping fit. My problem is the feeling that if I need to work hard on something, it makes me feel that I'm not very good at it. That's demotivating. Of course, it's great when it all comes together!

F: Now you play in theatres for musicals. You sit in the orchestra in the space in front of the stage – that's called the pit, isn't it? What's it like in there?

M: To the audience the pit seems very small, but actually most of them are bigger than they appear because they go back under the stage. It can feel crowded, though, and some musicians find it too claustrophobic. I prefer the fact that the audience can't really see me clearly – I'm kind of protected. If you're giving concerts in big halls, there's nowhere to hide. Although the pit looks dark from the auditorium, where the audience are sitting, we can actually see everything we need to.

F: Is there anything people may not know about being a pit player?

M: Having a good musical technique goes without saying, and you should be able to cope with a range of musical styles – but I guess that's true of any musician, really. In auditions you probably have to play music you haven't seen before – that's called sight-reading. But one personal quality people don't think of is patience – there's loads of hanging around to put up with. More predictable is being a team player. There's no room for ego in the pit!

F: Don't you get bored playing the same music every night? And what happens if you're ill on the night?

M: Oh, we have understudies to call on in an emergency. Pit playing's exhausting, and if you're worn out, you can't do your best. I accept it if I need someone to step in and am grateful – I can't worry that I'm not pulling my weight and working as hard as everyone else. We rehearse a lot, and I also do recordings with other groups in my spare time, so I work long hours. I never get tired of playing the same show every night, though – each performance feels different, even when the notes are the same!

F: How important is the conductor to a pit orchestra?

M: Very! He can see what's happening on stage and we can't, so he coordinates everything. It's not only that he keeps us together, like in a regular orchestra – sometimes he asks us to repeat a bit of music, or play more slowly because a singer has made a mistake. Everyone on stage has to see him too, so he stands quite high, which can make it difficult for us at the back of the pit, so sometimes there are small screens to help us.

F: Is there anything you've learnt you'd like to pass on to others?

M: We're only contracted to work in the evenings – or occasional matinées – so there's time to do other stuff – like record soundtracks for films. That's useful, and adds variety to a job that risks becoming boring if you're involved in a long-running show. You must build a good reputation, so you'll be asked to do other shows when one finishes. The standards demanded are incredibly high, but it's a small world so it's very social.

SPEAKING
Part 1
Practice task | Ex 1

 S01
See page 75.

How did you do? | Ex 3b

 S02

Question 1

Where are you from?

Student A: I come from Milan, which is a large city in the north of Italy.

Student B: I come from Barcelona, which is in Catalonia in Spain.

Question 2

Do you have a favourite colour? (What is it?) (Why?)

Student B: I don't have one and, to be honest, I don't think about it very often – but if I did, it would be green because I love the countryside.

Student C: My football team wears red and black, so I would say that they are my favourite colours.

Question 3

Can you tell us about your family?

Student A: I have quite a big family, with a brother, a sister and three cousins. We all live near each other and we're good friends.

Student C: My mum is a doctor, and my dad is a teacher. I don't have any brothers or sisters.

Question 4

What do you enjoy doing at the weekends? (Why?)

Student A: I really enjoy going shopping with my friends, and we spend a lot of time in the big mall in my city. There are lots of cafés where we can sit and talk, too.

Student B: I watch a lot of television at the weekends because I live a long way away from my friends, so I can't meet them very often.

Question 5

Are you interested in any sports? (Why? / Why not?)

Student A: No, not really – I prefer to listen to music and watch television.

Student B: I don't really like sport because I'm not very good at it. I'd rather listen to music.

Question 6

Can you speak any other languages apart from English? (What are they?)

Student B: I don't really like speaking languages much, but I'm trying hard and one day I'd like to learn Chinese, though I don't speak it now.

Student C: Not at the moment. I really enjoy learning English, because I like the pronunciation of the language, and I'd like to get really good at that before I start any new language.

EXAM TASK

 S03

See page 77.

SPEAKING

Part 2

Practice task | Ex 1

 S04

See page 78.

How did you do? | Ex 2a

 S05

Student A

In the first photograph there's a man choosing fruit. He's wearing a blue T-shirt and I think he's in a supermarket. There's a lot of different fruit for him to choose from, but he's choosing a large fruit – I'm not sure what it's called. In the second photograph the people are outside in the fields picking oranges from the trees. The man is wearing a striped jumper and the girl has a blue blouse and jeans. The weather looks nice. I guess they're choosing the best fruit to pick. I like to pick oranges because I like being outside in the fresh air.

Student B

Both photographs show people choosing fruit, but they're in different situations. In the first photograph a man is in a supermarket and he's choosing fruit to buy and eat. There's a lot of different fruit for him to choose from, although he seems to have chosen some already because he's putting it into a bag. On the other hand, the people in the second photograph are working in an orchard choosing fruit to pick so they need it to be ripe and in the best condition. They're only picking oranges, no other fruit. The man probably wants the best value for money, and he's going to enjoy it himself whereas the people in the second photograph might be experts who are choosing the fruit to sell. They need to be very careful about the fruit they choose because it must be ripe.

Strategies and skills:
Comparing different but related situations | Ex 4

 S06

Both photographs show friends who are enjoying a snack together, but they're in very different places. What's common to both photographs is what they're doing – the friends are eating and talking in casual situations. The first photograph shows two women sitting in a café in a city, talking together. However, the other photograph shows a group of people sitting on the beach, having a picnic or a barbecue. Another difference between the photographs is the clothes they're wearing – the group on the beach are dressed very casually but the women are wearing thicker clothes and it looks colder in the city. In the first photograph the women are enjoying each other's company because they're talking a lot. They look interested in each other and what they're talking about. They seem to be spending time together during the day, and maybe they're best friends. On the other hand, in the second photograph, the friends are enjoying relaxing out in the fresh air by the sea. They look happy together – perhaps they're on holiday. The whole group seem to be enjoying a day out. In both photographs the people are enjoying time away from work or college.

Strategies and skills:
Making speculations | Ex 6

 S07

Question 1: What are the people enjoying about studying outside?

Student A: They might be enjoying the fact that they're studying away from the classroom, and that they can work together if they want to.

Question 2: What are the people finding difficult about studying outside?

Student B: It's possible that it's difficult for them to study outside because it might be difficult to concentrate, and the sun might get in their eyes.

Question 3: Why have the people decided to study outside?

Student C: They could have decided to study outside because it's more relaxing for them, or because it's the weekend and the weather is too good to stay inside.

EXAM TASK

 S08

Candidate A, your photographs show people enjoying painting in different situations.

I'd like you to compare the photographs and say what you think the people are enjoying about painting in these situations.

Thank you. Candidate B, do you enjoy painting?

Candidate B, your photographs show people feeling tired in different situations.

I'd like you to compare the photographs and say why you think the people are feeling tired in these situations.

Thank you. Candidate A, have you ever been cycling in the mountains?

SPEAKING
Part 3
Practice task | Ex 1 and Ex 2

 S09 and S10

Examiner: Some people think that doing sport is the best way to stay fit and healthy, and other people disagree. Here are some things they think about, and a question for you to discuss. First you have some time to look at the task.

Now talk to each other about whether doing a sport is the best way to stay fit and healthy.

Student A: So what do we think about sport? Is it really a good way to stay fit and healthy? What do you think?

Student A: I don't really like sports, to be honest. In my opinion, eating the right food is just as important – there's no point if you spend hours jogging or something like that and then eat loads of chocolate. It seems to me that you take away any positive aspects of the sport. Do you think the same?

Student A: I think that's a good point. I don't enjoy sport much – probably because I never get chosen! But let's think about another problem of doing sport, and that's getting injured. What do you think about that?

How did you do? | Ex 3 and Ex 4

 S11 and S12

Examiner: Some people think that doing sport is the best way to stay fit and healthy, and other people disagree. Here are some things they think about, and a question for you to discuss. First you have some time to look at the task.

Now talk to each other about whether doing a sport is the best way to stay fit and healthy.

Student A: So what do we think about sport? Is it really a good way to stay fit and healthy? What do you think?

Student B: Well, I like sport so I guess I have to say yes. My thinking is that it makes you move, which is important for keeping healthy, and it's fun, too. I really enjoy being competitive, and I play a lot of different sports like football and tennis with my friends. Do you agree with me?

Student A: I don't really like sports, to be honest. In my opinion, eating the right food is just as important – there's no point if you spend hours jogging or something like that and then eat loads of chocolate. It seems to me that you take away any positive aspects of the sport. Do you think the same?

Student B: I see what you mean! But it's perhaps important to do both – do sport and also eat well. I can imagine that sport isn't much fun if you're not very good at it, though – it must be very frustrating if you never get into any teams. Then you aren't motivated to do it, and you don't stay fit and healthy – don't you think that's a negative point?

Student A: I think that's a good point. I don't enjoy sport much – probably because I never get chosen! But let's think about another problem of doing sport, and that's getting injured. What do you think about that?

Student B: Yes, it's true that it's a risk but you can take care not to get injured – like doing proper exercises to warm up your body first. In my opinion, you get all the benefits without the risk of injury.

Student A: OK – but does that also mean that it's a good way to actually <u>stay</u> fit and healthy? That's what the question is asking us, and I'm still not convinced.

How did you do? | Ex 5a and Ex 5b

 S13 and S14

Examiner: Now you have about a minute to decide what the best reason is for choosing <u>only</u> to do sport to stay fit and healthy.

Student B: So, now we've got to decide what the best reason is for just doing sport to keep fit and healthy. I think that I would say that the best reason is the fun that you get from it. It's very boring if you just go to the gym.

Student A: I can't disagree with that! I find the gym incredibly boring! But what about another thing we haven't mentioned before – the mental benefits of exercise. Although I don't like sport, I do find that if I go running, then my brain works better – and, actually, I feel happier. So I'm keeping fit and mentally healthy, too. I feel that's the best reason.

Student B: Yes, you're right – and we've decided that's equally important as physical fitness. So if we take both mental and physical fitness together, then that's definitely the best reason for doing sport. Is that all right with you?

Student A: I'll go along with that.

Strategies and skills:
Asking for and giving opinions | Ex 3 and Ex 4

 S15 and S16

Student A: OK – so let's think about this question. I love taking photographs, but not necessarily everywhere. What's your opinion?

Student B: My view on it is that it's not a good thing – you can't enjoy the moment when you're thinking about the photo you're taking. Don't you think that it takes away from the enjoyment of a special event? You have to be in the moment to really enjoy it.

Student A: The point I'm making is that you want something to help you remember it afterwards – that's the best way to have happy memories. It's very easy to forget things – like, I can't remember the first live music concert I went to. I wish someone had taken photos then.

Student B: OK – I accept that, and it's a good point, but it seems to me that everyone takes photos nowadays just because everybody else does – it's seen as the right thing to do. The reason I think that is because the last concert I went to all you could see were the phone screens being held up as people filmed the band. It spoiled it for everyone else.

Student A: You make a good point, plus it's hard to decide what to photograph when there are different things going on! Any ideas about that?

Student B: Not really – I'm no good at taking photos anyway!

Strategies and skills:
Showing how far you agree or disagree | Ex 7a

 S17

One

F: You know what? I think that sportspeople are paid far too much money for what they do. After all, they're only on the pitch for a short time! I work for eight hours every day!

M: You said that sportspeople are paid too much, and I think the same.

Two

M: I think that everyone should be able to drive a car in the modern world.

F: When you said that everyone should be able to drive a car, I wasn't sure about it.

Three

F: For me, listening to music is a great way to relax.

M: Thinking about what you said about music being a great way to relax, I definitely find that myself.

Four

M: In my opinion, everyone should travel less because of the damage it does to the environment.

F: Sorry, but I understood what you meant by damage to the environment was that it's actually harmful to the places people visit. I can't go along with that.

Five

F: I hate the adverts that are on television all the time – they're so boring.

M: So, just to make sure I've understood, you think that the adverts are boring, is that right? I completely agree with you!

Six

M: We work too hard nowadays – we should all have more holidays!

F: I guess what you mean is that we should work less and holiday more! That sounds really good to me!

Strategies and skills:
Negotiating towards a decision | Ex 9

 S18

One

M: So, we've talked about all the options and we have to make a decision. I'd like to choose this one – is that all right with you?

F: Absolutely – I'll go along with that.

M: Great – then that's decided.

Two

F: You said that you thought this was the best one. Shall we agree on that?

M: Yes, I think we've definitely reached agreement on that.

F: OK.

Three

M: Any idea which one to choose? How do you feel about it?

F: Well, we both have a different opinion on what's best.

M: We'll never make a decision, then.

Four

F: I'd go for this one. Do you feel the same?

M: It's not an easy decision to make – I'm not sure that's the right choice.

F: Well then, I'm sorry, we'll just have to agree to disagree.

Strategies and skills:
Negotiating towards a decision | Ex 11

 S19

One

M: OK – so in my opinion, taking away pressure is the most important reason for planning things in advance. Not knowing is really stressful.

F: I was thinking about looking forward to something, but I guess you're probably right.

M: So is that our final decision, then?

F: Yes, that's the best choice.

Two

F: We said that driving in towns wasn't good for the environment.

M: Yes, and I still think that's the most important reason for cycling, because of the pollution from cars. I really worry about the environment a lot.

F: We've both decided on that, I think.

Three

F: It's really hard to work abroad, I think, but it's good if you want to understand another culture.

M: Not everyone wants to do that, though – for me it's having new experiences.

F: But not everyone wants to do that – I don't, for one!

M: Oh dear – we won't be able to agree, then.

Four

F: I don't think it's important to go to the theatre.

M: But we have to choose the main reason. I'd go for fun.

F: What happens if you don't think it's fun? I'd rather go to the cinema.

M: Well, we can still choose one – what about learning new things?

F: All right – it's as good as any, I suppose.

Five

F: I think they're all important – there's no one reason.

M: Me too! But if we have to choose one, what do you think?

F: Staying healthy is important to me, and if I can cook, then I know exactly what I'm eating.

M: I think that's a good reason, but I like the idea of being independent …

F: Yes, me too – but health comes first really.

M: OK. Then, I think we've managed to come to a decision.

EXAM TASK

 S20

See page 88.

SPEAKING

Part 4

Practice task | Ex 1

S21

See page 89.

How did you do? | Ex 2 and Ex 3

S22 and S23

One

Examiner: Some people say that doing exercise helps people feel positive. What do you think?

M: I definitely agree with that. I know that if I go out running, I feel great when I get back. It seems to work even if I'm tired!

F: I know what you mean – isn't it something to do with chemicals released in the brain if you do exercise?

M: I think you're right but I'm not sure what the science behind it is!

Two

Examiner: In your opinion, does using social media help people have a positive attitude to life?

M: Social media can create problems. If people post photos of themselves having a good time, it can make you feel a bit jealous.

F: You say it can make you feel jealous, but actually those photos are often not the whole truth. People try to pretend they're having a better life than they really are.

M: You're right about that.

Three

Examiner: How important is it for people to show their feelings?

F: It's really important, and I think women are better at it than men. If you can share your feelings with friends, it stops you thinking too much and getting depressed.

M: You said that women are better at showing their feelings, and I guess that used to be true, but maybe it's changing. I talk to my friends about lots of things – certainly more than just sport!

F: OK – I accept what you say.

Strategies and skills: Giving full answers with examples and justifications | Ex 3

 S24

One

I really enjoy travelling abroad – I think you learn so much about other cultures. Once, when I went to Paris, I visited every art gallery I could find, and that gave me a life-long interest in art.

Two

It's difficult to say whether I always wanted to become a teacher. You see, what happened to me was I couldn't decide what to do and my parents suggested it. I love it, though.

Three

There are so many disadvantages about living in a city. Speaking for myself, though, I really like all the things I can do like going to theatres, so I prefer it to the countryside.

Strategies and skills: Adding ideas and developing a discussion | Ex 8 and Ex 9

 S25 and S26

One

Examiner: Do you agree that social media is essential for keeping up with friends?

M: I think social media's very important for that, because it's so easy to make arrangements that way.

F: Yes, and another point about what you've just said is how convenient it is because you know that friends will see everything immediately.

M: And if I could add something to that, it saves time as well.

Two

Examiner: Do you think the time people spend using social media would be better spent doing other things?

F: It can certainly waste a lot of time – I like having time to do other more interesting things, like sport.

M: I've got an example of that to add to what you've said – my friend spends all his time on his phone and he should be spending more time doing healthy things like exercise. I know that!

Three

Examiner: How important is the internet for finding out about the news?

F: Personally, I don't follow the news much. I find it rather boring.

M: Really? It's not the same for me – I love it. I don't have time to read newspapers, so social media is a great way of keeping up with it. I don't know what I'd do without the internet.

EXAM TASK

 S27

See page 91.

Practice Exam

LISTENING

Part 1

 PE01

1 You hear two people talking about a film they've just seen.

F: Well, what did you think?

M: Actually, it wasn't as bad as I'd thought it might be. The plot was pretty dramatic, and had a few good surprises. I was certainly on the edge of my seat.

F: I got lost several times, to be honest. On the other hand, the writing was exceptional – I could more or less believe in everything they were saying.

M: I think the writers deserve some kind of award – so often a script isn't credible.

F: And then it relies on the actors to bring it to life, which isn't always possible.

M: Some were rather second-rate, though there were a couple of good performances – like, the mother was terrific.

2 You hear two friends talking about an arrangement they've made.

F: So are you OK for tonight? Remember we're meeting Clarrie at six at the restaurant so we can eat together before going to the show.

M: I know that's what we planned, but I'm having second thoughts. It's going to take her ages to get there, given that she's working on the other side of town, and we don't want to be held up waiting for her and miss the show. I know she said it'd be OK, but you know what the traffic's like at that time of day. Perhaps we should consider meeting up later?

F: I'll give her a ring tonight to check.

3 You hear a man telling a friend about a graphic design course he's doing in his free time.

F: How's the course going at work? It's advanced graphic design, isn't it?

M: Yes, and it's OK, thanks – I'm certainly finding out about a whole new set of programmes I'd never even heard of.

F: Are you pleased you're doing it, then?

M: Well, it's not exactly going to get me a promotion, because lots of people have already done it. To be honest, I'm only doing it because my manager made it clear that she expected it. I guess it might do me some good in the long run – more money, maybe, though I don't think that'll happen any time soon.

4 You hear a girl telling a friend about going away to college.

M: So are you ready to start college next week?

F: I'm packed, and quite excited about going to live in student accommodation, but Mum is quite upset cos I'll be leaving home. I'll be back at weekends, though.

M: It's not that far away, is it?

F: No, though none of my school friends will be there, so I'll have to be sociable, which'll be fun. I guess the thing is not knowing how hard the course will be – I've heard that the tutors there expect high standards, and everyone else will be really good.

M: I'm sure you'll be fine. It's a whole new step in life!

5 You hear an announcement about a concert.

Welcome everyone to the Central Arena for our concert tonight. It's going to be spectacular! All the performers are ready and waiting to go, keen to start entertaining you – and just to let you all know that, due to fantastic ticket sales, we've added another night to this sell-out tour, so pass the word around your friends! All the details will be posted at the doors on your way out. Don't forget that anyone who has a voucher for a free snack should follow the signs to the café right now – you won't want to miss the start of the show because you're standing in a queue!

6 You hear a boy telling a friend about his tennis lessons.

F: So how are the tennis lessons going?

M: Not too bad, thanks – I have one every week, which is good, though to be honest the instructor can't really go into much depth because of the lack of time. He gives me lots of practise instead, which I enjoy, and I really try hard to do what he wants. The only problem is that all I want to do is find out how to win – not have the absolutely correct technique, so my priority is a bit different.

F: That's important, though, isn't it?

M: I guess so – but I don't have time for it.

7 You hear a girl telling a friend about a holiday in a national park.

M: How was your holiday?

F: Amazing! I'd seen pictures and read up about it, so I knew all the stuff we could do there, but the grandeur of the landscape took my breath away. The lodge we stayed in was out of this world – it was far more luxurious than I'd imagined, so we spent loads of time there.

M: Did you see lots of animals?

F: Well, not as many as I'd hoped, but a friend who went last year warned me that it was just a question of luck. But I've still got some nice photos that I took when I was walking in the hills.

8 You hear a man telling a friend about an advertisement he saw on television.

M: So, I was watching television last night, and this advert came on – I've seen it before, in fact I usually turn the sound off, but for some reason last night I watched it carefully. And you know what – apart from the reasonably amusing little story in it, which surprised me considering the bad impression I usually get from such ads – I'm not sure that what it says is accurate. And, after all, that's the one thing they should watch out for! I might contact the company and tell them.

F: You should – that sort of thing is very annoying!

That is the end of Part 1.

LISTENING

Part 2

 PE02

Jane: Hi everyone, I'm Jane Wilson, and I've been an actress since I was very young – not as you probably imagine in films or on stage, but in television commercials. Whatever your ultimate ambitions, it's a great job in itself with loads of advantages, like the amount of experience you gain and the good salary. But more than anything it provides you with the chance to make new contacts who will be useful later on. Some actors see it as a step to bigger and better things, while others (like me) are quite happy with it as a full-time career.

It's a common misunderstanding that acting in a commercial is just the same as any other acting. You have far less input into the role you're taking on. Although an advert often tells a story, and you may have some dramatic scenes, you have no time to work on a character like you do in a film, which is a shame; in fact, as commercials are so short, you have to really target your feelings to get the message across quickly.

Working on commercials demands a very specific skillset; you need to act to a camera, and follow instructions precisely while staying relaxed and natural – not an easy combination! One thing I wish I'd done more work on is voice control because this really helps build acting skills and confidence, so work on this in your classes.

What about when you want to start looking for work yourselves? Don't go for every role that comes up. Directors of TV adverts tend to have a certain look in mind, and won't consider anyone who doesn't fit this. Make sure you have a collection of photos to send out when applying for auditions – this saves time in the long run.

Most of the hundreds of jobs I went for in the beginning weren't right for me – like building materials or cars, but the worst one was when I applied to be in a commercial selling baby food when I didn't look old enough to be a parent! But you live and learn.

It's a very competitive world. Although you want to have an impressive CV, you may be surprised when I say don't include every commercial you've ever made. I did that, and then couldn't understand why I was never invited to audition to advertise chocolate even though I seemed to be considered endlessly for things like washing powder or soap. Then I discovered that I'd done one for a particular sweet company ages ago so no similar companies wanted me!

If you're invited to an audition, never turn it down. I did once because I was tired, and that particular company didn't ask me back. It's a small world, and you get a reputation for being awkward or unhelpful if you reject offers. So, I think taking every opportunity is common sense. Turn up looking professional – ideally do plenty of research first so that you appear knowledgeable about the product. Always arrive early, and don't be afraid to ask questions. But don't be disappointed if you're not successful - it's all good experience.

Once you have a job, make sure you're easy to work with. No one has time for an actor who isn't a team player – having a likeable personality is a useful asset. And key to the whole thing is flexibility - one week you might be playing a nurse, the next a taxi driver! You just go with the flow. When I started I was told that filming adverts was stressful because you only have a short time to impress people – I'd say it's exciting, although actors I know find it tiring. It's great to see the final version on television, though!

It's also fun to see some of the tricks of the advertising trade at first hand. People know about using mashed potato instead of ice cream, because it won't melt under the lights, but I did one where they actually used brown shoe polish on bread to make it look more appetising. I hadn't seen that before!

So – any questions?

That is the end of Part 2.

LISTENING
Part 3
 PE03

Speaker 1

I'd been doing my current job for ages, and was pretty good at it – I was in line for promotion and felt fairly settled. It was a close friend who pointed out the ad in the paper for a job with the football club I'd supported for years – he said it'd be right up my street. It wasn't my main area of expertise – in fact, it was in the Public Relations department, but I decided to give it a go. The interview was tough, so I was thrilled when I got the email offering it to me. I've just started, and it's going to be fine.

Speaker 2

I went straight into a job with a local firm immediately after school, and it was going quite well. I was managing a couple of junior staff members, and enjoyed that – I felt that I was being fast-tracked for bigger and better things. On top of that the salary was higher than many of my contemporaries were getting – but the downside was I was working far longer hours than they were. I felt I was missing out on that social side of life, so I applied for and got a job which was less demanding. I'm happy with my decision.

Speaker 3

I'd not worked particularly hard at school, and wasn't sure what I was really suited for. It isn't easy when there are so many possibilities out there! My parents guided me towards a college course in architecture, which was quite interesting but didn't really motivate me. I did start working in that field, but got frustrated quite quickly – every day seemed to be the same. I saw an ad for a social worker working with disadvantaged teenagers, and thought that would push me to achieve more even though it would be a drop in income. I've been doing it for a month, and it's looking good so far.

Speaker 4

I've always been close to my parents, so working up the road from them seemed ideal at first. The particular job turned out to be a dead-end, though – there weren't many chances to get ahead, and I was nervous about getting stuck there. I needed to grow up a bit, show that I was able to take charge of something myself. OK, it was convenient living at home – cheap, meals constantly provided, loads of social opportunities – but it was too easy. I moved to another town, got a job and was making enough to afford my own flat. It's working out pretty well, and I don't think my parents miss me!

Speaker 5

I was getting along nicely at work, even though it wasn't fulfilling any life-long ambitions. I'd just been made a manager, so the salary had gone up, and everything seemed to be going smoothly. I was quite good at balancing work and social life too. Everyone said I had it made, but I felt bored. I decided to change everything and take a job abroad, in spite of all the advice to the contrary. I think I just wanted to show everyone that I knew better than them – and, actually, I'm loving life on the other side of the Atlantic.

That is the end of Part 3.

LISTENING
Part 4

 PE04

M: Today we're talking to Lina Beecham, who works as an animator in films. Welcome to the programme, Lina. Was animation something you've always wanted to do?

F: Well, I began drawing when I was two. Other toddlers were just scribbling, but I was trying to create pictures. My first drawing of our family car was primitive, but my parents loved it – in fact they still have it! I can't remember which cartoon film I saw first, but after that I never wanted to do anything else. My classmates were doing sensible subjects like computer science, and didn't understand why I always had a sketchbook with me.

M: When was the first time you drew something professionally?

F: It wasn't animation. I was 13 when one of my mother's friends asked me to illustrate the children's book she was writing. At the time I was incredibly proud and felt like a real artist. Now, looking back at the drawings and knowing that people can still buy the book, I go red when I think that they're still out there – they're quite childish. I did put it on my CV later, which may have helped get me into art college.

M: Did you always rely on your natural talent or did you have a lot to learn?

F: The actual drawing side came naturally, but I had to study technique at college. I didn't realise how much better I could be. I learnt how to construct a drawing properly, and to eliminate basic errors. The best thing was learning to capture the finer details of whatever I was drawing. To be honest, I'd never been too bad at that – my classmates often wanted me to sketch them, and they could always recognise themselves – but it helped me develop a more expert approach.

M: Now you work in film animation. What's it like working with other animators?

F: There are lots of us on a film and we're quite competitive. I guess that's inevitable with creative artists! An animated film has to be tightly controlled – everything has to be consistent and there's loads of detailed planning. We're allocated a particular character or storyline to develop but keeping everyone informed of what we're doing is critical. Without that there would be chaos!

M: Is there anything you don't enjoy about your job?

F: Animation is very time-consuming. Because it's so tightly planned, it's hard to express yourself freely, and some people

do get frustrated by that. It's a different approach from working with live actors, and you need a great deal of patience. I remember once having difficulty with a particular drawing of a fox – I couldn't get it right – and it was hard to keep going with it. But even though you can't stop thinking about it, you can't give up either.

M: Is there anything of yourself in the characters you create?

F: Well, you're creating a character from nothing and the audience has to connect to it emotionally. You have to create that connection through your drawing, and it has to be real. So, just like an actor does, you bring your own experience and perspective to it. It's good to be able to talk to other people about it too, though, and think it through properly from the outset so the character develops consistently.

M: You've just directed an animated film. How different was that from being an animator?

F: As an animator, you're involved at a basic level, bringing the story to life and focusing on the detail. As a director, you're more concerned with the overall impact of a film, and you also worry about quality control. In a way it's pleasing if an animator can work through their own vision, but a director has a lot more things to think about, not least financial. That's very complex – you're balancing so many different things. But it's been so useful for me to experience that role, although I'm happiest at my drawing board!

M: Thanks for joining us, Lina.

That is the end of the test.

SPEAKING
Part 1

 PE05
See page 108.

SPEAKING
Part 2

 PE06
See page 109.

SPEAKING
Part 3

 PE07
See page 111.

SPEAKING
Part 4

 PE08
See page 111.

READING AND USE OF ENGLISH
Part 1 Multiple-choice cloze

1

Students' own answers

2

1 D **2** C **3** B **4** A

3

1 3 **2** 1 **3** 4 **4** 2

4

1 'Great' has the meaning of big and good or impressive. 'Big' refers to physical size. 'Severe' suggests something bad. 'High' is used for prices.

2 'Cause' means to make something happen. It is followed by a noun, not a 'that' clause. 'Demand' means to require or need. 'Mean' indicates that something follows as a consequence. It is followed by a 'that' clause. 'Allow' means to make it possible for something to happen. It is used in the pattern *allow + someone + to*.

3 'Although' is used at the beginning of a sentence, or at the beginning of a second clause. 'However' is used between commas or at the beginning of a sentence. 'Despite' is followed by a noun. 'Instead' is followed by 'of'.

4 'Take off' means become successful. 'Get something off' means to remove it. 'Put something off' means to delay it. 'Make off' means to escape.

Strategies and skills
Phrases with prepositions

1a

1 interested (+ in) **2** get (+ to) **3** familiar (+ with) **4** recovering (+ from) **5** proud (+ of) **6** approved (+ of) **7** effect (+ on) **8** heard (+ of)

1b

1 'curious' + about, 'keen' + on, 'attracted' + to

2 'arrive' + at/in, 'find' + no preposition, 'reach' + no preposition

3 'informed' + about, 'interested' + in, 'knowledgeable' + about

4 'mending' + no preposition, 'improving' + after, 'gaining' + no preposition

5 'pleased' + with, 'satisfied' + with, 'content' + with

6 'liked' + no preposition, 'agreed' + to/with, 'accepted' + no preposition

7 'result' + of/in, 'solution' + to, 'end' + of

8 'recognised' + no preposition, 'noticed' + no preposition, 'realised' + no preposition

2

1 C ('in person' – face to face) **2** B ('by profession' – as a job) **3** D ('in common' – shared) **4** C ('To my surprise' – I was surprised by this) **5** D ('on the scene' – where a crime or accident has happened) **6** C ('by heart' – from memory)

3

1 out ('sell out' – sell all of something)

2 take ('take over' – dominate completely)

3 came up with ('come up with' – think of)

4 take ('take up' – accept)

5 up ('pick up' – learn)

6 shut down ('shut down' – switch off a computer)

4

1 B ('go ahead with' – start on something that has been planned)

2 C ('put off' – delay until another time) **3** D ('go up' – increase)

4 A ('get together' – meet up) **5** D ('go off' – stop working)

6 C ('get behind with' – don't do enough of something so you might be late finishing it) **7** B ('put up with' – endure)

8 C ('take after someone' – be like someone)

Verb patterns

5

1 to reserve ('manage to do' something)

2 that we had lost ('accept' + 'that')

3 moving ('consider doing' something)

4 Sam to be ('urge someone to do' something)

5 to help ('agree to do' something)

6 working ('imagine doing' something)

6

1 C ('decide to do' something; 'consider doing something', 'think about doing something', 'insist on doing something')

2 A ('find something + easy/difficult'; 'experience something', 'believe that something is …', 'realise that something is …')

3 B ('suggest that someone should do' something; 'urge someone to do something', 'tell someone to do something', 'persuade someone to do something')

4 C ('like to do something'; 'insist on doing something', 'imagine doing something', 'stress that' …)

5 D ('appreciate something'; 'benefit from (doing) something', 'approve of (someone doing) something', 'agree to (do) something')

6 D ('encourage someone to do something'; 'suggest that someone (should) do something', 'propose something/propose doing something', 'say that someone should do something')

Easily confused words

7

1 B (You 'post' photos, comments, etc. online. You 'send'/'mail' things to people by post. When you 'deliver' something, you take it to a place.)

2 C (You 'release' an album. You can say that you 'bring out' an album, but not just 'bring' it. You 'display' something in a place, for people to look at. When you 'present' something to people, you show it to them or explain it to them.)

3 A (To 'contain' something means to have it inside. To 'combine' things means to put them together. You can say that something is 'composed' of different things, but not that it 'composes' them. 'Consist' is always followed by 'of'.)

4 B ('Rays' is the correct word for talking about the sun. A 'bar' is a long thin piece of something. A 'light' is a lamp. A 'flash' is a sudden bright light that disappears quickly.)

5 D (A tourist 'destination' is a place that tourists often go to. A 'visit' is a time when you go to a place. An 'intention' is something that you plan to do. An 'aim' is something that you want to achieve.)

6 C (The 'view' from a place is everything you can see from there. A 'scene' is a place or situation where something is happening, e.g. the scene of a crime, or a part of a play. A 'sight' is something that you see, e.g. 'Bicycles are a familiar sight in the city'. A 'glance' is an act of looking at something very quickly.)

Verb collocations

8

1 keep ('keep something *secret/keep a secret*' – not tell people about something) **2** take ('take advantage of something' – behave unfairly to get what you want) **3** do ('do the job' – be adequate) **4** make ('make sense' – seem correct) **5** have ('have a word with someone' – talk to them) **6** come ('come true' – become a reality) **7** spend ('spend time doing something' – use your time in that way) **8** play ('play a trick on someone' – do something to them as a joke) **9** get ('get rid of' – throw away) **10** go ('go wrong' – create a mistake or problem)

9

1 c ('rather than' – instead of) **2** f ('as long as' – if/provided that) **3** a ('owing to' – because of, due to, thanks to) **4** e ('apart from' – except) **5** b ('despite' – in spite of) **6** d ('so as to' – in order to)

10

1 C ('rather' + *than*; 'instead' + 'of', 'whereas' is followed by a clause, 'by contrast' is followed by a clause)
2 A ('otherwise' – if this doesn't happen; 'however', 'although' and 'except' have the wrong meaning)
3 B ('in spite of' + noun; 'except', 'however' and 'although' are all followed by a clause)
4 A ('unless' – 'if' + 'not' (the sentence means 'I will only call you if there is a problem'); 'provided that' – if, 'except' is followed by 'if' or 'that', 'owing to' – because)
5 C ('as well as' + noun; 'in addition' is followed by 'to' or a clause, 'in particular' has the wrong meaning, 'what's more' is used at the beginning of a sentence and followed by a clause)
6 D ('Although' + clause, + clause; 'However' and 'Nevertheless' are used at the beginning of a sentence (not a clause), 'in spite of' is followed by a noun)

EXAM TASK

1 B ('in case' – because something bad might happen; 'even if' – whether or not, 'provided that' – only if, 'whereas' introduces a contrast)
2 B ('as well as' – adding a similar idea; 'although' needs to be followed by a clause, 'in spite of' and 'in contrast' introduce a contrast)
3 A ('known + as; 'called' is followed by a noun or pronoun, 'named' is followed by a name, 'entitled' is used for books, films, etc. and not usually for people)
4 A ('views' – opinions that are expressed; 'wishes' – things that someone wants, 'requests' – things that someone asks another person to do, 'decisions' – things that someone decides to do)
5 C ('a month's/week's/year's) supply' – a fixed collocation; 'donation' – an amount of money that you give, 'number + of' – used with countable nouns, 'delivery' – something that is delivered to a place)
6 D ('consider' someone to be something'; 'decide', 'accept', 'realise' that someone is …)
7 A ('make sense' – a fixed phrase meaning 'to seem like a good idea')
8 C ('get on with' – continue with; 'go through with' – finish something, 'put up with' – tolerate something bad, 'get away with' – avoid punishment for something)

READING AND USE OF ENGLISH

Part 2 Open cloze

1
Students' own answers
2
1 been **2** this/that **3** whose **4** more
3
1 Which answer is part of a verb tense? 1
• Which tense is it? (present perfect continuous)
• Why is this tense correct here? (a past action that is continuing in the present)
2 Which answer is a relative pronoun? 3
• What noun does it refer back to? (people)
• Why is this pronoun correct here? (it refers to possession)
3 Which answer is a comparative structure? 4
• Which word before the gap helps you decide it should be a comparative structure? (far)
• Why is 'less' not correct? (wrong meaning)
4 Which answer is a reference word, which refers to an earlier idea? 2
• What idea does it refer back to? ('a power nap can make up for a bad night's sleep')
• Why is 'these' not correct here? (because it is plural, and we need a singular reference word)

4

Gap 2 can be filled by two possible words because *this* and *that* have a similar meaning, and are both grammatically correct in the sentence.

Strategies and skills

Present tenses

1
1 been (present perfect continuous)
2 is (present simple passive)
3 are (present continuous)
4 do (present simple negative)
5 has (present perfect passive)
6 has (present perfect simple)

Future forms

2
1 will be able (future form of 'be able to')
2 be watched (future passive)
3 will have left (future perfect)
4 will be travelling (future continuous)
5 will have to (future form of 'have to')
6 have been living (future perfect continuous)

3
1 be (future continuous) **2** have (future perfect)
3 be (future form of 'be able to') **4** been (future perfect continuous)
5 be (future passive) **6** have/need (future form of 'have to'/'need to')

Conditional forms

4
1 A (past perfect, third conditional)
2 B ('would' – second conditional)
3 A (present simple, first conditional)
4 B (present simple, zero conditional)
5 C ('unless' – *if not*)
6 C ('wish' + past perfect)
7 A ('if' – zero conditional)
8 B ('wish' + 'would')

Relative clauses

5
You know because in most cases the word before each gap is a noun or pronoun, and after the gap there is another clause (a relative clause). Sentence 5 is slightly different. There is not a noun or pronoun before the gap because the non-defining relative clause refers to the whole meaning of the first clause, not one particular word.

6
1 where (referring to 'city')
2 who/that (referring to 'someone')
3 when (referring to 'day')
4 whose (referring to 'Ana')
5 which (referring to the fact that the show had already started)
6 which/that (referring to 'course')

Comparative forms

7
1 f ('how' – used to emphasise a quality)
2 d ('so tired that' – very tired and so …)
3 a ('by far' + superlative – the biggest, best, etc., by a large amount)
4 c ('far' + comparative – much bigger, better, etc.)
5 b ('such a good actor' – a very good actor)
6 e ('the' + comparative + 'the' + comparative – the more one thing is true, the more the other thing is also true)

8

1 more ('far' + 'more' + adjective)
2 such ('such' + 'a')
3 most ('one of the most …')
4 how ('how' + adjective + someone 'is to do' something)
5 so ('so' + adjective 'that …')
6 by ('by far the' + superlative)

Reference words and impersonal structures

9

1 that ('that' – conjunction)
2 this ('this one' – referring back to this email)
3 It (impersonal structure)
4 what (impersonal structure)
5 there ('there was' – past form of 'there is')
6 that ('that' – referring back to the fact that Marta had failed to answer her phone. 'This' is also possible here.)

Quantifiers

10

1 few ('few' – small number + plural countable noun)
2 much/any ('not much' – a small amount, not any – none + uncountable noun)
3 little ('very little' – a very small amount + uncountable noun)
4 none ('none' – not any)
5 over ('well over' – many more than + plural countable noun)
6 of ('plenty of' + uncountable or plural countable noun)

Linking words and expressions

11

a sentences 1, 3 and 4
b sentences 2 and 5
c sentence 6

12

1 A ('Although' – used before two contrasting clauses)
2 B ('Besides' – used at the beginning of a sentence, followed by a comma)
3 C ('despite' – used before a noun)
4 B ('However' – used at the beginning of a second sentence, between two contrasting ideas)
5 A ('too' – used at the end of a sentence)
6 A ('while' – to indicate two actions happen at the same time)

13

1 since ('ever since' – since)
2 though ('even though' – although)
3 only ('if only' – if)
4 well ('as well as' – also)
5 spite ('in spite of' – despite)
6 rather ('rather than' – instead of)
7 apart ('apart from' – except)
8 due/owing ('due to'/'owing to' – because of)
9 case ('in case' – because something might happen)
10 order ('in order to' – to)

EXAM TASK

1 has (present perfect tense)
2 In (fixed phrase – 'in response to')
3 where (relative pronoun referring to a place)
4 of (quantifier – 'plenty of')
5 unless (conditional sentence)
6 up (phrasal verb; 'pick something up' – learn it)
7 is ('What' + impersonal structure)
8 for (phrasal verb; 'look out for' – try to find)

READING AND USE OF ENGLISH
Part 3 Word formation

1

Students' own answers

2

1 scientific **2** appearance **3** healthily **4** impossible

3

1 1 **2** 3 **3** 2 **4** 4

Strategies and skills

Negative prefixes

1

un-: uncertain, unpleasant, unsatisfied
in-: inaccurate, informal
im-: imprecise, impatient
ir-: irregular, irrelevant
il-: illegal
dis-: disorganised, dissatisfied

Noun suffixes

2

-ance/-ence: appearance, assistance, independence, performance
-ment: agreement, employment, encouragement, improvement
-ness: happiness, illness, kindness, nervousness
-ion: collection, decision, destruction, explanation, variation
-y/-ity: collectivity, popularity, safety, similarity, variety

3

2 assistant **3** consumer **4** comedian **5** economist **6** employer, employee **7** instructor **8** scientist **9** politician **10** tourist
We use the suffixes **-ian, -ant, -er, -ist, -ee, -or**

4

1 c **2** e **3** i **4** g **5** j **6** a **7** d **8** h **9** f **10** b

5

1 retirement (retire + -ment)
2 competitions (compete + i + -tions)
3 appearance (appear + -ance)
4 success (succeed → success (irregular))
5 satisfaction (satisfy + ac + -tion)
6 supporters (support + ers ('many' requires plural form))
7 performance (perform + -ance)
8 ambition (ambitious + -tion)

Adjective suffixes 1

6

-al: natural, traditional
-ful: careful, helpful, stressful, successful, wonderful
-ing: daring, embarrassing, exciting
-ive: creative, effective, impressive
-less: careless, helpless
-ous: ambitious, dangerous

7

1 artistic (art + ist + -ic) **2** scientific (science + tif + -ic)
3 commercial (commerce + i + -al) **4** enthusiastic (enthusiasm + t + -ic)
5 spectacular (spectacle + u + -lar) **6** twentieth (twenty + i + -eth)

8

1 fascinating (the exhibition creates the feeling) **2** delighted (the feeling of being accepted) **3** amazed (the feeling created by his speed) **4** entertaining (the show gives the feeling) **5** disappointed (the feeling caused by the results) **6** challenging (the feeling created by the exercises) **7** excited (how they felt when they saw their cousins) **8** interesting (the book gives this feeling) **9** embarrassed (how certain things make you feel as a teenager) **10** revealing (the article is revealing)

Adjective suffixes 2

9

-able: comfortable, employable, profitable, reliable
-ant/-ent: confident, patient, pleasant
-y: healthy, noisy, tasty

10

1 uncomfortable (un + comfort + -able – the seat wasn't comfortable but I still enjoyed the film) **2** unexpected (un + expect + -ed – things occurred that had not been planned for and so they were not expected) **3** fortunate (fortune + -ate – we managed to catch the train as luckily it was late) **4** unhealthy (un + health + -y – food like cakes and chocolate are not good for you) **5** effective (effect + -ive – there are better ways to express how we feel) **6** unlucky (un + luck + -y – we played well enough to win, but we didn't, so were *unlucky*) **7** disorganised (dis + organise + -d – he is not organised) **8** unsuccessful (un + success + -ful – not a success, so no interview)

Adverbs

11

1 increasing (also possible: increased), increasingly (increasing + -ly)
2 comfortable, comfortably (comfortable + -ly)
3 desperate, desperately (desperate + -ly)/despairing, despairingly (despairing + -ly)
4 occasional, occasionally (occasional + -ly)
5 traditional, traditionally (traditional + -ly)
6 accidental, accidentally (accidental + -ly)
7 original, originally (original + -ly)
8 personal, personally (personal + -ly)
9 successful, successfully (successful + -ly)
10 imaginative, imaginatively (imaginative + -ly)

12

1 personally (adverb – the pattern is adverb + adjective)
2 original (adjective – the pattern is adjective + noun)
3 successfully (adverb – the pattern is adverb + verb)
4 accidentally (adverb – the pattern is adverb + verb)
5 dramatic (adjective – the pattern is adjective + noun)
6 traditionally (adverb – the pattern is adverb + passive verb)
7 increasingly (adverb – the pattern is adverb + adjective)
8 imaginative (adjective – the pattern is adjective + noun)

Verb suffixes and prefixes

13

1 advertise (the pattern is 'to' + base form of verb + noun)
2 frighten (the pattern is 'to' + base form of verb + object pronoun)
3 criticised (the pattern is 'being' + past participle)
4 enabled (the pattern is noun phrase + verb + object pronoun)
5 realised (the pattern is subject + verb + 'that' clause)
6 tighten (the pattern is 'to' + base form of verb + object pronoun)

EXAM TASK

1 location (the pattern is – 'the' + noun + for)
2 popularity (the pattern is – 'its' + noun)
3 substantial (the pattern is – verb + adjective + noun)
4 Scientists (the pattern is – plural noun + plural verb)
5 carefully (the pattern is – adverb + verb)
6 divers (the pattern is – adjective + plural noun + plural verb)
7 effective (the pattern is – adverb + adjective)
8 strictly (the pattern is – 'be' + adverb + passive verb)

READING AND USE OF ENGLISH
Part 4 Key word transformations
Practice task

1

Students' own answers

2

1 have given up trying
2 not used phrenology since
3 was believed to be

3

1 3 **2** 1 **3** 2

Strategies and skills

Past tenses

1

1 S (The speaker was in the habit of playing a lot of tennis at college.) **2** S (The speaker has lived in Paris since 2012 and still lives there now.) **3** D (A – We have been friends for ten years up until this point in time; B – We became friends ten years before a specific point in time that has been referred to previously.) **4** S (The father was in the habit of telling the speaker to do their best at school.) **5** S (The speaker last saw George two years ago.) **6** D (A – Joan started to prepare the meal after we got home; B – Joan was already cooking the meal when we got home.)

2

1 have been living here for (present perfect continuous + 'for' – an action that started in the past and still continues)
2 would visit our grandparents every ('would' – a repeated action in the past)
3 didn't use to enjoy ('used to' – a habit in the past)
4 had never met Charles (past perfect – an earlier action in the past)
5 has stopped trying (present perfect – a recent past action)
6 haven't taken an exam (present perfect – a recent past action)

Reported speech

3

1 Sam to check ('advise' + object + 'to' + base form)
2 me not to sit ('warn' + object pronoun + negative base form + 'to')
3 Marta of stealing ('accuse' + object + 'of' + -'ing')
4 me to come/go ('invite' + object pronoun + 'to' + base form)
5 what I was doing at ('ask' + reported question with 'what')
6 she could use ('ask' + reported question with 'if')

Comparative forms

4

1 wasn't as long as (shorter than I expected)
2 a faster runner than (Marlon is slower)
3 was more successful than (the second film was less successful)
4 such a big (the house was big; there is no comparison)
5 the most interesting (superlative – 'the most')
6 much cheaper than (the last hotel was less expensive)

Passive forms

5

1 is being opened (present continuous passive)
2 was given a ticket by (past simple passive + 'by' to say who did the action)
3 had been decided that (past perfect passive)
4 will be informed (future passive with 'will')
5 is expected to start (present simple passive)
6 is supposed to be (present simple passive)
7 believed/thought to have been (present simple passive)
8 get my computer repaired ('have'/'get' something done)

Conditionals and *wish*

6

1 both (She will only come to the party if she can get a taxi home.) **2** B (an obligation or condition; A involves a possible outcome) **3** B (Lily's train was delayed, she was late; A – the train wasn't delayed) **4** both (The snow prevented us from going shopping.) **5** A (She was sorry she had spent a lot of money; B – She was unsure about the amount of money she spent (and was surprised it was a lot.)) **6** B (I am not happy it is raining now; A – I am not happy there is a lot of rain in general.)

Grammar and vocabulary changes

7

1 no point in taking ('no point' + 'in' + '-ing' form)
2 had been on time (third conditional)
3 so difficult that I could ('so' + adjective + 'that')
4 has been learning French for (present perfect continuous + 'for' – an action that started in the past and continues in the present)
5 more interesting than (comparative – 'more' + adjective + 'than')
6 advised us not to stay (the pattern is 'advise someone (not) to do something')

Paraphrasing

8

1 B ('put out' – leave outside e.g. 'put out the rubbish'; 'put down' – put something you are holding onto the floor or another surface) **2** A ('get part of' – obtain a piece of; 'give part of' – offer a piece of) **3** C ('turn away' – move your face or body to another direction; 'turn off' – switch off) **4** A ('give away' – donate; 'give out' – distribute) **5** A ('There isn't a point of'/'There's a point for' are not correct) **6** C (when something 'gives off' a smell, it means you can smell it; when you 'give in', you agree to something or admit defeat)

9

1 S (I will never speak to Carol again.) **2** D (A: the break was unintended; B: the break was intended) **3** D (A: people couldn't park; B: people could park) **4** S (They had spent all the money.) **5** S (In the end, we escaped.) **6** D (A: he ignored the children; B: he watched or listened to the children carefully)

EXAM TASK

1 accused me of not telling ('accused' + verb pattern: 'accuse someone of (not) doing something')
2 should not have left (past modal form with 'should' + 'not' + 'have' + past participle)
3 a better dancer (irregular comparative of 'good')
4 is thought to be (present simple passive)
5 wish I had gone ('wish' + past perfect to express a past regret)
6 looking forward to meeting ('look forward to' + '-ing' form)

READING AND USE OF ENGLISH

Part 5 Multiple choice

Practice task

1

Students' own answers

2

1 C **2** D

3

1 1 B **2** C **3** D **4** A
2 C matches 2 exactly ('remind us that we are only a tiny part of the life on this planet' – shows us we are not the most important thing on Earth)
3 B does not match 1 (The text describes what Antarctica is like, but it does not say it is unique.)

D does not match 3 (The text mentions the main British research station, but does not say that most scientists in Antarctica are British.)
A does not match 4 (There is nothing in the text to say that Antarctica is important for scientific studies.)

4

1 Britain first established research stations in Antarctica in the 1940s, and from the start, a no-women rule was strictly followed. As late as the 1960s, **(B)** female scientists who applied for posts in Antarctica were banned from joining male colleagues on trips to the continent. Unbelievably, one female scientist received a letter of rejection stating that there were no facilities for women in Antarctica, including no shops or hairdressers! **(C)** This trivial-sounding excuse revealed **(D)** a deeper, widely held belief that somehow Antarctica was only for men. This is not surprising when you consider that the history of the continent is made up of **(A)** heroic accounts of adventurers like Robert Scott and Ernest Shackleton, tales in which men relied on their strength and determination in a battle to survive. It was only in the 1980s that women finally overcame these prejudices and joined the teams of researchers in the remote stations.
2 D matches (most people found it impossible to believe that women could live there – 'a deeper, widely held belief that somehow Antarctica was only for men')
3 A does not match exactly (the text says that there were stories about men who relied on their strength, but it doesn't say that only men had this strength.)
B doesn't match (the text says that women applied for jobs there but were refused.)
C doesn't match (the text mentions excuses, but it doesn't say that women accepted them easily.)

Strategies and skills

Identifying attitude and opinion

1

1 No ('only too aware of the difficulty of beating our heavily favoured opponents.')
2 Yes ('I couldn't believe the volume of noise the fans created as they cheered and screamed …')
3 Yes ('I couldn't help feeling that the reality didn't quite live up to my expectations.')
4 No ('I felt more sorry for the other passengers than I did for the parents, whose efforts to control their child seemed far from adequate.')
5 No ('I didn't hesitate to follow my fellow travellers across it.')

2

1 A ('I was beginning to think that maybe skiing wasn't for me')
2 C ('the plot was as much of a mystery to us as it had been at the beginning')
3 B ('I began to wonder what the experience would be like')
4 A ('and was delighted to find that')
5 B ('some of the group members were definitely beginning to get on my nerves')
6 B ('Not many people could claim such a varied and interesting work history')

Deducing the meaning of unfamiliar vocabulary

3

1 a large number (The writer was alarmed, and the word 'all' is used.)
2 a negative feeling (The writer has not managed to become a professional singer after ten years.)
3 an indirect way (The writer changes to a more direct approach and asks a direct question.)
4 feeling better (The writer refers to losing and being disappointed, then becoming confident and optimistic.)

5 money (There is a contrast between the writer's limited amount of money and their prosperous friends.)
6 positive (The final hotel was good; better than the others.)

4

1 A (The writer knew there would be better bargains (lower prices) elsewhere.)
2 C (The voices were behind a closed door and unclear, so the writer couldn't hear them very well.)
3 B (Others would 'jump on the bandwagon with their own versions' (of our products) – i.e. copy our products and aim to benefit from our success.)
4 B (The writer 'wasn't exactly thrilled', and hadn't seen her aunt and uncle for 15 years, so wasn't sure it would be a pleasure.)

Matching meaning

5

1

A True (They wanted to find suitable team members.)
B False (It was a big challenge, i.e. difficult.)
C True (They had to be physically fit.)
D True (They needed people whose personalities and habits wouldn't drive them mad.)

2

A False (It advertised to attract visitors.)
B True ('Tourists are now flocking to the island in such numbers …')
C True (The island now faces a crisis.)
D False (They are destroying the peacefulness, but the text doesn't say they are damaging the landscape.)

3

A False (The text mentions that Joe was excited, but not the writer.)
B False (The writer saw them 'as clear as day'.)
C True ('The first indication we had … was the occasional "plop" as they dropped back below the surface.')
D False (They quickly disappeared beneath the waves.)

4

A False (She had a passion for photography before she went.)
B False (Her passion for landscape photography took her there.)
C True (She discovered her love of whales.)
D False (The text doesn't mention this.)

6

1 It was long and difficult, by plane, by road, then on foot ('flown from London to Rwanda'; 'driven nearly 200 kilometres … on rough tracks'; 'fought my way on foot through eight exhausting kilometres of hot and humid rainforest').
2 No, only that the journey on foot was exhausting.
3 He was a young researcher, and this was his first experience of seeing an active volcano.
4 He felt excited and slightly nervous ('The thrill of finally arriving was mixed with a certain nervousness').
5 There were explosions and some smoke and flames.

7

C is the correct answer ('The thrill of finally arriving was mixed with a certain nervousness on realising the awesome natural power of what was in front of us').
A is not correct (the writer mentions the hot and humid conditions, but this was before he arrived at the volcano.)
B is not correct (although the writer mentions being relieved that he wasn't alone, he does not say he was relieved that he had arrived.)
D is not correct (the writer mentions feeling relieved that he wasn't alone, but he doesn't mention feeling lonely.)

Understanding reference words

8

1 A waiters ('skilful **waiters** hurried around handing them large plates') B customers ('There were **customers** … , waiting patiently as skilful waiters hurried around handing them (**customers**) large plates') C customers ('There were **customers** … , waiting patiently as skilful waiters hurried around handing **them (customers)** large plates')
2 A excited ('the **sense of excitement** that we felt') B the mist ('There was a slight mist in the air … , but that (**the mist**) only added to the sense of excitement') C the mist ('There was a slight **mist** in the air … , but **that (the mist)** only added to the sense of excitement')
3 A young people ('**Young people** queue up … , dreaming of the chance to become celebrities') B young people ('**Young people** … , dreaming of the chance to become celebrities' – wanting to achieve their ambitions to become celebrities) C young people ('**Young people** queue up … , dreaming of the chance to become celebrities, but **few (young people)** ever achieve their ambitions.')

9

1 B ('It takes years to **learn to keep control of the class** and become a confident and effective teacher')
2 A ('**Getting to my house** is simple.')
3 C ('For this reason, many **actors** give up and turn to alternative careers')

EXAM TASK

1 B is correct ('the main motivation, which is simply the pleasure of running.' A is not correct – 'most runners have at least some desire to win, … but (this is) secondary to the main motivation.' C is not correct – 'There's also the personal satisfaction of pushing your body to its limits. … but (this is) secondary to the main motivation.' D is not mentioned.)
2 C is correct ('when I crossed the finish line, **it** (completing the marathon) didn't feel like such a big achievement.' When you replace 'it' with the nouns in A, B and D, the sentence doesn't make sense.)
3 C is correct ('the tough thing about ultra running is getting up day after day and persuading your tired, aching body to perform again. This was what really tested me.' A is not correct – this was one challenge, but she suggests her body adapted quickly. B is not correct – 'Covering more kilometres in a day wasn't a huge problem for me.' D is not correct – the writer says her training programme involved running in the heat and rain, but doesn't say she found this difficult.)
4 B is correct ('They were all very friendly and keen to offer help and support, which I hadn't expected.' A is not correct – the journey had been long but straightforward, and she had got a reasonable amount of rest. C is not correct – the tents were quite big and fairly comfortable, so she wasn't disappointed. D is not correct – 'the forecast was good, so it wasn't a huge concern.')
5 A is correct (We can understand the meaning in contrast to the things the writer says she did expect, i.e. 'I knew I would have to deal with …', 'I was also well prepared for …')
6 B is correct ('having a go at one of the toughest challenges in the world … is hardly something to be ashamed of.' A is not correct – she says she is not going to try again. C is not correct – 'I travelled home with no medal, but by no means defeated.' D is not correct – 'I am not sorry that I took part …')

READING AND USE OF ENGLISH
Part 6 Gapped text
Practice task

1

Students' own answers

2

1 C 2 A

3

1 'This new kind of outdoor teaching establishment' refers back to 'beach school'.

2 'They' refers back to 'children'. 'Also' refers back to the idea of children becoming more confident and independent – 'also' adds a second, similar idea (they pay attention and achieve good results academically).

Strategies and skills

Understanding reference devices

1

1 urban foxes ('The population of **urban foxes** in London … . Although **they** are a familiar sight in all parts of the city centre')

2 Tahiti ('set off on his first voyage of exploration, to the South Pacific island of **Tahiti**. It was **here** that he carried out observations')

3 popular myths ('There are many **popular myths** concerning diet and exercise. **One of the most widely believed** is that limiting food intake …')

4 keep your money, valuables and documents in different places ('One useful tip … is **to keep your money, valuables and documents in different places**. **Doing so** means that you reduce your risk …')

5 clearing up the beach ('the race was on **to clear it all up**. **This** was far too challenging a task … .')

2

1 here (Tahiti)

2 one of the most widely believed (popular myth)

3 they (urban foxes)

4 Doing so, This (keeping money etc. in different places, clearing up the beach)

3

1 A is correct ('Both of these' refers back to the two ideas mentioned: sleep is more important for the body and people can train themselves to need less sleep.)
B is incorrect ('their' does not refer back to anything.)

2 B is correct ('It' refers back to ice cream.)
A is incorrect ('this one' does not refer back to anything – it would need to refer back to a countable noun.)

3 A is correct ('there' refers back to 'suitable places'.)
B is incorrect ('this … place' does not refer back to anything.)

4 B is correct ('It' refers back to cross-country skiing.)
A is incorrect ('Here' does not refer back to anything.)

Text structure and cohesion

4

1 c ('It has also won him ten awards' adds to the sentence about 'His talent for acting'.)

2 a ('September is equally beautiful …' adds to the information about 'June'.)

3 b ('However, upstairs …' contrasts with the information about 'The downstairs rooms …'.)

4 e ('But can they ever cope … ?' questions and contrasts the statement that 'Robots can certainly help children …'.)

5 f ('As well as these attractions, it is also …' adds to the information about places of interest on the island.)

6 d ('Yet on closer inspection, you can see it is …' adds additional and contrasting information to 'From a distance, the rock looks completely bare.')

5

a Similar (equally, and, too)
b Contrasting (However)
c Similar (also)
d Contrasting (Yet)
e Contrasting (But)
f Similar (As well as, also)

6

1 c – similar ('It' refers back to 'plastic')

2 f – contrasting ('Other kinds' refers back to 'some kinds')

3 a – contrasting ('this awareness' refers back to 'understanding')

4 e – similar ('In addition to this, plastic fibres form part of …' refers back to 'plastic is used')

5 b – similar ('They' refers back to 'Many people')

6 d – contrasting ('these materials' refers back to 'Alternatives to plastic')

7

1 Other factors to consider are (introducing more than one factor – the range of courses on offer/the number of teaching hours; 'The next one is' would introduce only one more factor.)

2 In extreme cases (introducing a strong example of the fear of heights; 'This is because' would introduce a reason, not an example.)

3 This is why (introducing a reason; 'Instead of this' would introduce an alternative.)

4 This means that (introducing a consequence; 'Other problems include' would introduce more examples.)

5 This is because (introducing a reason; 'Doing so means' would introduce a consequence.)

8

1 This is because (The second sentence provides an explanation.)

2 My favourite is (The second sentence provides a specific example with a reason.)

3 In some cases (The second sentence provides additional general information in the form of a possible result.)

4 What fascinated me more was (The second sentence provides additional information on a specific aspect.)

5 That is why (The second sentence provides a reason.)

Rephrasing, exemplifying and commenting

9

1 In other words,
2 Clearly,
3 For instance,
4 To put it simply,
5 For example,
6 It was frustrating that

10

1 B ('In extreme cases' gives an example of the danger that the first sentence mentions.)

2 A ('Other features include' introduces some more examples of features that the scooter has.)

3 A ('What interested me more' comments on the idea of visiting the library, and reinforces the idea in the first sentence of not being keen on visiting the markets.)

4 B ('In other words' introduces a rephrasing of the idea in the first sentence.)

5 A ('Unfortunately' introduces a contrasting idea and a comment by the writer.)

EXAM TASK

1 C ('a painting robot' refers back to the idea of 'machines' in the previous sentence. 'It' in the following sentence refers back to the robot.)

2 D ('They' refers back to 'humans' in the previous sentence and is followed by 'Their' in the next sentence.)

3 A ('This' refers back to the process of searching for and scanning images.)

4 G ('This' refers back to the single image. The idea of the image is continued in the following sentence.)

5 B (The previous sentence suggests that computer images have a lot of good and interesting qualities. 'But' introduces a contrasting idea, that they are not really art.)

6 F ('More importantly' adds more detail about why art is only for humans.)

READING AND USE OF ENGLISH
Part 7 Multiple matching
Practice task

1

Students' own answers

2

1 Helen

2 Katya

3 Helen

4 Katya

3a

a 2: failed to persuade a family member to do things differently? ('I tried to discourage him' suggests the writer tried to put her brother off the idea of a surprise party; 'he refused to change his mind' suggests he disagreed, so we can conclude that she failed.)

b 4: felt happier after revealing the secret? ('To my huge relief' suggests the writer was tense, or not happy, keeping the secret, and was relieved to tell the truth; 'Once we'd had a good laugh, we thoroughly enjoyed …' suggests the writer was happier after revealing the secret.)

3b

1 don't use

2 a whole chunk

3 the context

4a

1: 'A neighbour spotted me searching through my cousin's wardrobe and reported what she thought was a break-in. Two hours later, I was finally released.'

2: 'I was uneasy at the idea of going into my cousin's flat when no one was there. I should have spoken up, because it turned out I was right to be worried.'

4b

1 No, the answers don't occur in the same order as the options.

2 We know she wishes she had been more forceful because she says 'I should have spoken up'. She felt 'uneasy' (nervous) about going into her cousin's flat.

3 A neighbour saw her and called the police (reported what she thought was a break-in); the writer was released (by the police) two hours later.

Strategies and skills
Reading for specific information

1

1 'But I forgot the most important rule: don't overtrain too early on. I picked up an injury on only my third week of training.'

2 'spending three days hiking in the beautiful Tuscan landscape'

3 'Disaster struck when it came to my first solo number and the words completely went out of my head. … the memory of that put me off acting for months.'

2

1 A Paris ('choosing somewhere to sit outside in the sunshine and enjoy a delicious lunch')

2 C New York ('there's no better city for an exciting evening out watching a play or a musical')

3 B Barcelona ('It's definitely worth considering a trip beyond the city limits for a day, to find some outstanding beaches.')

4 A Paris ('take in the glorious scent of the roses.')

5 B Barcelona ('take advantage of the excellent metro system to get around the city quickly')

6 C New York ('Make sure you get a few selfies to impress your friends!')

Understanding implication

3

1 B (The writer had always loved sailing and jumped at the chance to work on a yacht – this suggests the job suited her perfectly.)

2 C (The website wasn't getting many hits, so the writer contacted a friend to add some videos. This suggests the writer wants to improve the website, to increase the number of hits.)

3 A (The writer mentions looking at all the things you want to take, and thinking about whether you need them. This implies it is important to not take too many things, but to travel light.)

4 B (The writer says that his friends had no money worries, but things weren't quite as simple for him. This implies he had some money worries.)

5 B (The question 'What was I thinking?' suggests that giving up the job was perhaps not a sensible decision. This implies the writer has doubts about her decision.)

6 C (The description of the flat suggests it is not very appealing (it is small, with a hard bed and bare walls). The question 'Was this really going to be my home …?' implies that the writer is disappointed to be living here.)

Paraphrasing in questions

4

1 a A 'heavy snow started coming down. We were concerned about losing our way and getting stuck on the mountain overnight'; B 'But we weren't sure of the best route to climb, and some parts of the rock looked too soft to hold our ropes securely.'

b A 'when heavy snow started coming down. We were concerned about losing our way and getting stuck on the mountain overnight. This was when I realised I should have checked the weather forecast more carefully before we set out.'

2 a C 'there certainly wasn't time for all the nights out that some of my friends had talked about.'; D 'my evenings were full in the first few weeks with countless "meet and greet" get-togethers'

b D 'my evenings were full in the first few weeks with countless "meet and greet" get-togethers – all with discounts on the prices, which was a nice surprise.'

3 a E 'he studied for a degree in photography'; F 'After graduating from college with a BA in fashion design'

b F 'she soon found that a degree wasn't in itself enough to get her noticed by employers, and she needed to do a few seasons as a volunteer helper at fashion shows before a career opportunity came along.'

Recognising attitude and opinion

5

1 C ('I spent far too much money, unfortunately, but that's the only thing I would change.')

2 F ('But make sure you know exactly what you want, or you're likely to end up spending a lot of money on things you never use.')

3 A ('I was slightly cautious about taking on such a challenging walk.')

4 D ('If you've got some time on your hands, it's well worth taking the train up to Mallaig, as it's one of the best ways to enjoy the stunning scenery.')

5 E ('But I can't get over the behaviour of the fans. Five minutes into the game and people start shouting and screaming in ways they would never think of doing in other situations.')

6 B ('I was shocked when my boss called me into her office one day and told me that someone had made a complaint about me.')

EXAM TASK

1 B ('I happened to be in Madrid this summer with some friends, so we decided at the last minute to check out the Mad Cool Festival.')
2 A ('for over three hours, in the heat of the day. I was wearing jeans and heavy boots (just in case of rain!)')
3 D ('We decided to abandon camping and treat ourselves to a decent night's sleep in an eco-lodge at a nearby farm. Good decision!')
4 C ('it's impossible to escape the music and crowds, which I found tough.')
5 A ('so make sure you get plenty of sleep before you go.')
6 A ('The whole place was packed with people, which made for a totally crazy atmosphere – it was amazing to be in the middle of it.')
7 D ('I was expecting the acts to be mainly older, established bands, but in fact there was a bit of everything, from electronic to hard rock and rap, and some local talent, too.')
8 C ('I wish I'd been more organised and bought my ticket in advance – buying on the day was really stressful.')
9 B ('it's amazing to see so many well-known bands, but it led to some tough choices when acts were scheduled at the same time.')
10 C ('the highs were meeting people from all over the world and chilling out with mates in beautiful surroundings.')

WRITING

Part 1 Essay

Practice task

1
See the example essay on page 42.
2
Students' own answers
3
Students' own answers

Strategies and skills

Audience, structure and tone
1
Introduction: 4
Paragraph 2: 2
Paragraph 3: 1
Paragraph 4: 3

2
Yes, it covers all the points.
The writer's conclusion is that it is not possible to live in the modern world without a mobile phone.

3
1 formal (e.g. 'I believe they are now a necessity', 'Furthermore')
2 doesn't use (e.g. 'they are now', 'it is not possible')
3 serious (e.g. 'In conclusion, I believe …')
4 an academic (The essay is for 'your teacher' and its purpose is to discuss the statement in a balanced and formal way.)

4
1 c **2** a **3** d **4** f **5** b **6** e

Writing introductions and conclusions
5
1 A and C
2 B and D

6
1 C is the best introduction (It makes general statements to introduce the topic and mentions some of the ideas which will be developed in the essay. A mentions personal experiences, rather than making general statements.; B gives two contrasting opinions, but they are too detailed, rather than being a general statement about the topic.)
2 B is the best conclusion (It sums up arguments on both sides, and expresses a personal opinion. A makes some general statements, and then introduces a new idea ('it is cheaper to watch films at home'); C expresses personal opinions, but does not sum up the arguments in the essay.)

Connecting ideas in a paragraph
7
1 While (Introduces an idea which is then contrasted in the following clause.)
2 as well as ('in addition to')
3 In addition to this (Refers back to the idea in the previous sentence and adds to it.)
4 However (Introduces a contrasting idea.)
5 Despite (Introduces an idea that will be contrasted in the next clause.)
6 Furthermore (Adds another (more) important idea to an argument.)

Language for structuring your essay
8
First point: Firstly, First of all, The first reason is
Further points: Another reason is, Next, Secondly,
Last point: Finally, Lastly, Last but not least,
Conclusion: All in all, In conclusion, To sum up,
In the model essay, the writer uses: Firstly, Another reason is, Lastly, In conclusion,

9
1 First of all (It introduces the first point. The phrase 'all in all' is used to make a conclusion.)
2 Another reason is that (It introduces the next point. 'Last but not least' would introduce the last point.)
3 Finally (It introduces the last point. 'Next' is used to introduce another point, generally.)
4 To sum up (It introduces the conclusion. 'Lastly' would introduce the last point.)

Complex sentences
10
1 people should eat less meat **as** it is
2 **more** facilities in cities than (there are)
3 to study at home **rather than** going
4 you a lot, **so** I think all young people should be
5 **If** the book is successful, (then) you can
6 might disappear forever, **which** would be

Impersonal sentences
11
1 Countries all over the world (more general than 'where I live')
2 an extremely popular place (less personal than 'I love going to the beach')
3 people of all ages (more general than 'My family')
4 are known to cause stress (less personal than 'I always get really worried about')
5 It can be difficult for people (more general than 'I find it hard')
6 Fear of losing friendships (less personal than 'I'm scared that I'll lose my friends')

EXAM TASK

Example answer

Most towns and cities have a wide variety of sports facilities, but people usually have to pay to use them. I believe it would be a good idea to make these facilities free for everyone.

Firstly, it is known that keeping fit is one of the most important things for health. If everyone can do regular exercise, the population in general will be fitter and healthier. This is good for the whole community.

Next, sports centres are places where people can go to meet others and make friends. In cities, a lot of people are lonely and struggle to make new friends. If sports facilities were free, these people would find it easier to join in and socialise.

Finally, it is not fair that only people with money can use sports facilities and get fit. Everyone should have the same opportunities to improve their health.

In conclusion, I would argue that health is a basic human right, so everyone should be able to use sports facilities equally. I think the whole community would benefit if these facilities were free for everyone to use.

183 words

WRITING
Part 2 Article
Practice task

1 and 2

Students' own answers

3

1 Perhaps we should stop giving gifts completely and donate the money to charity. Problem solved!
2 I was given some jazz music by a so-called friend who forgot I hate it!
3 We all like giving gifts, don't we?
4 I think if you can't choose something appropriate, it's better not to give anything.
5 Is it really necessary to give gifts at all, though?
6 In my country we give gifts on birthdays or anniversaries.
7 But
8 incredibly important

Strategies and skills

Engaging the reader

1

1 A (A is more interesting than B, which is a statement of personal fact) 2 A (A is more eye-catching and makes you wonder what 'it' is, while B is a statement of personal fact) 3 B (B is more eye-catching and addresses the task more directly) 4 B (B uses more interesting language than A to say the same thing) 5 A (A is more eye-catching and suggestive of the following content than B) 6 B (B uses more interesting language than A)

2

Example answers

1 Do older people appreciate gifts more than younger people?
2 Is it a good idea for people to stay active, even if they hate it?
3 Do many young people try to help others?
4 Is it actually important to own something special?
5 Is it possible to forget something like that?
6 It's a good question, but is there an answer?

3

A is better. It makes the reader think, talks to the reader directly, asks a rhetorical question and doesn't just describe the place, but keeps the reader waiting to find out more.

4

1 I expect you were imagining
2 take part in
3 energetic
4 spectacular
5 incredibly
6 trendy
7 chat
8 guess

5

1 c
2 a
3 e
4 b
5 f
6 d

6

A is best. It uses interesting language, a rhetorical question and addresses the reader directly.

EXAM TASK

Example answer

My best ever holiday!

Most people enjoy holidays, but are holidays actually important? They may not always be successful. Things happen, like bad weather or an argument with a family member, so I had mixed feelings about them. Then, one year I went to South America. That changed my opinion!

We'd always spent family holidays visiting grandparents who lived by the sea. But one year my parents decided to try something new and visit some distant relatives who live in South America. Well, I've never had such a fantastic experience.

The long flight there was tough, even though I killed time by watching four very boring films on the way. Once we arrived, though, it was all worth it! We saw amazing sights, ate fantastic food and experienced a completely different culture. My favourite part was seeing huge waterfalls that seemed to go on forever. It took ages to sort out all my photographs! The added bonus was meeting relatives I'd never seen. We were there for two wonderful weeks.

Has it affected me? In my opinion it's been life-changing, and opened my eyes to new experiences. I'll never forget it!

190 words

WRITING
Part 2 Email/Letter
Practice task: informal email

1 and 2

Students' own answers

3

1 It was so good to hear from you.
2 I hope these ideas are useful.
3 I've been very busy at college so I haven't got round to writing to you either!
4 Best wishes,
5 because it's very sociable
6 I've been thinking about activities you could do.
7 Or a sing-song; that'd be good if you had the barbecue.
8 But I guess you've thought of that already.

Strategies and skills

Common expressions – informal language

1

1 Hi Emily – great **to** hear from you!
2 I can**'t** wait to see you!
3 I hope that ~~is~~**has** helped you.
4 How about go~~ing~~ to the beach?
5 Hope to **hear~~ing~~** from you soon.
6 Get ~~you~~ **back** to me soon!
7 I'm free ~~every~~**any** time you need me.
8 All **the** best,

Using contractions

2

1 I haven't finished.
2 You'll enjoy the party.
3 Don't forget to write.
4 I won't be able to see you.
5 I wouldn't enjoy it.
6 It'll be a good party.
7 It's a good idea.
8 Wouldn't you like to come?

3

1 **I'm** sure **you'll** enjoy a barbecue.
2 **You'll** find loads of things **you'd** enjoy doing.
3 The only problem **I've** got is the weather – **it's** going to rain!
4 **You're** more likely to have a good time if the **party's** planned.
5 **I'm** sorry that I **haven't** got round to replying.
6 The weather **can't** be ignored because **it's** very changeable.
7 Unfortunately, I **won't** be able to come but **it'll** be fun anyway.
8 **I'm** happy to accept whatever **you'd** like to do.

EXAM TASK

Example answer

Hi, Jack,

It's always good to hear from you. I guess you can predict that where I live everyone's crazy about playing football – we've got loads of teams here, from under-eights up to adults. There's a local club where teams play matches against other towns. I'm not so keen, actually, but I think I'm unusual!

Apart from that, people here play tennis, and there's also a popular running club. That's actually my thing – I go running every weekend, and I want to run a marathon one day. I think it's popular because it's easy to do, and, unlike football, you don't have to be part of a team. It's not so competitive – you can run races if you want to, but most people do it just to keep fit.

You asked about professional sport on television. Well, obviously it's mostly football, which is on every week, but to be honest I find it rather boring. Luckily, I can watch loads of other professional sports instead, like cycling and sailing – that might surprise you, but it's really fascinating.

Let me know if you need any more information!

Write soon!

190 words

Practice task: formal letter

1 and 2

Students' own answers

3

1 I would be grateful if you could contact me during the evenings from 5 p.m. to 8 p.m. My telephone number is 077994466773.
2 Yours sincerely,
3 Although I have not worked in a restaurant before,
4 I … would like to apply for the job of waitress in your restaurant.
5 I am able to work two or three evenings every week
6 Dear Mrs Jones,
7 My French is very good, and I also speak a little Italian.
8 I'm good at dealing with people, as I run a social club … I am a team-player

Strategies and skills

Common expressions – formal language

1

1 put forward
2 One possibility is to
3 Can I ask for your opinion of
4 I'd like to request
5 increase
6 inform you of
7 am looking forward to seeing
8 How are you

2

The correct order is: C, B, A, D
C tells us about the writer and their interest in writing novels; B explains why the writer is interested in the course; A explains how the course would be of benefit to the writer; D concludes the letter with the hope that the writer will be accepted onto the course.

EXAM TASK

Example answer

Dear Mr Rawlings,

Thank you for your letter which I received yesterday. I am very pleased to have won the competition, and am writing to provide the information you have requested.

I would like to go to Paris in June as the weather would be warm then. However, I do have some questions.

First of all, I'd like to know more about the accommodation. I would enjoy staying with a family so that I can practise my French, but I would like to know where the family live. Is it in the centre of Paris? If not, then I would prefer to stay in a central hotel. I have never been to Paris before, and I'm looking forward to seeing as many of the sights as possible.

Secondly, could you confirm that the flights are direct and I would not have to change planes anywhere? I am not keen on flying, so I only want to take one return flight.

You also asked me to tell you about special requirements I have. Actually, I am a vegetarian, so it is important that I can get meals that don't include meat.

I would be grateful if you could reply as soon as possible.

Yours sincerely,

WRITING

Part 2 Review

Practice task

3

1 The story was a romantic one of two teenagers …
2 I went to see 'Sing-along' at the Theatre Royal.
3 and in fact I saw it twice!
4 However, the songs were still fun.
5 If I had to pick something I didn't enjoy, it would be some of the scenes with the family in Paris.
6 Would I recommend this musical? Definitely!
7 It looked really difficult.

Strategies and skills

Developing ideas in a paragraph

1

1 A ('The event had been sold out for months'. There is no mention of the theatre being popular.)
2 B ('They only gave it one star.' There is no mention of the writing specifically.)

3 A (The singing was very good ('superb'), but the acting wasn't so good ('let the production down'). However, the review doesn't say that the acting was 'very bad'.)

4 B (The badly planned layout of the seats (i.e. the poor design of the theatre) was the reason that the stage was difficult to see.)

5 B (The writer couldn't 'get into it' and the characters were not interesting ('there was nothing about them that could hold my attention'). They don't mention if the game was difficult to play or not.)

6 A (The good reputation of the course helped to get the writer their job ('because it was recognised by so many employers who knew how good it was'). The writer does say they enjoyed it, but doesn't say it was useful for this reason.)

2

1 example (the information gives ways in which the review was negative)

2 effect (the information describes the effect on the writer; 'it still had a cosy feel to it that I really liked')

3 reason (the information explains why the film is about loyalty)

4 effect ('As a result')

5 reason ('This was due to the fact')

6 reason ('This was caused by')

7 effect (the range of music had the effect of bringing new types to the writer's attention – 'it really opened my eyes and ears to new musical experiences')

8 example (the information gives a personal example of how the tickets were very expensive for most people – 'In fact, they were so expensive that I had to do hours of overtime to afford one')

3

1 C ('thrillers' – scary films. The paragraph talks about the effect on the writer's sleep and watching things on TV and in the cinema.)

2 D (The paragraph talks about characters and buying a copy (of a book). The writer liked the book.)

3 A (The paragraph talks about going online and playing (games) with other people.)

4 E (The information goes on to talk about activities and playing badminton.)

5 B ('It only opened last month'; you can get cakes and sandwiches.)

6 G (The paragraph talks about models and clothes, and explains why the writer thinks the show was successful.)

Using functions and making recommendations

4

1 explaining
2 describing
3 explaining
4 giving opinions
5 describing
6 giving examples
7 recommending ('I suggest that' + 'give it a go' – try it out)
8 recommending ('It's not to be missed' – you should do it)
9 explaining
10 giving examples

5

1 would (The writer is making a definite recommendation.)
2 strongly (The phrase: 'strongly advise')
3 definitely (The structure: 'you should definitely' + verb)
4 thoroughly (The phrase: 'thoroughly recommend')
5 seriously (The phrase: 'seriously consider')
6 regret (The structure: 'won't regret' + -ing form … 'as'/'because' …')

6a

Para 2 describing ('It's a kind of strategy game, which means …')
Para 3 explaining ('What I like about it is …')

Para 4 giving examples ('that's good fun', 'is great, too')
Para 5 explaining ('If I have a criticism, it is that it's …' 'and some people get annoyed that …')
Para 6 recommending ('I'd strongly recommend it to …')

6b

The writer recommends it, but only to people who enjoy gaming.

Using adjectives that indicate opinion

7

Strongly positive: brilliant, impressive, outstanding, remarkable, stunning
Positive: entertaining, memorable, useful, worthwhile
Neutral: acceptable, competent, convenient, odd, satisfactory
Strongly negative: horrible, ridiculous, upsetting

8

1 partly ('outstanding' – strong adjective. It does not collocate with 'partly'.)

2 absolutely ('absolutely' – strong quantifier; 'acceptable' – neutral adjective. The two do not collocate.)

3 slightly ('remarkable' – strong adjective. It does not collocate with 'slightly'.)

4 very ('ridiculous' – strong adjective. Therefore, 'very' is not needed and does not collocate.)

5 a bit ('worthwhile' – neutral adjective. Therefore it does not collocate with 'a bit'.)

6 truly ('satisfactory' – neutral adjective. Therefore it does not collocate with 'truly'.)

7 completely ('convenient' – neutral adjective. Therefore it does not collocate with 'completely'.)

8 greatly ('greatly' – strong positive quantifier; 'odd' – negative adjective. The two do not collocate.)

9 terribly ('terribly' – strong negative quantifier; 'entertaining' – positive adjective. The two do not collocate.)

10 completely ('completely' – strong quantifier; 'useful' – neutral adjective. The two do not collocate.)

9

1 stunning, odd, worthwhile
2 competent, brilliant, impressive
3 entertaining, outstanding, acceptable
4 impressive, stunning, convenient
5 remarkable, outstanding, memorable
6 odd, satisfactory, useful

EXAM TASK

Example answer

I'm not always a fan of outdoor events, partly because they're often spoiled by bad weather, but last week I attended a local sports tournament which I really enjoyed.

It took place on a site just outside town where there were football and hockey pitches, and next door to the local tennis club. There were three main sports competitions organised throughout the day, covering a range of sports. There were around eight teams playing football and six playing hockey, along with individual games taking place in the tennis club. There were also several running races going on around the outside of the site, and there were games for disabled people, too.

What was so great was the atmosphere, which was really positive, and all the extra things happening. For example, there were food stalls so no one went hungry, and bands playing a range of music. The only bad thing was how crowded the site became, but that was because everyone was having a good time!

I would recommend this event not only to sports enthusiasts, but to anyone who enjoys a good day out! I'll go again next year.

189 words

WRITING
Part 2 Report
Practice task

1 and 2

Students' own answers

3

1 The event raised nearly £500 for local charities.
2 I suggest that …
3 The aim of this report is to …
4 It is clear that …
5 They particularly enjoyed …
6 … where visitors are not usually allowed.
7 Introduction

Strategies and skills

Organising ideas in a report

1

1 C (the paragraph lists aspects of the current facilities the staff are happy with)
2 B (the paragraph gives information on problems with and complaints about the current facilities)
A is too general – neither paragraph deals with both advantages and disadvantages.
D is not accurate – neither paragraph makes recommendations for improvements.
E is too specific – neither paragraph focuses entirely on the cafeteria.
F is too informal – language in a report should be formal.

2

The list of points about the coffee bar could be presented as a bulleted list:
The main complaints about the coffee bar are:
• it is too small
• there are not enough seats
• it only sells unhealthy snacks

3

1 C (it is formal and clearly states the aim of the report; A is too informal; B does not mention that the report will make recommendations)
2 A (it gives some clear recommendations; B is too informal; C summarises the main findings but does not give any definite recommendations)

4

1 purpose of, I (states what the report is for)
2 sum up, C (summarises the report's findings)
3 intended, I (describes the purpose of the report)
4 Overall, C (draws a conclusion)
5 conclusion, C (draws a conclusion)
6 looks at, I (states what the report does)

Referring to research

5

1 b (collocation: 'carry out a survey') 2 c ('interview' + ('a number of) people') 3 a ('most' + 'of' + 'the' countable plural or uncountable noun) 4 d ('a survey of' + plural noun) 5 e ('the majority of' + plural noun)

6

1 majority ('the majority of' – most) 2 number ('a small number of' – a few) 3 None ('none of those' – no one) 4 All ('all those' – everyone) 5 quarters ('fifteen out of … twenty' is the equivalent of three quarters) 6 half ('eight out of … fifteen' is the equivalent of just over half)

Formal language

7

1 fortunate to have ('we are fortunate to have' – luckily, we've got) 2 popular with ('popular with students' – students love) 3 insufficient space ('there would be insufficient space' – there wouldn't be enough room) 4 enthusiastic about (loved) 5 concerned about (scared that) 6 cause of dissatisfaction ('one cause of dissatisfaction' – one thing everyone complained about)

8

1 is considered to be (present simple passive)
2 has been suggested (that) (present perfect passive)
3 are expected to (present simple passive)
4 was criticised (past simple passive)
5 was thought to be (past simple passive)
6 is thought to be excellent (present simple passive)

EXAM TASK

Example answer

<u>Introduction</u>
The aim of this report is to assess the current public transport system in Avebury. To do this, I carried out a survey of 150 local people.
<u>The current situation</u>
Avebury is a small town about 25 kilometres from Manchester. There is currently a regular bus and train service between Avebury and Manchester.
<u>Things that are working well</u>
The majority of those surveyed are satisfied with the current services. The general feeling is that
• the trains and buses run on time.
• there are usually seats available.
• they are usually clean and free from litter.
<u>Criticisms of public transport</u>
Many younger people complained that the buses and trains stop too early in the evening. The last bus or train to Avebury is at 9 p.m. In addition, young people felt that using public transport is expensive for those who travel to and from work every day.
<u>Conclusion and recommendation</u>
It is clear that the bus and train services are popular. However, I would suggest that buses and trains should run later at night, and there should be cheaper tickets for those who travel regularly to and from work.
190 words

WRITING
Part 2 Story
Practice task

1 and 2

Students' own answers

3

1 Just as …
2 cheerfully
3 He had finally saved up enough money to buy the new computer game that he wanted, and he was looking forward to playing it with his friends.
4 was going, turned around, had moved
5 And Sam didn't mind at all that he didn't have his new game!
6 Sam was very surprised to see him. 'Hi,' he said.
7 Sam picked up his wallet and headed into town.
8 As they ate, …
9 long and boring

Strategies and skills

Sequencing events

1

1 then (next) **2** While (showing that two actions happened at the same time) **3** At first (at the start) **4** By the time (when) **5** during (while something was happening) **6** As soon as (immediately when) **7** until (an action continued and stopped at the point mentioned) **8** After (a preposition, followed by a noun)

Narrative tenses

2

1 ran (a main event) **2** were standing (a longer action) **3** was (a state verb) **4** was waiting (a longer action) **5** knew (a state verb) **6** hadn't told (an action that happened or didn't happen earlier) **7** had said (an action that happened earlier) **8** hoped (a state verb) **9** hadn't forgotten (an action that happened earlier)

Adjectives and adverbs

3

appearance: elegant, slim, tall (short, beautiful, handsome, thin)
feelings: delighted, enthusiastic, nervous (confident, confused, eager, cheerful)
places: crowded, noisy, peaceful (quiet, remote, beautiful, dirty)
weather: icy, sunny, stormy (hot, cold, cool, warm, boiling (hot), freezing, wet)

4

1 miserable (adjective describing a person – 'Tom') **2** peacefully (adverb describing an action – 'sleeping') **3** calm (adjective describing a state – 'being calm') **4** nervously (adverb describing an action – 'opened') **5** confidently (adverb describing an action – 'walked') **6** kind (adjective describing a behaviour – 'kind of you')

Direct speech

5

1 'My bus was late,' Molly explained.
2 'Leave me alone!' the man shouted.
3 'Where are you going?' Lily asked.
4 'The zoo is closed,' the woman told us.

EXAM TASK

Example answer

Amy picked up the map and set off on her bike. She and her friend Sara had found the map in an old, empty house. It showed the way to some caves, and Amy and Sara were excited at the thought of exploring them. Amy had told her mum about the map, but she kept it a secret from everyone else.
Amy met up with Sara along the road, and the two girls continued. While they were riding along, they chatted about what they might find. 'Maybe the caves were used by pirates,' Amy suggested. 'We might find some treasure!' At last they arrived at the right place. The entrance to the caves was hidden, and it took them nearly half an hour to find it. Inside, there was no treasure, just some piles of old boxes and a tiny kitten, which had lost its mother. Amy quickly phoned her mum. 'Mum, I've found a kitten. Can I keep it?' she asked. 'I guess so,' her mum replied. 'Why not?' So Amy rode home feeling happy, not with a bag full of treasure, but with a new pet, which she thought was even better!
190 words

LISTENING

Part 1 Multiple choice

Practice task

1 and 2

Students' own answers
1 A **2** C **3** B

3a

1 C (only the woman says this – the man doesn't mention it)
2 B (only the woman says this – the man says he didn't notice)
3 A (the man says the plot made him sad)
4 A (the woman says that it made her cry)

3b

Both 3 and 4 are paraphrases for the idea of 'upsetting' in option A. Neither speaker actually says they found it 'upsetting,' but what they do say indicates how they felt about it.

4a

1 C (the importance of preserving it – 'losing their habitat … its survival is crucial')
2 B (identifying species of wildlife that live in it – 'certain predators')
3 A (describing the factors that threaten it – 'another hazard')

4b

1 C is the correct answer. (The speaker says that species are losing their habitat and survival of the reef is crucial for them, so she's emphasising its importance.)
2 B The speaker mentions predators that are attracted to the reef, but isn't identifying different types of wildlife that live there.
3 A The speaker says that predators are another danger to creatures living in the reef, but she isn't describing all the factors that endanger the reef itself.

5a

A: 'though, inevitably, it's kind of taken over my life: I knew I'd miss going out in the evenings with you guys.' This is wrong because he knew it would be time-consuming.
B: 'though some of the lectures aren't as fascinating as they looked in the prospectus!'
C: 'I knew it would be demanding, though – I've never done anything like it before.' This is wrong because he expected it to be difficult.

5b

Option B is correct because he finds the lectures more boring than they appeared.

Strategies and skills

Listening for agreement

1

1 D (the woman thinks communication should be through a phone call, but the man says a phone is only there for social media.)
2 D (the man thinks there are too many updates, but the woman thinks they're useful.)
3 S (they are both disappointed that the show was cancelled.)
4 D (the woman thinks relationships change, but the man thinks they stay the same.)
5 S (they both think that money changes people.)
6 D (the woman found the film exciting, but the man found the characters distracting.)

Identifying a speaker's purpose

2

1 advising ('It's probably better')
2 requesting ('Can we … ?')
3 complaining ('I have never had such a badly cooked … !')
4 suggesting ('it might be a good idea')
5 warning ('if that happens, we could find … difficult')
6 outlining ('The first part … takes place')
7 encouraging ('I'm sure it'll be successful')
8 criticising ('but you never do')

Identifying attitude and opinion

3

1 B ('I'm spending hours …')
2 A ('do you really think we should go there then?')
3 A ('I'm going to get a second opinion')
4 B ('wasn't really worth watching')
5 A ('I would have preferred not to be interviewed')
6 B ('there are so many people watching')

Identifying feelings

4

1 B ('I can't believe … it's unacceptable!')
2 B ('It's so hard … such a lot of noise … !')
3 A ('I really can't wait')
4 A ('It's a good thing I …')
5 C ('I guess it's not impossible if …')
6 B ('do I really have to … ?')

EXAM TASK

1 A (agreement – 'M: But it looked horrible – so cramped and basic. F: Well, that's probably just what it'd be like in space … maybe they were able to ignore all that.')
2 B (agreement – 'F: You could really feel the tension and excitement … – that was awesome. M: Imagine if we'd actually been there and experienced that!')
3 A (feeling – 'F: It's a shame not everyone's taking part in the campaign – we need to have better publicity about it, really.')
4 C (purpose – '… would you mind giving them a call then to cancel it?')
5 C (opinion – 'Now I have to sing what will sell commercially, which isn't my scene, but it's a start and I can't expect to have it my own way.')
6 A (agreement – 'M: It brightened up my day, anyway – you shouldn't be so miserable about it. F: I admit I did smile – and I guess we all need cheering up sometimes.')
7 C (main point – 'I was quite taken aback by what I found, and felt that it would be more useful to explore that, so my original concept changed.')
8 A (feeling – 'F: I let the team down a bit though – I didn't do so well personally … I had no idea about some of the questions.')

LISTENING

Part 2 Sentence completion

Practice task

1

Students' own answer

2

1 chemistry ('At school I loved maths and my teacher suggested I should study technology at university, but I chose to do chemistry, thinking I would teach it as that's what both my parents did.')
2 (weekly) market ('I sold my icecream to friends, in the local cinema and most successfully in the weekly market where all the young ones loved it.')

3 washing machine ('My mum calls it a magic box, though I think it's more like a washing machine when you see it, as it's big and white.')
4 proud ('That doesn't worry me, and I'm proud that my product is natural and organic, …')
5 rose ('I can produce flavours like rose, though, and people always enjoy that in the summer'.)

3

1 friend ('my friend suggested I should study technology')
2 most successfully ('most successfully in the weekly market')
3 mother ('My mum calls it a magic box')
4 doesn't ('our menu is constantly changing. That doesn't worry me, and I'm proud that my product is natural and organic')
5 can't ('I've heard of companies making flavours such as pumpkin pie, … but, because of my philosophy of keeping things local, I can't do that. I can produce flavours like rose, though, and people always enjoy that in the summer')

Strategies and skills

Listening for cues

1

1 Jason was surprised that …
2 Jason uses the word _____ to explain …
3 Jason was very interested in the theory that …
4 the biologist considered the way he tried to photograph tigers as …
5 Jason was thrilled …

2

1 considered the way he tried to photograph tigers
2 surprised
3 (Not used)
4 uses the word _____ to explain
5 very interested in the theory
6 thrilled

3

1 dogs ('I couldn't believe that people preferred them to dogs')
2 beard ('Then they've got what I'd describe as a beard on their face') **3** mountains ('it's now thought that some could also be living in mountains. I found this a fascinating idea') **4** opportunity ('This created what he thought of as his opportunity') **5** red panda ('Not even the picture of a rarely seen red panda could cheer him up, although it was a delight to me.')

Listening for specific details

4

1 adjective (he is describing a noun) **2** person (a person would make a suggestion) **3** thing (an uncountable noun is needed to fill the gap, so it is a thing) **4** plural noun ('**are** the biggest danger' – a plural noun is the subject)

5

social (There are a lot of adjectives, but Joe says that 'social' is what he really enjoys about the job: 'that's what I really enjoy about it.')

6

a Four people are mentioned: sister, mother, cousin, friend.
b Only the friend 'came up with the idea of going there together', so the friend 'suggested it'.

7

preparation – 'that' refers back to 'it'. It also refers forwards to the idea that it is necessary if you don't want to fail, i.e. succeed.

8

humans – 'because' is important as it introduces the reason that Sally is upset, which gives you the answer.

Identifying feelings
9

1 unhappy (If you find something 'upsetting', you are unhappy about it.) **2** expect ('I had no idea that' – I didn't expect) **3** unsure ('confused about whether it was a good idea' – not sure) **4** more interested in ('really attracts me … more than …' – more interested in … than …) **5** keen to do (be up for something – keen to do something) **6** amused by ('makes me laugh' – I am amused by)

Identifying and eliminating distractors
10

I work as a prompter in a theatre – not a job that many people know much about! I specialise in opera, and I have to follow the performance on stage and whisper the words if one of the singers forgets them. It sounds **boring**, and it can be **demanding**, but I find it very **rewarding**, even though there are some downsides – as with any job I suppose.
I have to sit in a small space just below the stage for several hours – it's pretty cramped and can be uncomfortable. I get used to that, and do **exercises** for my **legs** and back to keep flexible. It doesn't matter what **clothes** I wear because no one can see me, though unfortunately that does make me a bit lazy with how I look! So what do I need to do my job? I must be **musical**, which I am, so it's difficult to stop myself singing along with the people on stage! I also have to have a lot of **patience**, but I guess it's **concentration** that tops the list.
The singers have to rely on me, so they can be **relaxed** on stage. This feeling of **trust** between us develops over time, and I regard it as special. I love being able to contribute to a great performance. I don't do it for thanks, but it's always nice when the singers acknowledge what I do. Sometimes they turn and give me **applause** at the end of a performance, and sometimes they give me **flowers**. The nicest thing was a letter from a singer who had retired, telling me how much he had valued me during his time on stage!

11

1 'boring' and 'demanding' are both adjectives, but don't describe how Sue feels – she says that the job sounds boring and demanding, but she finds it 'rewarding'.
2 'exercises' and 'legs' are potential distractors, but Sue says that her 'clothes' are not important ('it doesn't matter what clothes I wear')
3 Sue mentions being 'musical' and 'patience' but it's 'concentration' that 'tops the list,' so is most important.
4 'relaxed' is an adjective, but it doesn't relate to the relationship Sue mentions. 'Trust' is a noun, and it introduces the relationship that Sue regards as 'special'.
5 Sue mentions 'applause' and 'flowers' as examples of things she appreciates.

EXAM TASK

1 documentary ('then, a bit later, I saw a documentary which showed how they live and what they do. From then on I was hooked.')
2 communities ('I prefer to think of them as communities because they all work for each other!')
3 farm animals ('You may know that some crops like blueberries and almonds depend almost fully on bees for pollination, but I'm very sure you hadn't thought about farm animals. Much of their food, like clover, also needs bees to pollinate it.')
4 red ('It seems odd to me that they can't see red, because it's so strong – but if there are bees around anything of that colour, it's probably because the centre of the flower is actually yellow.')
5 upsetting ('Conservationists are apprehensive, and say it's worrying, but I actually find it upsetting')
6 hotels ('My personal suggestion is to create a shelter for bumblebees – just a pot or a box. Some people call them hotels, which makes me smile.')

7 average temperatures ('When I started beekeeping, I quickly discovered that if average temperatures go up, flowers come out earlier. This creates a mismatch between the time when the flowers produce pollen and when the bees are ready to collect it. Unfortunately, I can't do anything about that!')
8 bears ('It's probably perception. Just like spiders or snakes, some people find the appearance of bees frightening, because they're not cute and cuddly, and would rather give bears their support instead. I find this sad.')
9 gloves ('My gloves are what make me feel safest when I'm dealing with my bees, and I never forget them.')
10 hairspray ('Personally, I'd say definitely avoid hairspray – you don't want bees around your head.')

LISTENING
Part 3 Multiple matching
Practice task

1

Students' own answers

2

1 A 2 E 3 C

3a

1 A ('parks' and 'open areas' relates to 'green spaces')
2 D ('groups of visitors' relates to 'tourists')
3 C ('buses and trams' relates to 'public transport')

3b

A ('I would have liked there to be more parks' – he is disappointed by the lack of green spaces. Only A matches.)
D ('I thought the whole place had a buzz about it … visitors everywhere only added to that' – he liked the tourists. This doesn't match D.)
C ('I think that was my fault' – he's not frustrated by the transport system. This doesn't match C.)

4

'a great weekend' (they enjoyed it)
'difficult to take in' (they didn't enjoy seeing it)
'not always for the better in my opinion' (disagreement/ disappointment; they didn't feel it was an improvement)
'the air quality, caused by the buses and cars, was particularly poor – I didn't expect that' (surprise)
The speaker expresses surprise when they say 'I didn't expect that'.

5a

She is frustrated by the transport system (C) ('the buses were a nightmare! You waited for half an hour and then three came at once!')

5b

She is pleased with the atmosphere ('I loved the atmosphere'). She feels impressed by the view of the city ('which was amazing') but not by the architecture.

Strategies and skills
Identifying attitude
1

1 B ('really helpful') **2** A ('what we can achieve') **3** A ('good fun', 'very supportive') **4** B ('really difficult', 'makes us work even harder') **5** B ('as engaging as this') **6** A ('how much more I want to learn')

Listening for gist

2a and 2b

1 C ('… really historic houses. They had so much more character and interest than boring modern purpose-built resorts.') **2** A ('which can be good and bad') **3** B ('I then have to do the cooking, so I don't get a break. On the other hand, it's more convenient … so it's actually fine with me!') **4** F ('I can't say the same about the staff, though, and in fact I mentioned this to the manager at the end of our stay.') **5** E ('but our aim was to see animals and there weren't that many around. … maybe we picked the wrong time of year.')

Interpreting opinion

3

1 B ('… a saying that honesty is the best policy … but aren't there occasions when bending it a little does no harm?') **2** B ('I went for black and white ones thinking that they'd be more vivid than the usual colour ones. I regret that decision now!') **3** A ('I always avoid the huge centres with their chain stores. You find the same things in them all, which is less satisfying than the unusual stuff you can pick up in the smaller independent shops.') **4** A ('I don't get it at all, even though I know it's popular.') **5** A ('There's been talk of improving the flow, but that's all – we're still waiting for any sign of it.') **6** B ('That doesn't mean I put it all away, though – I want to have some fun as well!')

EXAM TASK

1 H ('if we can just tell the truth and not try to hide things, then those pressures fall away')
2 D ('what works for me is just being with people who I value and love – I'd rather invest in them and know that I'll always have friends and family around me')
3 E ('Dealing with pressure is such a difficult thing, and learning how to maintain that calmness is really the answer to everything.')
4 A ('Whenever I've achieved something, I have to set myself another target, something different to aim for')
5 F ('But I've discovered that what I really value is making people's lives better – I want to make a difference to them.')

LISTENING

Part 4 Multiple choice

Practice task

1

Students' own answers

2

1 B **2** C **3** A

3a

C

3b

B

3c

No

4

'So if that's what they want, I know I have to give them the support they obviously require' – She understands that they need advice. She doesn't 'regret' the type of books they buy, but recognises they might not get it right: 'so they may not make the right choice'. She doesn't dislike the way they shop, she describes it: 'When these people shop for a book they don't browse through all those on offer'

5

She talks about pleasing people: 'but I have to accept what I see as a fact, which is there's no other possibility to keep everyone happy'

Strategies and skills

Identifying the main idea

1

1 A ('I tend to buy books spontaneously – I don't waste time trying to decide … . Does that mean I make bad decisions when I buy a book? Probably not, … I rarely regret my choice.')
2 B ('What I mean is, buying engineering books for boys and dolls for girls may be storing up trouble for the future.')
3 B ('it's a fact that we buy and throw things away without much thought, and maybe we don't value the things we have as much as we should. When I was younger I used to save up to buy something new and I kept it for a long time.')
4 A ('But what that means is that our homes become full of stuff we've bought impulsively, without thinking, and now don't know what to do with. Decluttering and throwing away things we don't need should become a priority, but it's not an easy thing to do.')
5 A ('This could be because they can't afford to buy things, but that's unlikely. It's more that their priorities have changed. Young people choose to buy experiences rather than material goods.')
6 B ('We're surrounded by advertisements everywhere … . Almost every site we visit online has adverts, and they're targeted towards our own particular interests. It's hard to filter them out, to ignore the tempting goods they offer.')

2

1 what often happens is (the usual outcome is)
2 the fact is (a general statement)
3 One thing is (an example)
4 the main one is (the most important is)
5 the key (the most important)
6 in fact (actually)

3

1 because (conjunction before a clause giving a reason or explanation; 'for example' introduces an example)
2 thanks to (this means owing to/because of (a reason); 'which leads to' introduces a result or consequence)
3 for instance (introduces an example; 'as' is incomplete – the phrase is 'such as' which also introduces an example)
4 problem ('but' + 'the problem is' contrasts with the imaginary situation – 'I'd love to play'; 'the reason is' would not provide the contrast)
5 that's why (phrase introducing an intention or reason; 'that's because' introduces an explanation)
6 the result of that (introduces the outcome or consequence of an action; 'the reason for that' introduces an explanation for an action)

Understanding opinions

4

1 A (The speaker is saying that it is only possible to have a few good friends. If you know a lot of people, it is impossible to know them very well and therefore they can't be good friends. So, having fewer (good) friends is preferable to knowing a lot of people – who are not good friends.)
2 B (The speaker suspects that when someone doesn't express what is on their mind, there is something else interesting or important they are hiding – 'there is more involved')
3 A (The problem – 'argument' – is mainly due to the fact that the people involved have different personalities and is not a major disagreement over something. Therefore, it is not serious or even real – 'an actual problem'.)
4 A ('less of an issue than' – not as difficult as, i.e. 'easier to solve')
5 A ('various reasons' – a number of different reasons, i.e. not any one reason in particular)
6 B ('really interesting thing' – 'most important aspect')

5

1 inconvenient ('scheduled at the wrong time') **2** argue ('fall out') **3** deafening ('made it difficult to hear') **4** follow my dreams ('achieve my aims') **5** simplicity ('be so straightforward') **6** in the spotlight ('having no privacy/always on view')

EXAM TASK

1 B ('It was nice to make her feel good!')
2 A ('My problem is the feeling that if I need to work hard on something, it makes me feel that I'm not very good at it. That's demotivating.')
3 C ('I prefer the fact that the audience can't really see me clearly – I'm kind of protected.')
4 C ('But one personal quality people don't think of is patience – there's loads of hanging around to put up with.')
5 A ('I accept it if I need someone to step in and am grateful – I can't worry that I'm not pulling my weight and working as hard as everyone else.')
6 B ('It's not only that he keeps us together, like in a regular orchestra – sometimes he asks us to repeat a bit of music, or play more slowly because a singer has made a mistake.')
7 A ('You must build a good reputation, so you're asked to do other shows when one finishes.')

SPEAKING

Part 1 Interview

Practice task

1

Students' own answers

2a and 2b

1 C **2** A **3** B **4** C **5** C **6** A

3a

1 A 1; B 2	**4** A 2; B 1
2 B 2; C 1	**5** A 1; B 2
3 A 2; C 1	**6** B 2; C 1

3b

Example answers

1

A I come from Milan, which is a large city in the north of Italy.
B I come from Barcelona, which is in Catalonia in Spain.

2

B I don't have one and, to be honest, I don't think about it very often, but if I did it would be green because I love the countryside.
C My football team wears red and black, so I would say that they are my favourite colours.

3

A I have quite a big family, with a brother, a sister and three cousins. We all live near each other and we're good friends.
C My mum is a doctor, and my dad is a teacher. I don't have any brothers or sisters.

4

A I really enjoy going shopping with my friends, and we spend a lot of time in the big mall in my city. There are lots of cafés where we can sit and talk, too.
B I watch a lot of television at the weekends, because I live a long way away from my friends, so I can't meet them very often.

5

A No, not really – I prefer to listen to music and watch television.
B I don't really like sport, because I'm not very good at it. I'd rather listen to music.

6

B I don't really like speaking languages much, but I'm trying hard and one day I'd like to learn Chinese though I don't speak it now.
C Not at the moment. I really enjoy learning English, because I like the pronunciation of the language, and I'd like to get really good at that before I start any new language.

Strategies and skills

Extending your answers with appropriate detail and examples

1

'Otherwise' doesn't mean the same as 'because'. It is used to explain what will happen if you do not follow an order or suggestion.

2

1 I like films **since** they provide escapism.
2 I haven't been abroad **as** I hate flying.
3 I can't practise my English more **owing to** (the) lack of time.
4 It's difficult for me to get to college **due to the fact that** the bus route has been changed.

3

1 for example
2 such as
3 for instance
4 like
5 for example
6 like
All the correct words introduce an example.

4

Example answers

Everyday life

1 I go to college by bus because it's too far to cycle and the traffic is very bad.
2 I like to do something different due to the fact that my work is boring so I need a change.
3 I don't have much free time. The reason is that I spend most of my time working, so I'm glad when I can get away on holiday and have a break.
4 If I don't, then I get confused, like I missed an appointment last week because I went to the office a different way.

Entertainment

1 I prefer to watch films at home since I like to have a snack while I'm watching and I don't like to disturb people around me in the cinema.
2 I really like documentaries, for example there was an amazing one about penguins last week.
3 I'd love to, but it's difficult where I live owing to the distance I live from the city centre – like it takes me an hour to get to the theatre.
4 We do share a lot of interests, but actually we do stuff separately as well, for instance I went to play tennis at the club because they prefer football.

Asking for repetition

5

1 b (question formation: 'could' + 'you say it again?')
2 d ('mind' + -ing)
3 f ('I'm not sure' + 'what' as pronoun + 'you said')
4 e ('I didn't hear' + 'what' as pronoun + 'you said')
5 a ('what' + question)
6 c (Follow-up sentence after 'Pardon'?; 'I'm afraid I didn't catch…')

Using a range of language

6

1 drove, visited	**4** sunny, relaxing
2 comfortable	**5** enjoy, prefer
3 decided on	**6** boring

Example answers

Future plans

What are you going to do this coming weekend?

I'm probably going to see my friends as I haven't seen them for a while. We might go to the cinema, or just sit and chat.

Where would you like to go for your next holiday?

I'd love to go to Canada because I haven't been there before and I've heard that it's beautiful.

Do you have any plans for your career in the future?

I'm not sure yet, but I'm thinking about becoming a teacher since all my family are teachers.

Education

What was your favourite subject at your first school?

It was maths, though I'm no good at it now.

Tell us about a favourite teacher from school or college.

It was my French teacher, who was great because she made the lessons so interesting. She used to show us films in French.

Do you often see your friends from school or college?

Oh yes – we all live in the same town, and so we often bump into each other.

Technology

Do you use the internet much for shopping?

I use it all the time as I hate going into crowded shops.

Do you ever switch off your mobile phone?

I try to because I know it's not good to use it too much, but it's hard. I always turn it off in the cinema or theatre.

Do you find out about the news on the internet, or another way?

Definitely the internet, due to the fact that it's the most up to date. My dad likes to buy a newspaper, though.

SPEAKING

Part 2 Individual long turn

Practice task

1

Students' own answers

2a

Which student:	Student A	Student B
describes the photographs?	✓	✓
compares the photographs?		✓
answers the question fully while talking about both photographs?		✓
talks only about the people in the photographs (not about themself)?		✓

2b

Student B gave the best answer.

Student A describes the photographs and doesn't compare them; Student B both describes and compares the photographs.

Student A answers the question briefly; Student B talks about both photographs when answering the question.

Student A gives their personal opinion about the situations in the photographs; Student B's answer only refers to the people in the photographs.

Strategies and skills

Comparing different but related situations

1

Students' own answers

2

Example answers

1 Both photographs show friends eating a snack together.

2 What's the same in both photographs is that the friends are eating and talking, and they're both quite casual situations.

3 The first photograph shows two friends in a café, sitting at a table while the second one shows a group of friends at the beach, sitting on the sand.

4 Another thing that's different is where they are. The two women are inside a café whereas the group of friends are outside at the beach.

5 The women are inside whereas the group of friends are sitting out in the fresh air at the seaside.

3

Example answers

1 In the first photograph the women are enjoying each other's company.

2 They look interested in each other and what they're talking about.

3 The women seem to be spending time together during the day – maybe they've met up for a shopping trip to the city.

4 In the second photograph the friends are enjoying a relaxing day out in the fresh air by the sea.

5 The friends look relaxed and happy – maybe they're on holiday.

6 The whole group seem to be enjoying a day out.

7 In both photographs the people are enjoying time away from work or college.

4

Students' own answers

Making speculations

5 and 6

Students' own answers

Organising a long turn

7

1 To begin with (starts off a description, presentation or discussion; 'At the beginning' would start off a narrative or recount.)

2 To compare them (announces the speaker's intention to compare two things; 'In comparison' compares something with something else already mentioned.)

3 On the other hand (introduces a comparison; 'Also' introduces a similar idea.)

4 As for (introduces a new point; 'Because' introduces a reason or explanation.)

5 For that reason (gives the result or consequence of the previous point. In this sentence, the idea is then expanded on by 'so they are finding it difficult …'. 'Since' introduces a reason for something, but it doesn't fit in this sentence because of the following 'so'.)

6 as (because; 'so' gives a result or consequence)

7 To finish (ends a description, presentation or discussion; 'To that end' would provide a reason.)

Answering the follow-up question to your partner's long turn

8

1 A The student gives a reason. (B doesn't answer the question.)

2 B The student extends their answer. (A's answer is too short and uses very simple language.)

3 A The student answers the question, and also refers to the photographs. (B answers with a statement of fact and doesn't refer to the photographs.)

4 B The student doesn't give too much information. (A goes on to talk about their family holiday, which doesn't directly relate to the question.)

Dealing with unfamiliar vocabulary

9

1 should know (modal + verb 'know' – ought to know)

2 gone blank ('my mind's gone blank' – phrase to say you suddenly can't think of or remember something)

3 call it ('what do you call it?' – phrase to say you can't remember a word for something)

4 what's (question form using 'what' to ask about a thing)

5 not sure ('not sure about it' – uncertain about, not confident of knowing something)

6 can't remember (have forgotten)

EXAM TASK

Example answers

Examiner: Candidate A, your photographs show people enjoying painting in different situations.

I'd like you to compare the photographs and say what you think the people are enjoying about painting in these situations.

Student A: Both my photographs show people painting, but they're in very different situations; the first obvious difference is that one is inside whereas the other is outside. The first photograph shows a group of children sitting round a table, and there's an older person with them – she may be a teacher so I think it's an art class. I think they're painting pots they've already made. The children are working together, choosing which colours to use. On the other hand, the second photograph shows a group of people who are being more practical and are painting the outside of a house. They've already chosen the colour, and are working hard to finish the job. Three of them are standing on ladders to paint the top of the walls. What the children are enjoying about painting is being creative, and making something that is completely their own. They may want to show their parents what they've painted, and they're probably feeling proud. The people painting the house are enjoying creating a home – maybe they're neighbours helping a young family to move into the town. They'll feel proud, too, when they've finished.

Examiner: Thank you. Candidate B, do you enjoy painting?

Student B: No, I don't really – I'm not at all creative, and was very bad at art classes when I was at school. It's not something I enjoy at all.

Examiner: Candidate B, your photographs show people feeling tired in different situations.

I'd like you to compare the photographs and say why you think the people are feeling tired in these situations.

Student B: OK, well, the photographs are very different, although what's common to both is that they show people who are obviously very tired. The first picture is outside in a forest– maybe a mountain road, whereas the second picture is in an office. The cyclist looks as if he's stopped for a rest, because he's bending over the handlebars resting his head on his arms. The woman looks tired – I can see her face – but she's continuing to work although she's finding it difficult. They're tired for very different reasons. The man's been cycling for a long time and he's got a heavy bag on the back of his bike which must make cycling more difficult. He's physically tired because of all this. The woman's clearly been working for a long time – there are loads of files and papers on her desk, so she's mentally tired. I think she needs to take a break from work and go and get some fresh air.

Examiner: Thank you. Candidate A, have you ever been cycling in the mountains?

Student A: Actually, I cycle a lot in my town because it's an easy way to get around, but I wouldn't like to cycle in the mountains. It would be too difficult!

SPEAKING

Part 3 Collaborative task

Practice task

1 and 2

Students' own answers

3

The following should be ticked:

- doing sport with friends is fun ('… and it's fun, too. I really enjoy being competitive, and I play a lot of different sports like football and tennis with my friends.')
- it's important to eat well and do sport ('In my opinion, eating the right food is just as important – there's no point if you spend hours jogging or something like that and then eat loads of chocolate. It seems to me that you take away any positive aspects of the sport.')
- it's easy to lose motivation ('I can imagine that sport isn't much fun it you're not very good at it, though – it must be very frustrating if you never get into any teams. Then you aren't motivated to do it')
- it's possible to avoid injuries when doing sport ('it's a risk but you can take care not to get injured – like doing proper exercises to warm up your body first. In my opinion you get all the benefits without the risk of injury.')

4

1 Yes (e.g. 'What do you think?', 'Do you agree with me?')

2 Yes (e.g. 'My thinking is that …' , 'In my opinion …'

3 Yes (e.g. '… play a lot of different sports like football and tennis with my friends.', 'I don't enjoy sport much – probably because I never get chosen!')

5a

Yes – they chose the mental benefits, along with being physically fit. ('B: So if we take both mental and physical fitness together, then that's definitely the best reason for doing sport. Is that all right with you? A: I'll go along with that.')

5b

The following should be ticked:

- Is that all right with you?
- I'll go along with that.

Strategies and skills

Asking for and giving opinions

1

Asking for opinion:

Any ideas about this one?

Don't you think that … ?

What do you think?

What do you think about that?

What's your opinion on this?

Giving an opinion:

From my point of view, …

It seems to me that …

My thinking is …

My view on this is …

The point I'm making is …

2

Example answers

1 For me, it's important to take photographs because I want to remember everything afterwards.

2 My opinion on taking photographs is that it's not a good thing as you can't enjoy the event at the time.

3 My point of view is that taking photos is more social since you can share them with friends on social media.

4 I see it like this. Taking photos is hard if you can't decide what to take photos of!

5 What I'm saying is, taking photographs all the time is bad, owing to the fact you end up photographing everything, and so nothing is special anymore.

6 I would say that taking photographs is hard, due to its complexity, and bad photos are not good to keep or share.

7 Let me explain. The reason I think taking photos at special events is bad is because you don't experience the event itself.

8 It seems to me that everyone takes photos nowadays because they want to share them on the internet.

3

1 Yes ('What's your opinion?', 'Don't you think that', 'Any ideas about that?')

2 Yes ('My view on it is that it's not a good thing – you can't enjoy the moment when you're thinking about the photo you're taking.'; 'The point I'm making is that you want something to help you remember it afterwards – that's the best way to have happy memories. It's very easy to forget things – like I can't remember the first live music concert I went to. I wish someone had taken photos then.'; 'The reason I think that is because the last concert I went to all you could see were the phone screens being held up as people filmed the band. It spoiled it for everyone else.')

4

Students' own answers

Showing how far you agree or disagree

5

1 B ('totally agree' and 'definitely' are stronger than 'partly agree'. The opinion in A is also qualified – 'but …' – which makes the agreement there even weaker.) **2** A ('Good point' and 'it's important' indicate strong agreement compared to 'I guess you're probably right' in B.) **3** B ('I think exactly the same' expresses much stronger agreement than 'Possibly …' in A, and 'it's a waste of time' adds another strong opinion to response B.) **4** B ('I can't go along with that' expresses strong disagreement compared to 'I have a slightly different idea … , to be honest' in A. B's added opinion 'it's really not a good use of time' strengthens the point.) **5** A ('How can you say that?' indicates disbelief that anyone could express such an opinion, so it expresses total disagreement. By comparison, B's 'I agree up to a point …' is much weaker.) **6** A ('I think the same' and 'it's key' both indicate strong agreement, while B's 'I guess you're probably right' indicates uncertainty.)

6

summarising	checking
I guess what you mean is …	Did you mean … ?
I understood what you meant was …	Do you mean that … ?
Thinking about what you said about …	Is that right?
When you said that …	Just to make sure I've
You said that …	understood, …

7a

1 You said that

2 When you said that

3 Thinking about what you said about

4 I understood what you meant; was

5 Just to make sure I've; is that right?

6 I guess what you mean is

7b

1 agree **2** disagree **3** strongly agree (*definitely*) **4** strongly disagree ('I can't go along with that') **5** strongly agree ('completely') **6** strongly agree ('really good')

Negotiating towards a decision

8

Negotiating: 1 c ('do you' + 'feel') **2** f ('think' + 'the same') **3** a ('make' + '(a) decision') **4** e ('all' + 'right') **5** b ('that' + 'what' + 'we think') **6** d ('shall we' + 'agree') **Reaching agreement: 1** f ('feel' + 'that's the best choice') **2** c ('go' + 'along with') **3** e ('come' + 'to a decision') **4** a ('reach' + 'agreement') **5** d ('decide' + 'on') **6** b ('our' + 'decision') **Inability to reach a decision: 1** e ('agree' + 'on') **2** d ('have' + 'an opinion') **3** f ('going to' + 'agree') **4** b ('not' + 'an easy decision') **5** a ('have to' + 'agree') **6** c ('think' + 'we'll never agree')

9

1 all right with you: go along with that

2 agree on that: agreement on that

3 feel about it: have a different opinion on what's best

4 an easy decision to make: agree to disagree

10

Students' own answers

11

1 A taking away pressure ('M: … taking away pressure is the most important reason … F: … but I guess you're probably right. M: So is that our final decision, then? F: Yes, that's the best choice.')

2 B environmental concerns ('F: We said that driving in towns wasn't good for the environment. M: Yes, and I still think that's the most important reason … F: We've both decided on that, I think.')

3 no decision ('M: Oh dear – we won't be able to agree, then.')

4 B learning new things ('M: what about learning new things? F: All right – it's as good as any, I suppose.')

5 B staying healthy ('F: Yes, me too – but health comes first really. M: Then I think we've managed to come to a decision.')

EXAM TASK

Example answers

Examiner: Some people think it's a good idea to have advertisements during television programmes, and other people disagree. Here are some things they think about, and a question for you to discuss. First you have some time to look at the task. Now, talk to each other about whether it's a good idea to have advertisements during television programmes.

Speaker A: OK – so we have to talk about advertisements during television programmes. Personally, I hate them because they interrupt the programme and if I'm watching a good drama, then it's really annoying.

Speaker B: I can see what you mean, but on the other hand advertisements do give you useful information – like about new cars on the market, or things like that. We need to have information about that kind of stuff.

Speaker A: True, but I don't want to think about that while I'm enjoying something else! I suppose you're right that they do give you a choice – you can see what's available. It's just that you can't turn them off.

Speaker B: That's a good point, and it isn't good if advertisements influence children who might see them – especially if they're advertising sweets or something like that. Children might be encouraged to eat too much sugar, then.

Speaker A: I agree about that. One point in their favour, though, is that the money that comes from advertisements can pay for really good programmes – so the quality of what we see goes up.

Speaker B: I hadn't thought of that, and you're right. On the other hand, it's not good if people feel pressure to buy something just because they've seen adverts for it – I mentioned cars before, but it could be anything. There are lots of advertisements for holidays at this time of the year and they're encouraging people to spend a lot of money – maybe they can't really afford them.

Examiner: Now you have about a minute to decide what the best reason is for not having advertisements during television programmes.

Speaker A: Well, I guess I've made my position clear – I hate the interruption to the programme.

Speaker B: Yes, but is that actually the best reason for not having them? You get annoyed, but other people might like them because of the information they get from them. For me, it's more about influencing children, and that's a really good reason for not having adverts on television.

Speaker A: I take your point. OK then, you also talked about pressure to buy. Would you like to choose that as our reason?

Speaker B: I'm not sure – people can resist the pressure. No, I think it's the children.

Speaker A: OK – I'll go along with that.

SPEAKING

Part 4 Discussion

Practice task

1 and 2

Students' own answers

3

1 Yes ('I know that if I go out running, I feel great when I get back. It seems to work even if I'm tired!')
2 They agree ('I know what you mean'; 'I think you're right')

4

1 'You say it can make you feel jealous'
2 'You're right about that.'

5

1 'If you can share your feelings with friends, it stops you thinking too much and getting depressed'
2 The man disagrees that women are better at sharing their feelings than men: '… I guess that used to be true, but maybe it's changing. I talk to my friends about lots of things …'

Strategies and skills

Giving full answers with examples and justifications

1

1 B ('plus' means 'and'; 'top of that' is an incomplete phrase – the phrase is 'on top of that'; 'as well' is not followed by 'then')
2 B ('on top of that' means 'in addition'; the other two options are not followed by 'that')
3 A ('there's also the point that' adds another reason; 'there's also' is not followed by 'true that'; 'plus' means 'also', so it would be a repetition)
4 C ('it's also true that' introduces another, similar idea; 'as well' means 'and', so it would be a repetition of 'too'; 'the point that' introduces a reason or purpose, not a similar idea.)

2

1 example (the phrase 'for example') **2** common (the collocation 'common knowledge') **3** look (the phrasal verb 'look at') **4** such (the phrase 'such as') **5** like (an informal way of introducing an example) **6** most (quantifier for the noun 'people')

3

Once, when I went to (Speaker 1: Once, when I went to Paris …)
What happened to me was (Speaker 2: …what happened to me was I couldn't decide …)

Speaking for myself (Speaker 3: 'Speaking for myself, though, I really like all the things …')

4

1 e (continues the comparison between exercise and eating) **2** b ('recycle' links with 'plastic bags') **3** c ('a good qualification' links with 'career') **4** d ('nice hotels' links with 'comfort') **5** f ('camping' links with 'the outdoor life') **6** a ('world temperatures are increasing' links with 'global warming')

Adding ideas and developing a discussion

5

1 add ('add something' + 'to')
2 come in (enter (a discussion))
3 interesting point ('That's a' + noun; 'make a point')
4 the same ('it's not the same' – it's different)
5 wouldn't ('would/wouldn't' for a hypothesis)
6 example ('an example' + 'of something')

6

Students' own answers

7

1 making arrangements easily, convenience of communication
2 enjoying things like sport instead, wasting time online
3 importance of knowing what's happening in the world, having time to read newspapers

8

1 making arrangements easily ('because it's so easy to make arrangements that way.'); convenience of communication ('how convenient it is because you know that friends will see everything immediately.')
2 enjoying things like sport instead ('I like having time to do other more interesting things, like sport.'); wasting time online ('It can certainly waste a lot of time')
3 having time to read newspapers ('I don't have time to read newspapers')

9

1 1
2 4
3 6

Responding to a difficult question

10

1 Correct
2 I'm sorry but I don't have ~~no~~ **any** ideas about that. (correct determiner)
3 That's a good question – but I don't know ~~how~~ **what** the answer is! (correct pronoun)
4 Correct
5 Could you repeat ~~again~~ the question, please? I didn't quite catch it. ('repeat' – say again, so 'again' here is not needed)
6 Let me ~~to~~ think about it. ('Let' + infinitive without 'to')

EXAM TASK

Example answers

1 Do you enjoy taking part in competitions? (Why? / Why not?)
Student A: Yes, I do. I think actually I'm pretty competitive – once I went on holiday and we were all just playing around with a bat and ball but I wanted to score the most points! So I guess that means I'm competitive.
Student B: Yes – it definitely sounds as if you are. I'm not, though – I don't think it's important to win all the time.
2 Do you think that being competitive is a natural quality, or can it be taught? (Why?)

Student B: Well, when Sara said before that she was pretty competitive that must show that it's natural for her. I don't know whether it can be taught though – some people just don't want to compete with others.

Student A: That's a good point, and I agree with what you said about me. I think I am naturally competitive, and I'm happy with that.

3 Some people say that young children should be encouraged to be competitive at school. What do you think?

Student A: That's a difficult question. I don't think I was actively encouraged at school, but maybe it would be a good thing for children because when they grow up the real world is competitive. You have to be the best.

Student B: Yes, I agree there. The reason I say that is because the business world is very hard, and you have to try to get to the top. Maybe for that reason it's a good thing to encourage children to be competitive at school.

4 Do you think it's necessary to be competitive to be successful in life? (Why? / Why not?)

Student B: I definitely think you do have to be competitive if you want to be successful, even though I don't particularly like it. If you're not, then other people do better than you in life.

Student A: So you think that being competitive is important – is that right?

Student B: Yes, I do – like when you go for a job interview there are always lots of other candidates for the same job. I tried to get a job once and there were about 20 other applicants. I didn't get it, unfortunately!

5 Is it possible to be too competitive? (Why? / Why not?)

Student A: I guess so – that's because you might want to win so badly that you don't think about other people's feelings.

Student B: And then you can hurt people – for example, you can make them feel stupid.

Student A: Just look at these television talent shows – people can get very hurt by what the judges say about them.

6 In your opinion, what does success really mean? (Why?)

Student A: That's a really difficult question! I'm not sure what to say.

Student B: Well, I think that people often think it means being rich, or famous, but in my opinion it's more than that. If I can be happy in relationships and be able to do what I want, then, for me, that's success.

Student A: OK – I accept that! But I think I would want more than that – I want to be the best in whatever job I do, and get to the top, so that's what success means to me.

READING AND USE OF ENGLISH

Part 1

0 B (similar meanings; 'view' - everything you can see from a high place, 'scene' - the place where something happens, 'glance' - the act of looking at something quickly)
1 A (verb patterns; 'suggested' + 'that', 'approved' + 'of', 'regarded' + 'as')
2 C (linkers; 'Although' is used at the beginning of two contrasting clauses, 'Despite' is used before a noun, 'Therefore' has a different meaning - as a result of this)
3 B (similar meanings; 'notice' - a written sign, 'display' - an arrangement of things for people to look at, 'logo' - a sign used by a company to identify its brand)
4 D (linkers; 'except' - not including, 'instead of' - as an alternative to, 'otherwise' - if something does not happen)
5 C (phrasal verb; 'take on' - compete with, 'take up' - start a new activity, 'take out' - take someone to a place, 'take in' - learn)
6 B (fixed phrase; in recent years)
7 B (similar meanings; 'the fight for something' - the campaign to achieve it, 'quarrel' - an angry conversation with someone, 'dispute' - a situation in which people disagree, 'conflict' - a situation in which people or countries are involved in a serious disagreement and likely to fight)
8 A (verb patterns; 'demand' + 'that', 'insist' + 'that', 'propose' + 'that')

Part 2

9 only/just (linking phrase: 'not only/just … but also')
10 as (comparative phrase: 'as … as')
11 have (present perfect tense)
12 be (passive with modal verb)
13 of (collocation: 'a range of')
14 no (quantifier)
15 more (comparative form)
16 this (reference word, referring back to the quality of 'being easy and cheap to mass-produce and transport')

Part 3

17 creative (**adjective** + noun)
18 quietly (verb + **adverb**)
19 researchers (a group of + **plural noun**)
20 musical (adjective + **adjective** + noun)
21 pleasure (verb + possessive adjective + **noun**)
22 communication (a form of + **uncountable noun**)
23 decisions (verb + all the + **plural noun**)
24 fascinating (the most + **adjective** + noun)

Part 4

25 advised me not to go
26 have my hair cut
27 (been) three years since
28 didn't mean to break
29 more difficult than
30 have turned down

Part 5

31 C ('Hearing him (my uncle) talking with passion about the joys of diving and the amazing things he had seen awakened something in me.' A The writer lived by the coast, but says he wasn't particularly interested in the sea. B The writer watched TV programmes **after** he had become interested.) D Friends challenged the writer to take up surfing, but he didn't.)

32 A ('but luckily the instructor stayed right beside us to make sure we were OK.' B The writer mentions the breathing equipment, but he doesn't say he felt confident about using it. C The writer mentions doing a real dive, but doesn't say he was excited about this. D The writer mentions not being very deep, but doesn't say he was disappointed about this.)
33 B (We can understand the context for the meaning because the writer talks about getting more experience and qualifications. We know that he already has the qualifications (he has therefore **achieved** them) as he became 'hooked on' diving as a result of this: 'After building up some experience in my local area and getting more qualifications, …')
34 C ('And the most amazing thing is their attitude to you as you make your way through their world, seeing you not as a threat but …' A The writer mentions the bright colours, but doesn't say this is the most surprising thing. B The writer says what the fish do 'they turn with lightning speed', but doesn't say this is the most surprising thing. D This is not mentioned.)
35 D ('But the oxygen tank on my back obviously caught its eye …' A The writer hoped the shark would not notice him, but in fact it did. B The writer says he knew the species could be dangerous, but it doesn't say this shark became aggressive. C This is not mentioned.)
36 A ('These (small pieces of plastic) cause problems with the underwater ecosystem and are particularly dangerous, as fish and other creatures can eat them …')

Part 6

37 F ('It' refers back to 'wood'. The sentence expands on the idea of why wood is not perfect. In the following sentence, 'these qualities' refers back to the ideas mentioned.)
38 C ('This high-tech material' refers back to 'modern wood' in the previous sentence. It mentions some of its qualities, which contrast with 'traditional wood' mentioned earlier.)
39 G ('It' refers back to the tower, and the sentence gives more information about it.)
40 A ('This' refers back to the fact that the material is good at keeping warmth inside a building. The sentence expands on this idea, and mentions an advantage of this.)
41 B ('They' refers back to 'environmentally friendly drinking straws' in the previous sentence. It is followed by 'they' in the next sentence.)
42 E (The idea of the 'digital world' is picked up in ideas later in the paragraph, e.g. that it allows electricity to pass through it, is an ideal material to use in electronic devices and is being used in computers.)

Part 7

43 B ('when I went to business school … that was when I made up my mind that I would do things differently.')
44 C ('we struggled to get people to invest in the business at first')
45 D ('I started suffering from anxiety … and I feel much better in myself, too.')
46 A ('I couldn't believe how quickly we built up our customer numbers.')
47 C ('I had managed restaurants before, so I set up the Street Café.')
48 B ('I know it wouldn't have been possible without the support and generous start-up loan my dad gave me.')
49 D ('I must admit I was nervous about giving up a regular salary')
50 A ('My colleague refused, saying we weren't allowed to sell or give the food away. That really annoyed me!')

51 C ('I would encourage more people to set up companies like this, although they should be aware of the long hours they'll need to put in at first!')

52 B ('we donate a solar-powered lamp to an African charity, for children with no electricity at home. Light is incredibly important because it allows kids to study and improve their lives')

WRITING

Part 1

1 Essay
Example answer

Visiting shopping centres and shopping online are both popular ways to buy things. While both have advantages, this essay will argue that online shopping is better.

The first reason is that shopping on the internet is considerably cheaper than going to shopping centres. Internet stores do not have to pay for expensive buildings or large numbers of staff, so their prices are often much lower than in shopping centres. Moreover, it is easier to shop around online and visit a larger number of stores.

Secondly, there is more choice online. Shops are often limited by space so can only sell a limited range of goods. Online stores are able to offer a much wider range of goods.

Lastly, it is much more convenient to shop from your own home. Visiting shopping centres takes time, and there are often traffic jams and queues. Furthermore, shops are not open all the time. With online shopping, you can relax at home and shop when it is convenient for you.

To sum up, online shopping offers a quick, cheap and convenient way to purchase things, so it is clearly better than visiting shopping centres.

Part 2

2 Report
Example answer

Introduction

The aim of this report is to assess the improved sports centre, identify any problems and make suggestions for further improvement.

Facilities

There are more sports available, due to the addition of an excellent badminton hall which can also be used for basketball and netball. Furthermore, the swimming pool has been extended and is now an impressive training facility. These are welcome improvements, and good for residents of the town.

Problems

The system for booking the squash courts does not work well, and there have been several examples of double-booking.

The swimming pool is not open often enough. It is frequently used by schools, which means the general public are unable to swim at those times. It also closes early at weekends.

Prices for using the centre are very high, even for students and senior citizens.

Suggestions

It would be better if the opening hours of the pool could be extended, particularly into the evenings so that people could swim after work. In addition, there should be discounts for the elderly.

Conclusion

The sports centre is a great benefit to the town, and these minor problems can be solved easily.

191 words

3 Review
Example answer

I'm not a good cook, so I recently went on a course to improve my skills. It lasted for two days and took place in a local hotel.

The classes were small, which meant that the instructor (Peter) was able to give us a lot of individual attention. He was excellent, and showed us how to make lots of tasty dishes as well as teaching us about unusual ingredients and how to use them. One example of something he made was a vegan casserole which was absolutely delicious!

The best thing about the course was learning to make meals that were not only healthy, but also quick and simple to prepare. Peter showed us how easy it is to cook good food, even if we lead busy lives. The only negative thing about the course for me was that it wasn't long enough!

I would definitely recommend this course. It is important for everyone to know how to cook, because it's unhealthy to eat fast food or ready-prepared meals all the time. People are afraid of cooking because they think it's difficult, but this course teaches you how easy it actually is!

192 words

4 Email
Example answer

Hi Tara,

I'm looking forward to coming! Congratulations on passing your driving test, too.

Thanks for organising the river trip, which sounds amazing. I'm sure I'll enjoy anything and everything you've planned, but one thing I really would like to do is visit the castle. I've seen pictures of it on the internet and it looks wonderful. Would that be possible, do you think? If you can drive, I guess it's easy to go nearly anywhere we want, which is fantastic! I'm happy about that because I hate travelling on buses.

I love museums, so I'd like it if we could fit in a couple of those, though I don't want you to be bored. You probably remember that I play tennis, so I'll bring my racquet in case we can have a game sometime. I hope the weather's going to be warm!

I'm glad you asked about food! Although I used to eat everything, I've been trying to cut down on red meat recently. Are there any restaurants that serve good vegetarian meals in the town? I hope you like that kind of food, too.

See you soon – can't wait!

Love,

190 words

LISTENING

Part 1

1

B ('**F:**   On the other hand, the writing was exceptional – I could more or less believe in everything they were saying. **M:**   I think the writers deserve some kind of award – so often a script isn't credible.')

2

A ('It's going to take her ages to get there, given that she's working on the other side of town, and we don't want to be held up waiting for her and miss the show.')

3

C ('To be honest, I'm only doing it because the boss made it clear that she expected it.')

4

B ('I guess the thing is not knowing how hard the course will be – I've heard that the tutors there expect high standards, and everyone else will be really good.')

5

A ('and just to let you all know that, due to fantastic tickets sales, we've added another night to this sell-out tour, so pass the word around your friends!')

6

C ('all I want to do is find out how to win – not have the absolutely correct technique, so my priority is a bit different.')

7

C ('The lodge we stayed in was out of this world – it was far more luxurious than I'd imagined.')

8 A

('I'm not sure that what it says is accurate.')

Part 2

9 contacts

('it's a great job in itself with loads of advantages, like the amount of experience you gain and the good salary. But more than anything it provides you with the chance to make new contacts who will be useful later on')

10 character

('Although an advert often tells a story, and you may have some dramatic scenes, you have no time to work on a character like you do in a film, which is a shame')

11 voice control

('One thing I wish I'd done more work on is voice control because this really helps build your acting skills and confidence, so work on this in your classes.')

12 photos/photographs/pictures

('Make sure you have a collection of photos to send out when applying for auditions – this saves time in the long run.')

13 baby food

('the worst one was when I applied to be in a commercial selling baby food when I didn't look old enough to be a parent!')

14 chocolate

('I did that, and then couldn't understand why I was never invited to audition to advertise chocolate even though I seemed to be considered endlessly for washing powder or soap.')

15 common sense

('If you're invited to an audition, never turn one down. I did once because I was tired, and that particular company didn't ask me back. It's a small world, and you get a reputation for being awkward or unhelpful if you reject offers. So, now I think taking every opportunity is common sense.')

16 flexibility

('And key to the whole thing is flexibility – one week you might be playing a nurse, the next a taxi driver!')

17 exciting

('When I started I was told that filming adverts was stressful because you want to impress everyone – I'd say it's exciting, although other people find it tiring.')

18 bread

('I did one where they actually used brown shoe polish on bread to make it look more appetising')

Part 3

19 E ('It was a close friend who pointed out the ad in the paper for a job with the football club I'd supported for years – he said it'd be right up my street.')

20 G ('I felt I was missing out on that social side of life, so I applied for and got a job which was less demanding.')

21 D ('I saw an ad for a social worker working with disadvantaged teenagers, and thought that would push me to achieve more.')

22 A ('I needed to grow up a bit, show that I was able to take charge of something myself.')

23 B ('I think I just wanted to show everyone that I knew better than them.')

Part 4

24 A ('after that I never wanted to do anything else.')

25 B ('I go red when I think that they're still out there – they're quite childish.')

26 A ('To be honest, I'd never been too bad at that – my classmates often wanted me to sketch them, and they could always recognise themselves – but it helped me develop a more expert approach.')

27 C ('but keeping everyone informed of what we're doing is critical.')

28 C ('I remember once having difficulty with a particular drawing of a fox – it wouldn't go right, and it was hard to keep going with it.')

29 A ('So, just like an actor does, you bring your own experience and perspective to it.')

30 B ('a director has a lot more things to think about, not least, financial.')

SPEAKING

Part 1

Example answers
Part 1

What did you do last weekend? (Why?)
I went to visit my cousin, who lives on a farm about an hour outside the city. We walked around the fields, and then had a barbecue in the evening because the weather was lovely.

Have you been to any special celebrations recently?
Yes – it was my parent's wedding anniversary last month. We all went out for a meal at a restaurant in the evening, and that was really nice. They got lots of presents!

Tell us about a film you've seen recently that you really liked.
I went to see a science-fiction film – I can't remember the title – but it was about life on another planet. I liked it due to the special effects which were really exciting.

Have you ever been to a live music concert? (Why? / Why not?)
No, I haven't been to a live concert, though I have seen one on television. And I have streamed some music from a live concert, too.

Do you like doing exercise in a gym? (Why? / Why not?)
I hate gyms because I can never use the machines properly! I prefer to do exercise outside in the fresh air, so I often go jogging instead of using a gym.

What's your favourite sport at the moment? (Why?)
Well, I really enjoy hockey, and I'm in a team in the local club. I don't really think I'm very good at it, though, and we lose a lot of matches!

How often do you watch sport with your friends? (Why? / Why not?)
I usually watch sport with my friends at the weekends. Sometimes we go to watch the local football team play, and at other times we watch things like important tennis games on television.

If you could be really good at one sport, what would it be? (Why?)
I'd really like to be good at football, owing to the fact that footballers get paid so much money! If I think about how much I'd enjoy the sport, though, I'd like to be good at swimming because that's something I can do all my life.

How do you generally travel to work or college? (Why?)
I often walk there if the weather is good, but it takes quite a long time. When it's raining, I catch the bus.

What do you like doing in the evenings? (Why?)
I usually watch television, or listen to music, and I like playing computer games, too. I prefer to go to bed quite late, so it's nice to relax in the evenings.

Is it important to you to have a regular morning routine? (Why? / Why not?)
I definitely do have a routine because it makes it much easier to get to work on time! Each night I choose the clothes I want to wear the next day, so I don't waste time thinking about it in the morning when I'm sleepy, and I always have the same coffee and one slice of toast for breakfast.

Where do you usually meet your friends? (Why?)
We tend to meet in the shopping centre because there's so much to do there – like there's a cinema, lots of cafés and other stuff. If the weather's nice we sometimes go for a walk, too.

Part 2
Candidate A
Both photographs show people having a meal together, but they're in very different places. The first group is in a restaurant, sitting round a table, eating a meal that looks quite formal, although they're not wearing smart clothes. They're talking and look quite relaxed – they must be friends because they're similar ages. The second photograph shows a family sitting outside in the garden, maybe having a barbecue, although I can't see it. There's a man who's giving an older man some food from a big bowl, so everyone is sharing the food, whereas in the first picture they all have their own meals that have probably been served by a waiter. Both groups of people look happy, so they're obviously all enjoying themselves in both places. I think the people in the first photograph are enjoying the food, but they're also enjoying sitting and talking together. I think that because they look as if they're listening to each other and laughing about something one of them has said. On the other hand, the people in the second picture look very relaxed and are enjoying spending some free time together in the sunshine, eating food they've prepared themselves.
Candidate B
I'd prefer to eat outside in the sun, because I love informal meals and I love being outside. It's a great way to spend time with friends.
Candidate B
Both photographs show people doing different things when they're on holiday in a city, and the people in both photographs are spending their time outside, not visiting museums or anything like that. The first photograph shows people who are clearly cycling round the city, and they've stopped for a break next to the river to take photographs. They're wearing warm clothes, so the weather seems to be cold. The people in the second photograph are on a sightseeing boat in an old city. I can't see their faces very clearly, but I'm sure they're having a good time, and the weather looks warm. In both photographs they've decided to do these things in the city because they want to find out more about it. It's probably easier for the group of cyclists to get round the city, and it's also quicker than walking. They're experiencing the buildings and life in the city close up whereas the people in the boat are seeing the old city from a different perspective. They're getting a kind of general idea of the type of buildings and the atmosphere of the city.

Candidate A
I'd prefer to cycle because I think you get a nicer experience, and you can do what you want. A boat tour follows the same route every time so you are just taken to different places whether you want to go there or not.

Part 3
M: OK, so we've got to think about whether it's a good idea for young people to plan their life and career when they're at school. It seems like a good idea to me – there are lots of advantages to planning life well ahead – like you waste a lot of time if you don't study the right things, or you're not thinking about the future.
F: That's true, but actually we've got to consider whether it's really necessary for students to plan their life and career, not just a good idea. Let's think about being able to change. You talked about studying the right subjects. Planning what to study may seem to be a good thing, but what happens if you change your mind about what job you want to do? If you've made a definite decision like studying science, then you're stuck. I think it's important to be able to change your mind later on.
M: You have a good point, and I agree with you. OK – so what about feeling pressure to make decisions? Do you think that's a negative point?
F: Yes, because there's so much pressure on young people nowadays – they have to look good, be good at everything – so they might find it hard to choose the right career as well.
M: But they need to feel that they're becoming independent – planning stuff is a good way of growing up.
F: I agree, but actually that happens so fast these days – don't you think?
M: I suppose so. And some young people do have unrealistic ambitions when they're very young – like I always wanted to be a footballer, but it was never going to happen!
F: I know what you mean – I wanted to be a singer!
M: So which is the most important reason for young people to plan their life and career? It's a tricky question, actually – I'm not sure that planning is right for everyone.
F: You have a good point there – everyone's different, and has different needs.
M: You're quite right – I totally agree with you. Of course it's never possible to plan for everything, so maybe just being realistic is actually the most important.
F: Well, In my opinion, it's most important to be able to do what you want, and if you don't plan, then you might not do that.
M: Actually, I think you're right. Let's choose that.

Part 4
How easy is it for young people to plan a career nowadays? (Why?)
In my opinion it's really hard to plan a career because there are so many different things you can do. On the other hand, it's actually hard to get a first job nowadays, and that makes it difficult, too. Some of my friends would like to follow a long-term career, but there's a lot of competition for jobs. which makes planning hard. They have to wait to see what comes up.

Can friends influence the choices young people make about life and work? (Why? / Why not?)
I think friends can influence lots of things like the music you enjoy or the clothes you wear, but I'm not sure that they influence a person's choice of career. That's a very big decision for most people to make, and unless friends have some experience, their opinion might not be helpful.

Do you think young people get the best advice about life or work from parents or teachers? (Why? / Why not?)

I guess it depends on what it is they want advice on. Both would be good for help with work questions, and teachers can help with the best things to study, but parents know you best. That means they can help you a bit more and talk to you about how you feel about things. Teachers are probably more practical.

Is it better for people to plan a career based on salary, or the satisfaction they would get from doing the job? (Why?)

That's actually a hard question. I want to say the satisfaction they'd get from the work, but salary is really important because we all have to earn a living. Maybe it's actually a bit of both. In my life, I want to enjoy my work but I also want to be rich!

In your opinion, what's the most important decision people have to make in life? (Why?)

Well, deciding on a career is quite important, but then you can always change your job. I think that choosing the person you marry is the most important decision you make – that's much more difficult to change!

Some people say it's often better to avoid planning anything at all, and just be spontaneous. What do you think? (Why?)

I'm a spontaneous kind of person, so I'd probably say just be spontaneous at all times – but, on the other hand, if you're not prepared for something, then it may go wrong. It's fine to be spontaneous in your free time, but work and other important things do need planning.

Alternative tasks for Practice Exam: Writing Part 2

2

Example answer

We all use technology, don't we? In fact, some of us might find it difficult to imagine a world without it! Most people would answer this question by saying 'my mobile phone', but let me tell you about my own favourite piece of technology.

Of course, it goes without saying that just like everyone else, I have a mobile phone, and I use it all the time. However, it can be annoying sometimes and you can't get away from the fact that other people can contact you anywhere, any time. Obviously that makes it convenient, but not necessarily lovable.

My own favourite technical device is my mini tablet. It fits into my bag, and I use it for everything, from checking information to buying tickets to shopping. I love it because the screen is so much bigger than a phone, but it's not as big and heavy as a laptop. I can do everything I want on it, and, more importantly, I can choose to not use it all the time.

Could I live without it? I guess so, because I could use my phone, but I wouldn't enjoy that so much!

193 words

3

Example answer

Dear Mr Evans,

I am writing in response to your advertisement in the local newspaper for a part-time assistant in the local tourist information office.

Firstly, I am 19 years old, and my English is good. I have been studying it for seven years, and am at Level B2. I have been living here for three years, and am very familiar with the town and the way of life.

Secondly, I am very keen on history, and in fact I have been studying it at college for the last year. I am particularly interested in the local area, and I would be delighted to help visitors learn more about the town. It has a rich past, with many stories I would enjoy telling.

Although I have not worked in a tourist office before, I love meeting people and am very sociable. I worked in a museum for a short time, and feel that this job would be perfect for me. I can work two or three days every week, and I would be free to start next Monday.

My telephone number is 08799446552204.

I look forward to hearing from you.

Yours sincerely,

191 words

4

Example answer

When Tom set off for school, he expected it to be just a normal day. The weather was hot and sunny, and he was feeling happy that it would soon be the summer holidays.

He was walking through the park when he saw a large crowd of people. Feeling curious, he walked towards them. As he got closer, he could see that there were film cameras and people in costumes. Then he recognised Daniel Harrison, a well-known actor. 'Wow,' he thought. 'This is exciting!' Suddenly, a woman came up to him. 'Do you fancy being in a film?' she asked. 'We need a few extra people for some crowd scenes.' 'Sure,' Tom said. 'OK. Ask your parents, and come back after school. We'll need you at about 4.30.' 'Great,' Tom said. 'Oh, and there's a party tonight for all the cast,' the woman added. 'You can come if you want, and bring your parents.'

As Tom set off for school, he couldn't wait to tell his friends that he was going to be a film star – and he was going to a party with Daniel Harrison!

186 words

These mindfulness practices can help you to stay calm and focused as you revise for your exams.

Important

If you feel that stress and anxiety are getting on top of you, speak to someone you trust. Opening up about how you feel can really help in dealing with what can be an intense time. If you have recently experienced the loss of a loved one, a traumatic event or have been diagnosed with a mental illness, or have any ongoing physical pain, it's really important that you check in with someone (such as a parent, teacher, counsellor or doctor) before doing these practices.

What is mindfulness?

Mindfulness is essentially awareness. It is about training your attention to notice your thoughts, feelings, emotions, sensations, physical reactions, and anything around you that is happening right now, without judging them. This can help you to make better, more skilful decisions. Your brain can be 'rewired' to work in more helpful or skilful ways. In many ways it's like brain training. Just as people go to the gym and lift weights regularly to build muscle, mindfulness helps train the brain by doing the practices daily.

Preparing for exams

Neuroscientists are starting to understand more about how mindfulness practice can help. Studies indicate that it helps in two main ways, especially when it comes to exams.

1 It helps to increase the density in the front of your brain. This is the part of the brain associated with memory, your ability to solve problems and to manage distraction.

2 It helps us to manage strong or difficult emotions. Feeling some stress and anxiety around exams is natural and, indeed, can help boost performance. It's when this becomes too much that it becomes a problem.

Mindfulness helps to calm activity in the part of your brain associated with worry.

Doing and being

Very often, it is easy to want to get straight into doing a task like revision just to get it finished and out of the way. This is called **doing mode** – it helps you to get things done, but not always to consider the best way of tackling the task. Mindfulness helps by giving you a moment to pause and enter **being mode**. This allows time for you to ground yourself and be fully focused on the present moment, so you experience things more fully. Usually this will help you to take a calmer and wiser approach to a task, which will mean you're more effective.

The pressures of revision and exams may make you feel that taking 'time out' from revision to do these practices is not possible. However, regularly doing even short practices where you can drop into 'being mode' can begin to give you greater mental space or clarity.

Mindfully making a drink

- What can you **hear**? For example, when making a drink, notice the sound of pouring the drink or boiling water.
- What can you **smell**? For example, for tea, coffee or juice, notice how the smells **change** as you make the drink.
- What can you **see**? For example, notice the colours and how they **change**.
- What can you **feel**? For example, the warmth or coolness of the drink in your hands.
- What can you **taste**? For example, when taking a sip of the drink, notice how it first tastes and any **changes** in taste.
- Enjoy **being in the moment** as you consume your drink.

This simple exercise can have a big impact. Many people find they notice and taste far more.

When you take time to slow down and live in a more moment-to-moment way, you are able to experience life more fully and appreciatively.

This can then help to create a greater sense of calm.

Being kind to yourself

Exam preparation can be a stressful time, so it's important to take some time out regularly to be kind to yourself: to recharge your batteries, give your brain some breathing space and acknowledge all the good preparatory work you're putting in. Take regular breaks and enjoy some 'downtime' with your friends and family to help recharge.

Practising mindfulness

Just like learning any new skill, for example playing a sport or an instrument, mindfulness is something that has to be practised daily to have richer benefits. Doing daily practices of 10 minutes or so can really help you to move your awareness to be fully in the present moment in a non-judgemental way, helping you to avoid overthinking, which can lead to worry, anxiety and stress.

> It is best to learn how to practise mindfulness through a course. There may be courses running in your area. An internet search will help you find a course local to you or one running online.

Good posture for practice

Getting your posture correct for doing mindfulness practice is really important. These practices are designed to be done in a seated position. They can also be done lying down.

Try to find a chair you can sit in that allows your feet to rest fully on the ground with your ankles, knees and hips all at right angles, with your back slightly away from the back of the chair.

The room you choose should be somewhere you won't be disturbed. Turn your phone onto silent or flight mode. Let the people you live with know that you'll be doing mindfulness practice so that they do not disturb you. Mindfulness can help you take a healthy, effective approach to your revision. But remember, you will still need to plan and revise!

Practice 1: Mindfulness of breath and body
The benefits

Very often our minds like to wander. In this practice, you focus your attention on your breathing and on different parts of your body. It's a bit like shining a torchlight so that you focus on just one thing at a time, feeling the sensations that arise. Practising this regularly helps the mind wander less, which leads to less worrying and helps with concentration. Remember – it is normal for your mind to wander while you are meditating as that is what minds do! You are just trying to train it.

The Mindfulness of breath and body practice will help you to develop your awareness and focus, which can help with revision. In addition, focusing on breath also has a calming effect (great if you are worrying about exams). Moving the focus to the body can also help to identify physical feelings caused by stress. Examples of stress in the body might be 'butterflies' or cramps in your stomach, your hands shaking, getting sweaty or your mouth going dry.

Guidance on the practice

If your mind wanders, try to bring it back with a sense of kindness. It doesn't matter how many times the mind wanders, it's bringing it back each time to focus on the breath or the body that's important, as you are increasing your concentration and training your attention each time. Don't be frustrated as it is just part of training your brain.

To access the audio file for Practice 1, please use the app.

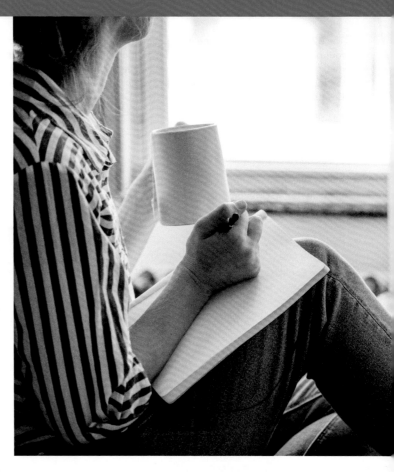

Practice 2: The three-step breathing space
The benefits

Worrying about what has gone on in the past or what might happen in the future cannot change events and distracts you from the present – from what you are doing now. The present is something that you can change, so that is where your focus should be. For example, worrying about your exams in several months' time won't be as helpful as revising now! The three-step breathing space practice helps you to fully ground yourself in the present and gives you a few moments to rest and recharge. The practice is structured a bit like an hourglass.

The three-step breathing space is a very useful practice if ever you start to feel stressed and want a pause to help you step back and get perspective.

Guidance on the practice

The great thing about this practice is that you can do it in three minutes or less. Use it to 'recharge' yourself while revising or ground yourself just before or even during your exam.

1 Firstly, you do a 'weather check' of the mind, to see what's going on, by observing your thoughts, giving you a more objective viewpoint of how busy or calm your mind is.

2 Then you turn your attention to your breath, helping to focus you in the present moment.

3 Finally, you expand out that awareness to sensations in the rest of your body, becoming aware of where you may be holding any emotions in the body as stress or tension.

To access the audio file for Practice 2, please use the app.

EXAM OVERVIEW

The **B2 First** qualification is one of the Cambridge English Qualifications and tests all areas of language ability. It is made up of **four papers**, each testing a different area of ability in English. The Reading and Use of English paper carries 40 percent of the marks, while Writing, Listening and Speaking each carry 20 percent of the marks. Candidates are awarded a score for each of the four skills and an overall score for the exam, plus a final grade (A, B or C). If a candidate's performance is below level B2, but is within level B1, the candidate will receive a Cambridge English certificate stating that they demonstrated ability at B1 level.

Reading and Use of English	1 hour 15 minutes
Writing	1 hour 20 minutes
Listening	40 minutes (approximately)
Speaking	14 minutes (for each pair of students)

All the examination questions are task-based. Rubrics (instructions) are important and should be read carefully. They set the context and give important information about the tasks. There is a separate answer sheet for recording answers for the Reading and Use of English and Listening papers.

Paper	Format	Task focus
Reading and Use of English 7 Parts 52 questions	**Part 1:** Multiple-choice cloze Choosing which word from a choice of four fits in each of eight gaps in the text.	Choice of vocabulary and relationships between words.
	Part 2: Open cloze Writing the missing word in each of eight gaps in the text.	Grammar, vocabulary and knowledge of expressions.
	Part 3: Word formation Choosing the form of the word given so that it fits into the gap in the text, with a total of eight gaps.	Grammatical accuracy and knowledge of vocabulary and expressions.
	Part 4: Key word transformations Using a key word to complete a new sentence which means the same as the one given, with a total of six pairs of sentences.	Grammatical accuracy and knowledge of vocabulary and sentence structure.
	Part 5: Multiple choice Answering six four-option multiple-choice questions based on a text.	Reading for detailed understanding of the text.
	Part 6: Gapped text Choosing sentences to fit into the gaps in a text, with a total of six sentences to place correctly.	Reading to understand text structure.
	Part 7: Multiple matching Deciding which of the short extracts or paragraphs contains given information or ideas and matching these with ten prompts.	Reading to locate specific information, detail, opinion and attitude.
Writing 2 Parts	**Part 1:** Compulsory task (essay) Using given information to write an essay of 140 to 190 words.	Focus on writing for an English teacher in a formal style.
	Part 2: Producing one piece of writing of 140 to190 words from a choice of the following: an article, an informal email or letter, a review, a report. In the For Schools exam, a story replaces the report.	Writing for a specific target reader, using appropriate layout and register.
Listening 4 Parts 30 questions	**Part 1:** Multiple choice Eight short recordings, each with a three-option multiple-choice question.	Understanding gist, detail, function, purpose, attitude, etc.
	Part 2: Sentence completion One long recording with ten sentence-completion questions.	Locating and recording specific information.
	Part 3: Multiple matching Set of five short recordings on the same theme to match to one of eight prompts.	Understanding gist and main points.
	Part 4: Multiple-choice (long text) One long recording with seven three-option multiple-choice questions.	Understanding attitude, opinion, gist, main ideas and specific information.
Speaking 4 Parts	**Part 1:** Interview Conversation with the examiner.	Giving personal information, using social language.
	Part 2: Long turn You talk about two photographs for approximately 1 minute.	Organising discourse in a 'long turn', describing, comparing, giving opinions.
	Part 3: Collaborative task A conversation with the other candidate based on some written prompts.	Sustaining an interaction, expressing, justifying and exchanging ideas, agreeing and disagreeing, reaching a decision.
	Part 4: Discussion Further discussion on topics related to Part 3.	Expressing and justifying ideas, agreeing and disagreeing.

Pearson Education Limited
KAO Two
KAO Park
Hockham Way
Harlow, Essex
CM17 9SR
England
and Associated Companies throughout the world.

https://english.com/portal

© Pearson Education Limited 2021

Written by Sheila Dignen and Jacky Newbrook

The right of Ashley Lodge to be identified as author of the mindfulness section of this work has been asserted by him in accordance with the Copyright, Designs and Patents Act 1988

First published 2021
Seventh impression 2024

ISBN: 978-1-292-39143-4

Set in Avenir Next LT Pro
Printed in Slovakia by Neografia

Acknowledgements
The publishers would like to thank Lynda Edwards for her feedback on the material through its development.

Image Credit(s):

123RF.com: Andrey Kiselev 74, Dmitrii Shironosov 82, grafner 81, jakobradlgruber 31, Vasyl Kosolovskyy 68;
Alamy Stock Photo: AA World Travel Library 76, Andrew Paterson 110, Andriy Popov 83, Brian Lawrence 110, Cavan Images 83, Darryl Brooks 10, Ellen McKnight 80, Frédéric Vielcanet 92, Hero Images 84, Iakov Filimonov 78, Jan Wlodarczyk 5, 18, Jeffrey Isaac Greenberg 7 79, Jim Cumming 31, Juice Images 79, Maria Kraynova 57, Nathaniel Noir 7, National Geographic Image Collection 26, Oleksiy Maksymenko Photography 80, PhotoAlto 80, robertharding 23, Roger Cracknell 01 / classic 41, Tetra Images, LLC 27, Valentyn Volkov 19, Wieslaw Jarek 77; **Getty Images:** ABGlavin / istock 24, Alexander Kirch / EyeEm 4, 16, aluxum / E+ 19, Cimmerian / E+ 12, Claudia Burlotti 71, Davis Lees 89, deebrowning / iStock 30, DjelicS / E+ 91, Elizabethsalleebauer / RooM 11, Erik Johansen 98, Fabio Biondi / EyeEm 32, Fotosearch 73, Fuse / Corbis 60, Geber86 / E+ 71, George Pachantouris 56, GMVozd / E+ 156, Hill Street Studios / Digital Vision 82, jeffbergen 51, John P Kelly / Stone 67, JohnnyGreig / E+ 63, kali9 / E+ 76, Kolbz / iStock 50, Kseniya Ovchinnikova 46, lzf / iStock 28, manonallard / E+ 71, Marco Bottigelli / Moment 48, Matteo Colombo / Moment 37, Michael Prince / Image Bank 55, Milo Zanecchia / Ascent Xmedia 25, MundusImages/E+ 157, ooyoo 21, Paul Bradbury / OJO Images 11, Paul Souders 90, PeopleImages / E+ 14, Peter Cade / Stone 22, petrenkod / iStock 4, 15, pixdeluxe 43, ppl58/iStock 64, praetorianphoto 9, Richard Bailey / Corbis 87, Richard Bailey / Corbis 44, Rimma_Bondarenko / iStock 4, 15, Robin Skjoldborg / DigitalVision 96, Ronnie Kaufman 74, Safique Hazarika Photography / Moment 66, Sang Ho Kim / EyeEm 52, semenovp / iStock 93, SM Rafiq Photography / Moment 13, Songsak Wilairit / EyeEm 34, Steve Prezant 85, Tetra Images 19, Tuul & Bruno Morandi / The Image Bank 86, Westend61 14, 71, zoranm 58; **Shutterstock.com:** 110, Dragon Images 78, Gudkov Andrey 94, Moviestore Collection 33, nuclear_lily 38, stockcreations 65, wavebreakmedia 110

All other images © Pearson Education